Mapping European security after Kosovo

MANCHESTER
UNIVERSITY PRESS

Mapping European security after Kosovo

edited by
Peter van Ham *and* Sergei Medvedev

Manchester University Press
Manchester and New York

distributed exclusively in the USA by Palgrave

Copyright © Manchester University Press 2002

While copyright in the volume as a whole is vested in Manchester University Press, copyright in individual chapters belongs to their respective authors, and no chapter may be reproduced wholly or in part without the express permission in writing of both author and publisher.

Published by Manchester University Press
Oxford Road, Manchester M13 9NR, UK
and Room 400, 175 Fifth Avenue, New York, NY 10010, USA
www.manchesteruniversitypress.co.uk

Distributed exclusively in the USA by
Palgrave, 175 Fifth Avenue, New York,
NY 10010, USA

Distributed exclusively in Canada by
UBC Press, University of British Columbia, 2029 West Mall,
Vancouver, BC, Canada V6T 1Z2

British Library Cataloguing-in-Publication Data
A catalogue record for this book is available from the British Library

Library of Congress Cataloging-in-Publication Data applied for

ISBN   0 7190 6240 3   *hardback*

First published 2002

10 09 08 07 06 05 04 03 02   10 9 8 7 6 5 4 3 2 1

Typeset in Times
by Graphicraft Limited, Hong Kong
Printed in Great Britain
by Biddles Ltd, Guildford and King's Lynn

Contents

List of figures	*page* viii
Notes on contributors	ix

Preface: Kosovo and the outlines of Europe's new order
Sergei Medvedev and Peter van Ham — 1

1 Kosovo: a European *fin de siècle*
Sergei Medvedev — 15
   Kosovo between *Idealpolitik* and *Realpolitik* — 15
   Kosovo between ethnic cleansing and allied bombing — 17
   Kosovo between (East)-modernity and postmodernity — 19
   Russia between *derzhavnost'* and the dollar — 23
   Behold, the new world order cometh — 27

2 Simulating European security: Kosovo and the Balkanisation–integration nexus
Peter van Ham — 32
   Introduction: writing security — 32
   'Security' as a political struggle — 33
   European security as a *tabula rasa* — 36
   Kosovo and the margins of modernity — 38
   Writing security on the Balkan screen — 40
   Kosovo: the pre-context of European security — 43

3 Kosovo and the end of war
Pertti Joenniemi — 48
   Introduction: deviant voices — 48
   War: a floating signifier? — 50
   War as usual — 54

	Towards a higher order?	55
	Dealing with a residual case	57
	Averting the mirror image	59
	Conclusion: war as a stranger	61
4	**Kosovo and the end of the legitimate warring state**	
	Iver B. Neumann	66
	Introduction	66
	The Copenhagen School and violisation	67
	War as legitimate violisation of politics	69
	The ontologification of war	73
	The other side	75
	Legitimising weapons, targets and victims	76
	Conclusion	79
5	**Kosovo and the end of the United Nations?**	
	Heikki Patomäki	82
	Introduction	82
	Principles of US foreign policy in the 1990s	83
	The UN after Boutros-Ghali: implementing the will of the US in Kosovo and elsewhere	93
	Conclusion: the dangers of hard will and narrow power	96
6	**Kosov@ and the politics of representation**	
	Maja Zehfuss	107
	Naming: reality and representation	108
	Derrida: reality as representation	110
	The reality of Kosovo	112
	The supplement: identity, credibility, cohesion	116
	Conclusion	117
7	**'vvv.nato.int.': virtuousness, virtuality and virtuosity in NATO's representation of the Kosovo campaign**	
	Andreas Behnke	126
	Introduction: reading preferences . . .	126
	Loading plug-ins: liberal truth against systemic anarchy	128
	Looking up host: www.nato.int	131
	Host found; waiting for reply . . .	131
	Reading file . . .	132
	Cache clean-up . . .	137
	'All video sequences are available in MPEG'	140
	Conclusion: vvv.nato.int: host not found . . .	141

8 Of models and monsters: language games in the Kosovo war
Mika Aaltola   145
  Introduction: Kosovo as a sign   145
  Repetition, variation and incantation   147
  The phantasmal background of political 'magic'   149
  Western *phantasmata* and Yugoslavian counter-'magic'   150
  Extending political order during the Kosovo war   153
  Concluding remarks: security in search of agency   156

9 'War is never civilised': civilisation, civil society and the Kosovo war
Mikkel Vedby Rasmussen   162
  Introduction   162
  Civilisation and civil society   163
  'Who are you?'   165
  The civilisation of civil society   167
  The cosmopolitan soul of Europe   170
  Concluding remarks   173

10 Chechnya and Kosovo: reflections in a distorting mirror
Christoph Zürcher   179
  Prologue   179
  Chechnya and Kosovo: the similarities   183
  Chechnya and Kosovo: the responses   187
  Epilogue: reflections in a distorting mirror   193

List of figures

1	NATO banner	*page* 131
	http://www.nato.int/kosovo/all-frce.htm	
2	F15/SAMs	132
	http://www.nato.int/kosovo/all-frce.htm	
3	Tank attack	140
	http://www.nato.int/kosovo/video.htm	
4	Tank attack	140
	http://www.nato.int/kosovo/video.htm	
5	Polysemantics of war images	192

Notes on contributors

Mika Aaltola Senior researcher on the project 'Openness in Finnish Foreign Policy', funded by the Academy of Finland, and assistant professor of international relations at the University of Tampere (Finland). His recent publications include *The Rhythm, Exception, and Rule in International Relations* (Studia Politica Tamperensis, 1999), and several articles on reality making, order creation and persuasion in international politics.

Andreas Behnke University adjunct at Stockholm University (Sweden), where he teaches international relations. His research interests include IR theory, critical security studies and NATO. His recent publications include articles on NATO's post-Cold War security discourse and on the securitisation of political issues.

Peter van Ham Senior research fellow at the Netherlands Institute of International Relations 'Clingendael', the Hague, and adjunct professor at the College of Europe, Bruges. His recent books include *European Integration and the Postmodern Condition* (Routledge, 2001); and (as co-author) *A Critical Approach to European Security* (Pinter, 1999).

Pertti Joenniemi Senior research fellow and programme director for Nordic–Baltic Studies at the Copenhagen Peace Research Institute (COPRI, Denmark). His publications are on region-building in the Baltic Sea and Barents areas, northwestern Russia, as well as the unfolding of political space in the northernmost part of Europe. He is co-editor of the *NEBI* (North European and Baltic Integration) *Yearbook*.

Sergei Medvedev Professor at the George C. Marshall European Center for Security Studies in Garmisch-Partenkirchen (Germany). He has held research positions in Moscow, Rome, Ebenhausen (Germany) and Helsinki. His research interests vary from semiotics and cultural anthropology to post-Soviet studies and European security. Recent publications include *Russia's Futures: Implications for the EU, the North and the Baltic Region* (UPI/IEP, 2000) and *Russia and the West at the Millennium* (forthcoming).

Iver Neumann Senior researcher at the Norwegian Institute of International Affairs (Oslo). His recent books (in English) include *Uses of the Other: 'The East' in European Identity Formation* (University of Minnesota Press, 1999); (as co-editor) *The Future of International Relations: Masters in the Making?* (Routledge, 1997); and *Russia and the Idea of Europe* (Routledge, 1996).

Heikki Patomäki Reader in international relations at the Nottingham Trent University. He is also the research director of the Network Institute for Global Democratisation. His most recent books (in English) include (as co-editor) *The Politics of Economic and Monetary Union* (Kluwer, 1997); *Democratizing Globalization* (Zed, 2001); and *After International Relations* (Routledge, forthcoming).

Mikkel Vedby Rasmussen Post-doctoral fellow at the University of Copenhagen (Denmark). He holds degrees from the University of Copenhagen and the London School of Economics. He currently works on a project on 'reflexive security' practices following the Cold War.

Maja Zehfuss Lecturer in international relations at the University of Warwick (England). She works on German participation in international military operations, constructivism and poststructuralism, and has published in *Zeitschrift für Internationale Beziehungen*.

Christoph Zürcher Researcher and Lecturer in international relations at the Institute of East European Studies of the Free University of Berlin (Germany). He is the co-editor of *Potentials of (Dis)Order: Explaining Conflict and Stability in the Caucasus and in the Former Yugoslavia* (Manchester University Press, forthcoming).

Sergei Medvedev and Peter van Ham

Preface: Kosovo and the outlines of Europe's new order

Introduction: 'Brother, can you spare a paradigm?'

Twelve years after the fall of the Berlin Wall, talk about the end of the Cold War continues to haunt the professional discourse on European security. The seemingly innocent reference to the post-Cold War era has turned into an almost standard opening line of most writings in the field. A remarkable uniformity of approach among different authors testifies not so much to the intellectual impotence of the trade as to a lack of reference-points in reconceptualising European security, compelling us to look back and attach our narratives to the Cold War as the last-known paradigm and a foolproof marker of Western identity.

Old mental maps are still very much in use for charting the new waters: bipolarity, systemic thinking and the mindset of inclusion–exclusion continue to cast their shadows beyond the Berlin Wall. The vacuum of Europe's nameless 1990s has attracted many new visions, and offers to fill the conceptual void left by the end of communism. Rosy scenarios along the lines of Fukuyama's 'end of history' were soon followed by the suggestion of the 'new pessimists' that we are instead entering a period of a 'coming anarchy' (Robert Kaplan), asking 'Must it be the West against the rest?' (Matthew Connelly and Paul Kennedy), or predicting a 'clash of civilisations' (Samuel Huntington).[1] When the United States proposed, in the early 1990s, to establish a new world order, it became clear that this new vision of the West's undisputed global leadership was too ambitious; this new world order was interpreted by many as just the new world's newest scheme by which to give orders. Understanding that its dream of a world society based on liberal values, democracy and a free-market spirit would be unattainable, the West soon succumbed to a defeatist notion of a new world disorder, 'accepting' that the 'other' does not think like 'us' – has not reached levels of civilisation and civil society similar to 'ours'.

In this story of post-Cold War conceptual confusion, the war in and over Kosovo stands out as a particularly interesting episode. 'Kosovo' obviously is more than a conflict, fight, clash or war over territory: it has been a battle over ideas, identities and interests. 'Kosovo' has been marketed as a turning-point in the development towards a new kind of Western mentality, as well as the culmination of a liberal sense of humanitarian solidarity confined to Europe's political space. Clearly, these events can also be read in a less positive manner, as testifying to Western arrogance, an over-reliance on the efficacy of high-technology and a lack of long-term visions and policies of peaceful engagement. But, however one wants to interpret 'Kosovo', it is certainly clear that political spin-doctors have been highly successful in selling this war/conflict, and that Western public opinion has been happy to buy the product/story.

What 'Kosovo' also offers is a template for academics, by which to test and taste a smorgasbord of new, often critical, ideas about European politics and security. Whereas some would label 'Kosovo' as politics-cum-war as usual, the vast majority (and certainly not a silent one, this time) seems to share the view that this event stands for 'something different'. NATO's war over Kosovo has called in question the orthodox understanding of what European security is all about. Perhaps appropriately, coming as it does at the beginning of a new millennium, 'Kosovo' testifies not only to the opening of a post-Westphalian era where aged notions such as sovereignty and territoriality have become uncertain, but to a potential post-Clausewitzian era in which 'hard' military power as the straightforward 'continuation of politics by other means' has proven to be ineffective, if not ultimately counterproductive. 'Kosovo' can therefore be called 'the first European war of the twenty-first century' (with the twentieth century ending in 1989), and seen as an example of how the West has been fumbling towards a new model of liberal order in Europe. 'Kosovo' symbolises and exemplifies the relevance of many 'end'-debates and 'post'-debates within the academic literature (i.e. the end of sovereignty, territoriality, geopolitics, modernity). The time perhaps is now right to provide an initial outline of the fuzzy borders of Europe's new political order which 'Kosovo' has helped to shape.

This book emerged from a desire to contribute to the debate on how 'Kosovo' (as well as the discourse on 'Kosovo' itself) has affected our understanding of a number of key concepts in European and global politics. It is not our intention to provide the reader with an 'unbiased' and detailed, let alone definitive, account of what preceded the Kosovo war, how it has been conducted and why, and how the aftermath should be evaluated (with all the comfortable benefits that accompany hindsight). There are quite a number of published works that try to do just that. The Kosovo saga is an ongoing story with its own ups and downs, ranging from ethnic cleansing and alleged genocide in the spring of 1999, to a quasi-successful popular revolution in October 2000, and the election of a democratic government in Belgrade in December of that year. These events form, of course, the background of the papers collected here. But rather than to rehearse or take sides on the debate on 'what really happened', the essays in this volume take a different route through the theoretical minefield of 'Kosovo', carefully watching out for the scholarly detonators and the metaphysical boobytraps. They are all interested in questions that go beyond practical, policy-oriented, concerns which may help decision-makers in avoiding (or preparing for) the next security crisis in Europe.

Mapping European security starts by asking how experiences in Kosovo have changed the discourse of European security. All chapters are based on the assumption that the conventional political paradigm needs to be challenged through a series of critical variants, although they do not follow a single agreed-upon theoretical approach to which they could all subscribe. But instead of mainstream notions like anarchy, balance of power and statal interpretations of European politics, this book calls for a reconceptualisation of security and the inside–outside dyad through the introduction of new sets of puzzles that concentrate on issues of identity, culture, language and the normative notions of global politics. There are now numerous critical approaches to (European) politics and the study of international relations in which this book is conceptually embedded. Constructivism, critical theory, postmodernism and many a feminist approach have unveiled the hegemony of mainstream social sciences and offered different readings of current events, recent history and their theoretical implications.[2]

This book makes an attempt to provide new and stimulating perspectives on how 'Kosovo' has shaped European post-post-Cold War reality (and a possible new European order-of-sorts). It will, of course, be impossible to press all these critical voices within the covers of one volume, and we therefore have no intention of offering a complete overview. It is our aim to contribute to the insecurity of the field of security studies by sidelining the theoretical worldview that underlies mainstream strategic thinking on the Kosovo events. Most of the book's contributions challenge the epistemological definition of the Kosovo game, arguing that we should be concerned both with the 'Kosovo out there' (i.e. far away in the exotic Balkans) and with the debate about what counts as security and how our definitions of security are shaped by various power/knowledge interests.[3] Our concern with 'Kosovo' is not rooted in a desire to offer 'problem-solving theory'. Rather, we are (as Ken Booth argued a decade earlier) interested in moving 'thinking about security in world affairs ... out of the almost exclusively realist framework into the critical philosophical camp'.[4] Most contributors to this book have adopted such a critical approach by re-essentialising and deconstructing orthodox assumptions about the nature of European (and global) security without, however, necessarily offering their own redefinitions.

The political and intellectual insecurity brought about by 'Kosovo' has much to do with a rising culture of virtuality to which most authors in this volume pay tribute. The Gulf war, which, according to Baudrillard's provocative statement, 'never took place', may still have been too far away in space and relevance.[5] But, in Kosovo, Europe found itself for the first time in the midst of a virtual war, based on aggressive strategies of simulation which were more typical of the new world than of the old continent. The war, originating in the United States-led revolution in military affairs and automated warfare, has made unprecedented use of airpower, thus largely disregarding and bypassing territorial (read: 'European') space.[6] On the 'home front', manipulation techniques of the media have alienated the audience from the 'felt presence' of war to the extent of turning 'Kosovo' into a media spectacle and a PR event. This has resulted in (what Walter Benjamin has called) the 'aestheticisation of war'.[7]

In 'Kosovo', Europe has for the first time faced the increased independent agency – some would say the dominant role – of technology and the media in security matters, turning the war into a form of symbolic exchange and 'European security' into a simulacrum. A remarkable disregard by policy-makers and military planners of the 'situation on the ground' has made the entire territory of Kosovo and Serbia redundant for war fought out on computer monitors and TV screens, in the realm of high-technology and high politics. The missing referents of war have highlighted a more general problem, namely the missing referents of European security and the constructed, simulated nature of the new project of producing a more robust European identity.

Although it is frequently claimed that 'Kosovo' heralds a new era of humanitarian and ethical politics within Europe, most of the contributors to this volume are far from assured that a system is emerging that can serve as a new grounding for Europe's political order. It is this quest for order and the mechanisms that are used by the West's political and military elites that attract most attention here. The cult(ure) of security rests on accepted claims about the nature and limits of the established political order, and the role of politics in shaping and changing this order. 'Kosovo' has again illustrated these power mechanisms, although the swirl of European integration, globalisation and fragmentation has altered the character of some more familiar procedures.

Indeed, 'Kosovo' has illustrated how security has been used to secure European sovereignty and its institutions. After the single European currency, 'security' has become Europe's next big 'new idea', although few have any clear understanding of how this new enterprise can/should be interpreted and realised. Perhaps by default, 'security' has become one of the keys tools for constructing Europe, a tool for claiming Europe's essential foundations through fixing the boundaries between inside and outside and the claim to organise, occupy and administer Europe's space. *Mapping European security* aims to investigate how 'Kosovo' has developed into this principal paradigmatic sign in the complex text of European security and asks how its very marginality has emphasised the unravelling fringes and limits of the sovereign presence of what 'Europe' thinks it stands for, and how it affects the discourse on European security.

Previews

The first two chapters of this volume offer a conceptual overview of the Kosovo debate, placing these events in the context of globalisation, European integration and the discourse of modernity and its aftermath. As its title suggests, the opening essay, by Sergei Medvedev, examines the latter aspect of 'Kosovo', interpreting it as a typical instance of late-modern decadence, a game of narcissism and simulation, resembling cultural paradigms of *fin de siècle* and the *Untergang des Abendlandes*. 'Kosovo' is an elusive phenomenon, evading the categorising discourses of modernity and postmodernity, sovereignty and integration, nationalism and transnationalism, *realpolitik* and *idealpolitik*, and other dichotomies. 'Kosovo' might have been advertised as heralding everything 'new', from 'humanitarian intervention' to the revolution in military affairs. Medvedev's deconstruction aims to ruin the binary opposition of 'old' and 'new' in relation to Kosovo, and to interpret it as an omen of uncertainty and indecision, a symptom of decay and of the protracted crisis of modernity.

Medvedev displays the failure of the old–new paradigm to analyse the actors of the Kosovo story and their respective discourses. On the one hand, 'Kosovo' has introduced the new element of *agency* into European security, whereby the main actors and driving forces of the West's war were not states, elites, bureaucracies or politicians, but means of communication – weapons and the media. He argues that Kosovo has ultimately blurred the distinction between weapons and the mass media. As 'smart' weapons started carrying on-board cameras, their purpose is transformed from destruction to entertainment. It was the media, in its military and journalistic guises, that produced and simulated the Kosovo war, which amounted to nothing more than a video-sequence, a computer game, a PR campaign, or at the very least a military parade, to be consumed by a (mainly) Western audience.

On the other hand, the 'new' discourse of European security that reveals itself through numerous media representations is in fact a traditional discourse of power akin to the Christian white man's discourse that has guided Western colonisation for the last 500 years under the banner of morality. The popular rendering of 'Kosovo' as the 'new' NATO versus the 'traditional nationalist' Milosevic is therefore a simulated binarity, luring the Western audiences into a false choice, and into accepting NATO bombings as a 'necessary evil'.

Peter van Ham has a different point of departure, arguing that the notion of 'European security' no longer follows the logic of representation (by which 'security' posits the state within legitimate boundaries), but now abides by a logic of simulation. Building upon the work of Cynthia Weber and Ole Wæver, he suggests that to tell stories about European security is to imply the very existence of 'Europe' as an object of reference. This is the alibi function of all discourses of European security, since to assume that 'something' is (possibly) threatened is to insist upon its very existence. 'Kosovo' and the European security discourse have discursively framed the diverse meanings of 'Europe', fixing its geopolitical boundaries by locating its practices and by speaking as if a stable European polity already exists. The 'enemy' of Europe's volatile identity has been defined as the 'unknown', the 'unpredictable' and the 'unstable'. The challenge for the EU has been to prevent a slow drift from a postmodern politics of diversity to a succumbing to the modern fear of fluidity and ambiguity.

'Kosovo' has been the ultimate marker of the strange-and-alien threatening contemporary European security by its ethnic and sectarian essentialism, its barbarian methods of 'ethnic cleansing', and its altogether premodern values, attitudes and practices. Van Ham suggests that by not accepting the rationales of European integration and European security, Milosevic's Serbia posed itself as the main challenge to the emerging new European order (NEO), and, by ignoring the logic of NEO realism, raised the key question which European policy makers and theorists have tried to ignore: on what stable foundations can European security be constructed? He claims that the Kosovo experience illustrates that the discourse on 'European security' has changed, once and for all, and that the 'signified' of statal security no longer dominates. Van Ham therefore concludes that 'Kosovo' has been both the *pre*text and the ultimate *con*text in which the contemporary reading of 'European security' is taking place.

These introductory chapters are followed by three chapters that examine Kosovo's impact on the idea of *war*. War is not merely armed conflict; nor is it merely politics by other means. War is one of the key events that shape and legitimise states in their quest for sovereignty and power (both inside and outside their boundaries). Pertti Joenniemi asks whether NATO's involvement in Kosovo was merely an 'air operation', a military intervention, or perhaps even an all-out war? He suggests that 'Kosovo' has played an instrumental role in changing the discourse on conflict within Europe, and that it signals a profound ontological clash by turning 'war' into an openly contested concept.

Joenniemi claims that 'Kosovo' has undermined one of modernity's central referents and that war now has to be envisaged without its traditional conceptual baggage (e.g. sovereignty and statehood). His essay suggests that the events in Kosovo have offered us war in a new guise: it does not stand out as a normal state of affairs, but occurs as an exception and a stranger. War represents a form of discontinuity of politics-as-usual and is something unexpected and unique within a broader political setting characterised by the general absence of securitisation. Cooperation within an imagined 'international community' has now become the norm, whereas local conflicts are depicted as exceptions, conducted by 'outlaws', which are automatically subject to Western-mediated remedies and 'normalisation'. Joenniemi claims that 'Kosovo' has been instrumental to the construction of a new doctrine of humanitarian intervention that is no longer 'modern' in the sense that it is not predicated on notions of sovereignty and a clear divide between inside/outside and friend/foe. Rather, he argues, it is premissed on ambivalence and ambiguity, caused by the blurring and transcendence of numerous political and conceptual boundaries, including the ones that are essential for the modern understanding of war.

Iver Neumann further investigates the claim of the West to have become the norm – and the only legitimate representative of 'humanity', thereby casting Serbia as the enemy not just of human rights but of 'humanity' as such. In exploring this claim, he goes to the origins of the notion of 'securitisation', citing the work of Carl Schmitt and several authors of the Copenhagen School (Barry Buzan, Ole Wæver). To their criteria of politicisation and securitisation, Neumann adds a category of 'violisation'. In Kosovo, certain national identities were violised, but at the same time for the West, war became a legitimate violisation of politics.

The central point of Neumann's chapter is the question of legitimacy: *who* can legitimately wage war, over *which issues*, and *by what means*? The answer to the first question in Kosovo was given in a legitimising speech act whereby the alliance of states appointed themselves as the representatives of humanity. As regards issues legitimising war, Neumann observes the late modern trend of replacing the left–right axis and the conflict of the classes by a national–post-national axis and the struggle between the local and the global. Liberal globalisation is left as the only political programme with a global appeal, and that is why 'NATO could so easily . . . pose as the representative of humanity as such. There simply was no force around to issue a counter-claim.'

The identity-driven violisation of politics has added an ontological dimension to war, eliminating the Hegelian understanding of war ('right against right'), and re-introducing the Catholic tradition of a 'just war'. Neumann's conclusions are unflattering for Western politicians, as he questions the morality of a no-own-losses war, which yields to the temptation of letting other people die instead. 'Humanity' was invoked in Kosovo as a political notion, a legal concept and, ultimately, as a speech act legitimising war and thereby replacing the legitimate warring state – but it has spectacularly failed, morally as well as politically, to legitimise the violence and death which followed its invocation. Neumann's quest for a 'political entity which may legitimately speak in the name of humanity' has so far proved futile.

In fact, many, including Russia, China and most Third World countries, would see such a political entity to be embodied in the United Nations – and the UN Charter as the only source of legitimacy for the possible use of inter-state violence. For them, 'Kosovo' may have seemed an unfortunate occurrence in which the UN was sidelined by NATO. However, as Heikki Patomäki argues in his chapter, 'Kosovo' was not an exception but rather the rule, an episode in the longer-term process of the domestication and marginalisation of the UN by the United States, underpinned by Manichean myths of good and evil and rituals of enemy construction. His analysis contributes to the discussion of the implications of US hegemony, originating in the debates of the late 1970s and the 1980s on hegemonic stability.

Patomäki starts by reconstructing the US–UN conflict in the 1990s, analysing the deep structures of US foreign policy discourse, and formulating its four guiding principles: unchallenged global leadership; the moralising production of myths and construction of enemies; maximising the support of public opinion; and supporting the global expansion of corporate capitalism. His analysis is particularly incisive in describing the crude ethics communicated by the globalising media, which follows the logic of selective sensations and a hierarchical valuation of human lives. The Americans and the Europeans are the most valuable, and get the most coverage; however, 'even poor and less valuable people can be covered if they die in large numbers in one spot at one time'. A particularly low value is attributed to 'evil-doers' in remote and unfamiliar places, whether presumed terrorists, fundamentalists or ethnic cleansers, who can be legitimately killed – indeed, they *have* to be killed in Western performative rituals of 'realism'.

Patomäki arrives at rather pessimistic conclusions, with respect both to the United States and to the role of the UN. For characterising the US, he uses Karl Deutsch's definition of 'hard will', which implies the ability to act 'in character', talking instead of listening. An ever-harder will on the part of the US and its increasingly 'narrow power' bring to mind the 'torpedo run by a pre-destined and a potentially destructive programme'. The UN after Kosovo holds out equally little promise to the world, as the moral basis of its pluralism and its basic legal procedures have been undermined. There are few signs indicating that the US would allow for a rejuvenation, empowering, or democratising of the UN system. Patomäki's radical proposal is to begin building a parallel and more efficient and more democratic global system than the UN, 'at first perhaps in spite of the will of the US and its closest ally, the UK'.

Whereas the chapters by Joenniemi, Neumann and Patomäki explore 'Kosovo' as a product of the decay of modern institutions and discourses like sovereignty, statehood, the warring state or the UN system, the subsequent three contributions explore the symbolic economy of 'Kosovo', treating it as a mere representation, a sign in the contrived text of 'Europe'. Informed by poststructuralist discourses, the contributions by Maja Zehfuss, Andreas Behnke and Mika Aaltola analyse the political implications of the crisis of representation, the virtualisation and visualisation of politics, and language games involved in enemy creation and identity construction.

First in this semiotic/linguistic cluster comes the chapter by Maja Zehfuss, looking into the political linguistics of Kosovo in a framework shaped by the texts of Ferdinand de Saussure and Jacques Derrida. She starts by observing a characteristic struggle over the name of Kosovo in the Western discourse: it could be the Serbian spelling of Kosovo, the Albanian spelling of Kosova, or the orthographic oddity 'Kosov@', a spelling suggested by the German Green Party in an attempt to avoid political partisanship inherent in the act of naming. This story attests to the fact that naming is a productive practice, an act of objectification, and eventually an act of assigning power positions: naming is empowering, and is therefore a *political* practice.

Moving on to poststructuralist ground, Zehfuss deconstructs the produced 'reality' of Kosovo, using Derrida's critique of Western logocentrism. For Derrida, any 'reality' is signified, and signs which were supposed to merely supplement 'reality' came to replace it. Attributing any positive value to 'facts of real life', and placing them at the heart of our normative discourses, are therefore political moves. Following this logic, Zehfuss shows how the 'reality of Kosovo' was constructed in the Western discourses. The 'real facts' like the 'genocide', the 'ethnic cleansing' and the 'humanitarian catastrophe' which served as a reason for Operation Allied Force, were supplemented by goals like upholding the credibility of NATO, ensuring the cohesion of the Alliance, and, more generally, the construction of a Western ('European') identity. However, in accordance with Derrida's logic, 'supplements' came to replace what were pictured as the 'real reasons' for the operation. This was exemplified by the practice of high-altitude bombing, which aimed to preserve NATO's cohesion, but ultimately exacerbated the plight of the refugees whom these bombs were supposed to protect in the first place.

In this sense, the claims of Western politicians – including former peace champions like the German Greens – that bombing was 'demanded by reality' were problematic since they posited 'reality' as something external to language. Zehfuss, instead, argues that 'Kosovo' was produced by the Western power discourse in the very act of naming, and in its numerous representations. In portraying Kosovo as an 'inescapable reality' and a no-other-choice situation, the West has in fact relieved itself of all responsibility for fellow humans.

Following Zehfuss's critique of the politics of the sign, Andreas Behnke proceeds to deconstruct the politics of the image. 'Kosovo' has been NATO's first virtual war using high-tech military equipment and computers to visualise the bombing raids (in the familiar 'before-and-after' pictures used during NATO's daily press briefing). Behnke asks how this 'virtual Kosovo' has affected NATO's policies as well as the public reaction to the war in general. He concerns himself with the 'virtualised' nature of the conflict and its representation in a virtual system of signifiers. Operation Allied Force has been part of a wider campaign in which the crucial battleground is the delocalised world of information networks, TV-screens, newspaper-articles and internet sites. It is on these grounds that the battles over legitimacy, effectiveness and consequences have been fought.

Behnke maintains that NATO's claim to represent a superior 'community of values' has been used to authorise the Alliance's exercise of military force against other, 'lesser', states. NATO has presented itself as an agent with a humanitarian purpose and almost untouchable moral values, untainted by politics, power and persuasion, attributes which have now been replaced by concepts such as morality, authority and force. In this sense, Behnke claims, NATO has conducted an epistemic war to secure its privileged moral status, fighting against the systemic anarchy of the international system and the inherent ambivalence and undecidability that necessitates (and even demands) the political designation of identity. By analysing the presentation of the Kosovo war on NATO's website, using images, narratives and videos, Behnke opens a new theoretical perspective on the visual/virtual side of the conflict.

In the last of three contributions on semiology, Mika Aaltola sees the events of 'Kosovo' as part of a long history of language games in relation to war, belonging and identity. He argues that the West has looked at the atrocities which have taken place in Kosovo as something fascinating and horrifying, events that by their exceptionality were testing and defying the moral order to be found 'at home'. Aaltola claims that it is at the periphery of the known world that the realm of marvels and wonders seems to begin. It is this world of 'magic' – the radically strange and bizarre – that is of interest to him in understanding what 'Kosovo' is all about. He argues that the periphery of (international) reality always has an inherently 'magical flavour' to it, mainly because it offers a template for understanding that element of global politics which deals with the art of producing and maintaining marvellous, striking and at times also surprising phenomena by ritualistic/performative methods.

For Aaltola, 'magic' implies a strong sense of forcefulness behind explicit words. In the case of 'Kosovo', the violence that was used was therefore not only the exercise of military force, but the (mainly rhetorical) sources of power themselves. During the Kosovo war, the spectrum of these 'divine' words (used by both sides) included 'freedom', 'liberty', 'hope', 'peace' and 'unity'. He argues that by their incessant repetition (with only marginal variation), these concepts have been sublimated and have acquired a powerful character reminiscent to the 'spirits' of medieval times. By drawing upon classical texts by Plato, Aristotle and Giordano Bruno, as well as by Wittgenstein, Aaltola makes it clear that 'Kosovo' has invoked a language game that has been essential to the creation of a legitimate political order in Europe.

This is the theme which Mikkel Vedby Rasmussen takes as the starting-point of his chapter, namely how the Kosovo war has informed us on the relevance of modish concepts such as identity and civilisation, and how the use of force can be instrumental in the construction of government in terms of civil society. Rasmussen links the public discourse on NATO's actions in

Kosovo with philosophical traditions such as the Scottish Enlightenment (and the writings of Adam Ferguson in particular), the work of Kant (and his conception of the pacific federation of liberal governments as the cosmopolitan purpose of history) and the recent debate on the role of civilisation introduced by Huntington. European politicians have frequently argued that NATO was using force against Belgrade to secure Western civilisation. But, using Foucault's notion of 'governmentality', Rasmussen suggests that we can better understand the notion of civilisation as the manifestation, rather than the explanation, of the West's construction of appropriate government in post-Cold War Europe. Therefore, NATO's war over Kosovo has illustrated the dominant belief in the West that the bombing campaign was *de facto* enforcing Kant's idea of a 'cosmopolitan system of general political security'.

As several other contributors to this book have argued, Rasmussen suggests that 'Kosovo' has helped to construct the nascent 'European identity', mainly in reference to the notion of cosmopolitan integration. Quoting the British Prime Minister Tony Blair, he suggests that the emerging definition of Western governmentality is captured under the heading of *globalisation*. This is illustrated by the fact that, during the war, the West could no longer define itself as a community of nation states, but that the very governmentality of the Western states had acquired a cosmopolitan nature. 'Kosovo' can therefore be considered in terms of the globalisation of domestic politics, an ongoing process that replaces the old rules of power politics with the novel convention of cosmopolitan community. To the West, both 'Kosovo' and the deepening of globalisation may be considered as proof that history is coming to an end and that a cosmopolitan system is emerging.

Globalisation is also a leitmotif for the final chapter in the volume, by Christoph Zürcher. He likens 'Kosovo' to Russia's war in Chechnya as two archetypal conflicts in a globalising world, involving three types of interdependent actors: nation states; identity groups; and international regimes. He explores the claims, rights and capacities of each of these actors. The similarities between the two conflicts range from their background – the institutional legacy of the socialist ethno-federations – to the new type of violence that likens Kosovo and Chechnya to many of the conflicts in Africa and Latin America in the 1990s. Zürcher quotes Mary Kaldor in calling this phenomenon 'new war', a type of organised violence that blurs the distinction between war, organised crime and large-scale violation of human rights. According to Zürcher, such conflicts share at least four common features: they involve identity groups and the state; the states involved are weak or virtually absent; the conflicts lead to the emergence of 'markets of violence' on which a few 'entrepreneurs of violence' engage in an economy of war, blurring the border between legal economy, organised crime and warfare; finally, these conflicts, and the actors, are embedded in transnational networks of images, resources and politics, linking the local wars with the globalising world.

Analysing the interventions by NATO in Kosovo and by Russia in Chechnya, Zürcher observes a remarkable lack of traditional *Realist* interests. Neither NATO nor the Russian federation went to war because its survival was actually threatened, or because of the relative gains to be made. Rather, both wars were supposed to cater to the expectations of domestic audiences, propping up the respective identity projects of 'European security' and 'Russian revival' under Putin, while at the same time 'sending the right message' to the opponent and to the world at large. As Zürcher succinctly puts it, 'winning these wars not only meant to outgun the enemy – it meant above all "selling" the conflict to the consumer, i.e. having the monopoly of interpretation'. This has been made all the easier by the blurred chain of command, and by what Zürcher describes as a lack of democratic control mechanisms in Russia as well as in NATO.

Into the unknown

Probably the most unfortunate similarity between Kosovo and Chechnya is that, although the high-intensity military phase is over, both conflicts are a long way from a lasting solution. In Kosovo, the tremendous war effort – at almost $1 billion a day, not to mention the $40 billion worth of damage to the Yugoslav economy – stands in stark contrast to the paltry results on the ground. Serb security forces have evacuated the province but remain essentially undefeated. Pictures on TV showed an orderly retreat of armed men, displaying Serb flags and V-signs. This army still has a potential use in oppressing dissent within Serbia or in waging an assault against Montenegro. Inside the province, the ending of the conflict has left Kosovo with what promises to be an indefinite and significant garrison of NATO-led troops, the KFOR; while the UN civil administration (UNMIK) is under-resourced. Though diplomats do not like to openly admit it, the 'international community' has established a strange kind of power-sharing arrangement in Kosovo between the UN and NATO, on the one hand, and the heirs of the KLA, including illegal guerrilla groups, on the other.[8]

Against the background of an expeditious return of over 800,000 Kosovar refugees – which should be rightly considered a major success of KFOR and UNMIK – the province has been cleansed of 230,000 Kosovo Serbs, Roma and other minorities (a UN estimate). Hundreds of Serbs are reported to have been killed or to be missing, while revenge attacks, ethnically motivated murders, bombings and arson have driven the vast majority of the remaining Kosovo Serbs and other non-Albanians in Kosovo into enclaves guarded by KFOR.

Of course, things have dramatically changed in Yugoslavia in the last months of the year 2000. Milosevic was defeated in the Yugoslav federal presidential elections in September; his refusal to accept the result led to the popular uprising on 5 October that brought to power the election winner Vojislav Kostunica. This was again followed by a landslide victory for Kostunica's Democratic Opposition of Serbia in the parliamentary elections on 24 December 2000, and the appointment of veteran opposition leader Zoran Djindjic as new prime minister. Milosevic has now left the political scene, and thus one of the NATO's main objectives ('We stay until Milosevic goes'), has been met. However, the irony of the situation is that finding a solution for Kosovo has become an even more complicated task, much more so than at the times of the straightforward 'the world v. Milosevic' stand-off. With a new and more legitimate government in Belgrade, Kosovo's hope for independence is weaker than in 1999–2000. No one seems to have a clear idea about Kosovo's future, and, like Bosnia, it is bound to remain a Western protectorate for many years to come. As Tim Judah has warned, in the long run, frustration over this contradiction could lead Kosovo Albanians into conflict with UNMIK and KFOR, if they come to be seen as occupiers.[9]

The insecurity in Kosovo is merely an episode in the wider security crisis faced by the West, the crisis of security referents, institutions and discourses. As happened so often in the 1990s, the invocation of the spirits of security, along with traditional mechanisms of power and Realist thinking, has proved ineffective. 'Kosovo' resists a solution purely in terms of security by a Foucauldian 'discipline and punish'. The question remains whether Europe will be able to learn from this failure and start to doubt the relevance of traditional thinking about security for the European project. 'Kosovo' has introduced new overtones into the European *Weltanschauung* and the ways in which 'Europe' asserts itself as an independent power discourse in a globalising world: increasingly diffident, looking for firm foundations in the conceptual void of the turn of the century.

Europe's security is back by popular demand, although it may just be an attempt to conceal the growing security gap and the increasing uncertainty of Europe in a world of late modernity. It is precisely the insecurity brought about by 'Kosovo' that makes military planners long for the strategic clarity of East–West confrontation; makes politicians yearn for the simplicity of Cold War zero-sum games; and makes academics repeat 'magic incantations' of security, relapsing into talk about the end of the Cold War twelve years after the fall of the Berlin Wall.

Peter van Ham and Sergei Medvedev
Garmisch-Partenkirchen, the Hague

Notes

The editors would like to acknowledge the George C. Marshall European Center for Security Studies for the opportunity to put this book together. The opinions expressed in this book are those of the individual authors, and all the usual caveats apply.

1 Robert Kaplan, 'The Coming Anarchy', *The Atlantic Monthly*, vol. 273, no. 2 (February 1994); Matthew Connelly and Paul Kennedy, 'Must it Be the West Against the Rest?', *The Atlantic Monthly*, vol. 274, no. 6 (December 1994); and Samuel Huntington, *The Clash of Civilizations and the Remaking of World Order* (New York, Simon & Schuster, 1996).
2 Ronnie Lipschutz (ed.), *On Security* (New York, Columbia University Press, 1995); Richard Wyn Jones, '"Travel Without Maps": Thinking About Security After the Cold War', in M. Jane Davis (ed.), *Security Issues in the Post-Cold War World* (Cheltenham, Edward Elgar, 1996); Keith Krause and Michael C. Williams (eds), *Critical Security Studies: Concepts and Cases* (Minneapolis, University of Minnesota Press, 1997).
3 Ronnie D. Lipschutz, 'The Insecurity Dilemma', in Lipschutz (ed.), *After Authority: War, Peace, and Global Politics in the 21st Century* (Albany, NY, State University of New York Press, 2000); Steve Smith, 'The Increasing Insecurity of Security Studies: Conceptualizing Security in the Last Twenty Years', *Contemporary Security Studies*, vol. 20, no. 3 (December 1999); and Bill McSweeney, 'The Meaning of Security', in McSweeney (ed.), *Security, Identity and Interests: A Sociology of International Relations* (Cambridge, Cambridge University Press, 1999).
4 Ken Booth, 'Security and Emancipation', *Review of International Studies*, vol. 17, no. 4 (October 1991), p. 321.
5 Jean Baudrillard, *La guerre du golfe n'a eu pas lieu* (Paris, Galilée, 1991).
6 CTHEORY interview with Paul Virilio, 'The Kosovo War Took Place in Orbital Space': Paul Virilio in conversation with John Armitage, available: http://www.ctheory.com/article/a89.html (accessed 28 December 2000).
7 Walter Benjamin, 'The Work of Art in the Age of Mechanical Reproduction', in Benjamin, *Illuminations. Essays and Reflections*, Edited and with an Introduction by Hannah Arendt (New York, Harcourt, Brace & World, 1968).
8 Jonathan Marcus, 'NATO's Incomplete Victory', BBC World News, 14 March 2000, available: http://newsvote.bbc.co.uk/hi/english/world/europe/newsid_671000/671432.stm (accessed 3 January 2001).
9 Tim Judah, 'Kosovo One Year On', BBC World News, 16 March 2000, available: http://news.bbc.co.uk/hi/english/world/europe/newsid_676000/676196.stm (accessed 3 January 2001).

1 Sergei Medvedev

Kosovo: a European *fin de siècle*

On a hot day in early June 1999, I was participating in a conference on European security in Berlin. The talk of the day was obviously the war in Kosovo. At the same time, at Unter den Linden, a few blocks away from the conference venue, a messy and joyful event was taking place – the Christopher Street Gay Parade, a prelude to the Berlin Love Parade held a couple of weeks later. As I left the conference hall and joined the crowds at Unter den Linden, it occurred to me that Kosovo and the Love Parade have a great deal in common. They are both carnivals of simulation and narcissism, glowing with flamboyant decadence. A techno-music parade and a military techno parade, a unified Berlin and a disintegrating Yugoslavia, rights of the gay minorities and rights of the Kosovo Albanians, are all signifying Europe at the end of modernity, a trademark European *fin de siècle*.

Kosovo between *Idealpolitik* and *Realpolitik*

Kosovo is the first war in history said to be fought in pursuit of principle, not interest. What is at stake is a radical revision of the moral (and, perhaps subsequently, the legal and institutional) basis of the international system. The Westphalian principle of sovereignty – originally created by monarchs to ensure their position against popular movements, and systematically (mis)used by rulers against their own subjects – is being eroded. In fact, the Weberian principle of the state as possessing a legitimate monopoly on violence seems to be failing. Sovereigns no longer hold this monopoly: it now belongs to the international community. The West has defined basic human rights as universal principles that transcend sovereignty.

In the new normative paradigm of *Idealpolitik*, sovereignty is no longer an ontological given, no longer inviolate. In some cases, it may be restricted (for example, Milosevic's token sovereignty over Kosovo or Saddam Hussein's over Iraqi skies); in other instances, it is simply revoked. As a result, sovereignty and governance arguably can be made more responsible and accountable, encouraging greater public participation and observance of human rights. (However, the question remains, responsible and accountable to whom? Is it to indigenous constituencies or to the moral authority of the West, which in some cases is external to domestic discourses?)

This seems well and good in theory, but the reality test has turned out to be much more confusing. To put it simply, interests of power have contaminated what looked like an attempt to execute normative *Idealpolitik*. In *The Twenty Years' Crisis*, E.H. Carr criticised the hypocrisy of the application of morality to the anarchy of international relations, and argued that it led to disaster by ignoring the real relations of power.[1] NATO's operation in Kosovo proved to be no different. *Idealpolitik* has been mixed (one could say compromised) with all sorts of traditional interests, strategies and mischief.

Interests at play in the conflict in Kosovo have been numerous and conspicuous. They have ranged from NATO's search for a post-Cold War role to play and for a clear enemy – to President Clinton's determination in his post-Lewinsky phase to show, *urbi et orbi*, that he was, after all, a morally responsible statesman. They have included the United States' wish to reassert its position in transatlantic relations in the wake of the Amsterdam Treaty and the arrival of the EMU; the desire of EU member states to prevent the influx of 1 million Kosovar refugees; the interests of the military industry and the interests of technology.

In the world of postmodern technology, hardware – computers, communication networks and state-of-the-art weapons – acquires a certain agency and generates interests of its own. Anton Chekhov said that if there is a shotgun hanging on the wall in the first act of a play, it is certain to fire in the third act. Likewise, B2 bombers, our civilisation's top guns, need to fly actual missions – and fly they did, taking off from a base in Missouri, refuelling over the Atlantic, bombing targets in Serbia, and returning to Missouri the same evening. As an American pilot declared in an interview, 'The great thing about flying a B2 is that you start in the morning, accomplish a mission, and you're back home in the evening, with your wife, your kids, and a cold beer.' 'Hi Dad!' – welcome to the world of postmodern warfare and computer morality. Never mind the cost-effectiveness of these B2 missions: they were all about media effectiveness and a display of technological supremacy. 'The medium is the message.' The B2 bomber as such is a message. It does not even have to do the dirty job of *dropping* bombs: all it has to do is fly, engaging in a communicative action rather than physical contact with the enemy. A fresh twist to the theme of technology as a relevant actor was added by defence analysts who suggested that some NATO members were using as many guided bombs and missiles containing chips with potential Y2K bugs as possible, rather than have them undergo a costly testing program.

The overwhelming interest in waging a war against Serbia, however, has belonged not to a specific agency, or a group, but to a certain power discourse – the post-Cold War dominant moral discourse of the 'West'. Claiming to have norms at its core (for example, NATO as a 'community of values'), this discourse is about expansion and power, much like the Christian white man's discourse that guided Western colonisation for the last 500 years under the banner of morality. After all, any ethical discourse is a discourse of power working by way of exclusion and retribution, by *surveiller et punir* (as per Michel Foucault), and the West's current moral assertiveness is little more than a new guise for a centuries-old tradition.

In seeking to establish itself as a norm for global conduct, the moral discourse of power is rather indiscriminate in respect of specific conflicts, instrumentalising them to its own advantage. In some cases, this discourse supports sovereignty (Kuwait); sometimes it supports human rights (Kosovo); and sometimes it supports neither (Turkish Kurds). The ethnic cleansing in Kosovo, real and terrible as it was, seems not to have been the overwhelming reason for Western intervention, but rather a convenient pretext. There was no contradiction between *Idealpolitik* and *Realpolitik* in Kosovo, as they were both manifestations of the same historical force, the same discourse of power. In Kosovo, it was principle exercised as power, and power disguised as principle.

Kosovo between ethnic cleansing and allied bombing

One of the great paradoxes of the war in Kosovo was that it was not just one campaign but two: there was the ethnic cleansing campaign in Kosovo and the allied bombing campaign against targets in Kosovo and all over Serbia. At times it seemed that these campaigns were taking place in separate dimensions. This was made particularly evident in daily television news reports. First, there would be a report on the arrival of thousands of new refugees at the Kosovo–Albania (or Macedonia or Montenegro) border. A correspondent in all-weather gear would be positioned before a backdrop reminiscent of scenes from *Schindler's List*: unending columns of refugees slowly walking along railway tracks. This would be followed by a smartly dressed correspondent at NATO headquarters in Brussels, going live to NATO's daily briefing, where an ingratiating and smiling Jamie Shea would provide the numbers of sorties flown and targets hit, and would assure us of the ever-increasing success of the bombing campaign. Sometimes, pictures from Serbian television would be included, showing destroyed bridges, factories and residential quarters, as well as people wandering amid the debris. (In Russia, the images were served in reverse order: first, the destruction in Serbia and then Kosovar refugees.)

It seemed that each campaign was following its own course. Serb troops were completing the ethnic cleansing of towns and villages in Kosovo, and

NATO aircraft were completing the orderly and meticulous destruction of Serbia's infrastructure. NATO was running short of targets and, at times, hitting the same site two or three times; meanwhile, it did almost nothing on the ground to stop the ethnic cleansing. At best, one can say that the two campaigns were carried out relatively independently of each other. At worst, one can argue, as did *The Economist*, that

> this was a war to stop ethnic cleansing, but the main effect was to intensify it. The bombing campaign accelerated the killing – no more than 2,000–3,000 people had died in the province before the bombing began, quite a few at the hands of Kosovar guerrillas – and it accelerated the emptying of the population at large. In humanitarian terms, the Kosovo campaign turned into a disaster.[2]

Indeed, it turned out to be a vicious circle and a self-propelled enterprise: NATO bombs accelerated ethnic cleansing, and the stronger outflow of refugees (escaping not only from Serb atrocities but from NATO bombs) prompted still more bombing. The entire population of Kosovo and civilians in cities all over Serbia became NATO's hostages and bargaining chips in a geopolitical game. Rather than helping the refugees, NATO seemed to be exploiting them in its narcissistic display of military power. In the seventy-nine days of the air campaign, the Alliance failed to pursue larger goals such as toppling Milosevic's regime, installing a new and more just order in the Balkans, or sending a strong message to the rest of the world. Later, as forensic evidence of the genocide in Kosovo was recovered, the news was met with horror in Western capitals, but also with a kind of relief, signalling the provision of retrospective moral justification for the bombing.

The first war in history said to be fought on moral grounds has been tainted by hypocrisy. It is hard to reconcile self-appointed 'normative politics' with the embracing of an ally like the Kosovo Liberation Army (KLA), an organisation with a well-documented history of terrorism, drug trafficking and ethnic cleansing. It is difficult to reconcile it with the use of cluster bombs that proved to be 'surgical' in the most direct sense of the word, that is, resulting in amputations. Likewise, it is hard to reconcile calls to abolish the death penalty (as the Council of Europe has urged of its member states) with the killing and punishing of innocent civilians for crimes committed by their leaders, which in effect was Europe's stance during the course of NATO's attacks. Even if one admits that the war in Kosovo had moral foundations, it was the morality of an action movie and a computer game, the morality of Western messianism and of 'chasing monsters' (Milosevic as the Fidel Castro of Europe), the Manichean morality of good–evil, inside–outside, us–them.

It is the binary mapping of the conflict in Kosovo (in which, for instance, an ambiguous force like the KLA fell into the 'us' category as Western journalists glorified these guerrillas on their mountain trails, while Russia, identified as a 'Serb ally', was relegated to the 'them' camp) that leads one to suggest that Europe was not simply looking to establish morality and justice, but rather to institute its own identity represented as morality. It was not that some pre-established European norms have compelled Europe to intervene in Kosovo, but the converse: the intervention in Kosovo was a means by which Europe could re-invent itself and imagine itself as a moral fortress. Europe needed Kosovo for the construction of its own identity and for the consolidation of the European project on a higher moral ground.

Kosovo between (East)-modernity[3] and postmodernity

To be fair, there was hesitation and confusion in Europe in reaction to the bombing. There was a certain degree of objectivity and balance in media reporting, and some astonishment at 'what we are doing'. But there was no audible protest. As cluster bombs were being dropped on the residential quarters of Serbian cities and 'collateral damage' was tolerated, Europe asserted its new identity. This was accompanied by a stunning 'silence of the lambs', the peace movements, the anti-war generation of the 1960s and 1970s, and of former NATO critics like the German Greens[4] who hastily developed their version of the concept of a 'just war'. It looked as if Europe had re-discovered atavisms of modernity, with essentialist narratives of identity, security, heroic politics and outright militarism. Wasn't it all about modernity, the war in Kosovo?

At first glance, it seems that 'Kosovo' was an outburst of modernity. Modern history was returning with a vengeance, in particular the Balkan history, with its post-Ottoman, post-Habsburg and post-Tito potential for conflict. The shadow of Kosovo Pole[5] suddenly loomed large over Europe, along with a number of other unresolved territorial disputes, unsettled borders and ethnic rivalries in East-Central and South-Eastern Europe. The conflict over Kosovo demonstrated that the east had not yet completed the tasks of modernity, that is, forming nation states, and defining borders. In the age of globalisation and European integration, it has turned out that pockets of violent modern nationhood still exist.

Indeed, the Balkans are often interpreted as the reserve of the archaic, reminding one of Jean Baudrillard's piece about a Stone Age tribe discovered in Papua New Guinea. As the story goes, the international community decides to completely isolate the tribe in order to 'preserve' its unique biosphere and to simulate the undiscovered. Likewise, the West could theoretically preserve the 'unique multi-cultural environment of the Balkans' as a UNESCO Heritage Site, a Jurassic Park of ethnic strife and territorial disputes.

On the other hand, the West, too, seems to have relapsed into modernity, making use of war and power politics, and waving national flags. British defence analysts on Sky News would jealously count the number of attack sorties flown by the Royal Air Force during the air campaign. As Maja Zehfuss mentions in chapter 6, the German press would proudly report that the German Tornadoes 'were flying in pole position'.

It would be too simplistic, however, to read the war in Kosovo as a sudden recurrence of modernity, nationalism and military security in late twentieth-century Europe. To begin with, Serbian, Albanian and other nationalisms are staged in a postmodern setting; that is, this is nationalism as a response to globalisation, integration and the emergence of transnational diasporas. Each of the nationalist movements in the region is surprisingly global, positioning itself in relation to the 'West', that is, the EU, NATO and the United States, but also in respect of Russia (as occasionally does Serbia). Ethnic leaders are vying for the West's attention, and their strategies are addressed to the 'international community' as well as to their direct opponents and domestic constituencies. That is to say, someone like Milosevic is hardly an archaic nationalist, obsessed with ethnicity, and intent on defying the West. On the contrary, he has proved to be a rather pragmatic politician, playing the strategy of a regulated conflict with the West, indeed using the West for the purpose of consolidating his own power. Provoking NATO's attack may have been Milosevic's strategic miscalculation, yet there is no denying that he had been playing with the global community as much as with Serbs' archaic instincts. Likewise, appeals to the world and international PR have become a major activity for the KLA and the Kosovar leaders.

Second, the war in Kosovo has marked a major infringement on the modern principle of sovereignty as the ultimate legitimate monopoly on violence. Milosevic was a classic sovereign: until the November 2000 revolution in Belgrade he was legitimate (elected), and he used various forms of violence against his Serbian and Albanian subjects. It was precisely this monopoly that was being challenged by the 'international community'. In addition, the West was repeatedly questioning the sovereign political choice of the Serbian nation, refusing aid to Serbia while Milosevic was in office. In a sense, one can call this limitation of sovereignty a 'humanitarian Monroe doctrine' (or a 'Brezhnev doctrine').

It is interesting, however, that the war in Kosovo has also infringed on the sovereignty of Western nations. It subjected their alleged 'national interests' to supranational purposes (NATO's search for action and leadership, preserving the transatlantic relationship and also attempting to shape Europe's security and defence identity and common foreign and security policy, etc.) and to transnational technologies. The leading actors in the war were not states (with the possible exception of the US, the last surviving nation state), but institutions. The story of the war in Kosovo has taken place not in the *realpolitisches* field of traditional state interests, but in the highly virtual institutional field of 'European security'.

Third, this simulated field features a new concept of agency that roughly corresponds to what the poststructuralist literary critics, following Roland

Barthes, call 'the death of the author'. The story of Kosovo had no author: it was written by impersonal forces like 'Europe', or the 'West', or the 'community of values', or the 'new world order'. Discourses have no face or personality, and war in Kosovo has been written by a collective body of the West, emerging in an electrified field of symbolic exchange and simulation. A remarkable thing about the war in Kosovo was that it materialised 'out of the thin air' of late modernity. It has had no author or mastermind behind it (even though interests have been involved), and NATO was no more than an instrument, an executor, a performer. In this way, the war in Kosovo has resembled Russia's war in Chechnya, especially its first episode in 1994–96. It was not known who made the decision and gave orders to start it, while the roles of President Yeltsin, the Security Council and the Ministry of Defence still remain unclear.[6]

The missing agency concept represented in the conflict in Kosovo goes some way in explaining NATO's spectacular planning failures and the general *ad hoc* and *ad libitum* mode of operation. When, early in the air campaign, it became clear that NATO had failed to deflect Milosevic from his course of ethnic cleansing, it seemed that the Allies had no plan whatsoever except to continue bombing with reckless abandon, as though driven by Napoleon's motto *On s'engage et puis on voit*. Given the improvisational nature of the bombing, and alarmed at the evident inefficacy of air strikes, NATO began to look for alternative mechanisms of conflict management and/or retrospective justification of its own action. It looked to the players it should have involved from the outset: the OSCE, the United Nations, the International Criminal Tribunal for the former Yugoslavia (the Hague Tribunal), and finally the EU and Russia.

Indeed, the Chernomyrdin–Ahtisaari mission virtually saved NATO, which by late May 1999 seemed hopelessly stuck in the Kosovo quagmire, unable to stop bombing, on the one hand, and unwilling to employ ground forces, on the other. Had a political solution not been mediated in early June 1999, it is hard to imagine the further course of events, especially given that the Allies, according to some reports, could have run short of munitions within the next month. The West's impersonal war machine had to turn for help to personal-style politics from the European peripheries (Finland and Russia); a marginal discourse was needed to save the grand narrative of the new world order.

Fourth, on the subject of de-personalised actors, one cannot fail to notice the immense role played by the mass media in the war in Kosovo. Just as in the Gulf War, this conflict was produced, fought and consummated in the field of televised images; that is, it was virtualised and simulated to a high degree. (Compare this with Jean Baudrillard's provocative statement that 'the Gulf War did not take place';[7] see also Andreas Behnke's and Iver Neumann's chapters in this volume). In a darkly ironic coincidence, shortly before the start of the air campaign, the movie *Wag the Dog* was released, featuring some imaginary – simulated – 'Albanians'. The media is the tail wagging the dog of world politics, or rather the media has become *the* dog, waiting, in Pavlovian spasms, for more food, like Kuwait or Kosovo or Chechnya, that it can digest and communicate in a politically relevant and melodramatic manner.

The mass media in question are total and global. Reports may be biased and distorted, but media as such do not belong to either side in the conflict. (For example, in 1994–96, the Russian media sided almost entirely with the Chechens, angering the Russian generals.) In arguing that Serb TV should be exempt from bombing, CNN was much more likely driven by hunger for information than by humanitarian concerns or professional solidarity.

Indeed, the media dominated the war in Kosovo. B-52 bombers joined the dissident Belgrade radio B92 as mass media devices. State-of-the-art military technology has become a department of the mass media. An analogy can be made with today's top racing cars that carry on-board cameras, and rather than mere racing their function becomes *showing* the race. (In this sense, it is preferable that a car sometimes crashes, providing a unique view from the cockpit, to be replayed in slow motion). By the same token, today's bombs and missiles with inbuilt cameras are designed to destroy but also to *show*, allowing the viewers to savour the entertaining process of destruction. The purpose of the guided missile that hit the bridge in Novi Sad was primarily communicative, in other words, it was (a) 'to send a message' to Milosevic and the world and (b) to televise the final approach of the missile to the target, followed by an eloquent blackout. The bombing of the Novi Sad bridge turned into a media spectacle, drawing hundreds of millions of viewers worldwide. Maybe in the future broadcasting companies will sponsor missiles and bombs with on-board cameras as they now sponsor Formula 1 cars.[8]

Since most contemporary wars are positioned in a global context, the art of 'sending messages' (not only to the enemy but to the world at large) plays an ever-increasing role in the conduct of war, sometimes eclipsing operational efficiency. In earlier times, it was mostly military parades that functioned as PR, but now war itself, like NATO's operation in Kosovo, can be turned into a PR campaign. Apparently, one of the reasons for starting the bombing in late March 1999 was the illusion of an easy victory – a victory that would fit nicely with the festivities surrounding NATO's fiftieth anniversary in April of that year. Witness Javier Solana's repeated pronouncements that the campaign would be over by the time of the Washington summit – NATO's birthday present to itself.

What likened NATO's air strikes to a PR campaign was the goal of zero casualties among the Allies, a figure which was quite normal for a parade (unless an unfortunate onlooker falls under a tank), but not in a war. This obsession with safety revealed a paradoxical aspect of the postmodern mind. On the one hand, Western man is ready, indeed willing, to wage wars, releasing his archaic instincts. But, on the other hand, his willingness to sacrifice himself has been irretrievably lost through forces of hedonism, consumerism and atheistic humanism. That was the main problem of the war in Kosovo, a campaign that the West wanted to fight wearing gloves. (Or, as a feminist critic of US power like Cynthia Weber might have suggested, wearing a condom.)[9] The reluctance to endanger 'our boys' culminated in an outspoken story about Apache helicopters. The twenty-four battlefield helicopters were heralded as ultimate weapons able to hunt down Serb tanks in Kosovo. It took a month to prepare their arrival, then they were flown into Albania with much pomp, but they never got off the ground for fear that they would have to fly too low, becoming vulnerable to anti-aircraft fire. The Apaches stood idle while the Serbs were completing the ethnic cleansing.

Kosovo was a truly postmodern war, an Oscar-winning action movie, a new 3D computer game where one could employ emotion and skill, and even be morally rewarded for defeating the evil – without risking one's life. However, there was blood behind the screens. There is a story by Jorge Luis Borges in which two kings play chess on a hilltop; at the bottom of the hill, two armies are fighting in accordance with the moves on the chessboard. One king gains the upper hand, and so does one of the armies. As the winning player declares checkmate, the other falls dead.

Postmodernism is an entertaining game on a computer screen, or on the chessboard, but, to our sheer confusion, there happen to be real people somewhere underneath. The more virtual a game becomes for 'us', the harder it turns out for 'them'. The safer an American pilot's flight in the high-tech skies over Kosovo, the bloodier is the mess on the ground (both from bombs and ethnic cleansing). The bigger the speculative flows on global financial markets, trading in virtuality, the more bitter are conditions for the 'real' economy in the Third World. Calls for curing the injustices brought on by global interdependence, such as making NATO answerable to the UN, or imposing the 1 per cent 'Tobin tax'[10] on global speculative transactions (see chapter 5, by Heikki Patomäki), will hardly change the fundamentally post-moral nature of the new world order.

Russia between *derzhavnost'* and the dollar

The war in Kosovo can be seen as the playing out of the competition between the two most publicised essays on international affairs of the last decade, Francis Fukuyama's *End of History* and Samuel Huntington's *Clash of Civilizations*. The prize in the contest was Russia. Had Russia chosen to join its Slavic/Orthodox brethren in Serbia in defying the West, Huntington would have prevailed. Had Russia, on the contrary, acquiesced with the military power, moral arguments and, most importantly, economic instruments of the West, the title would have gone to Fukuyama.

In the first round, it seemed that Huntington was pulling ahead. The reaction in Russia to the start of the NATO air campaign was overwhelming and unanimous. Deep political divisions and partisanship were put aside in the protest against NATO and the show of solidarity with the Serbs. The West had given Russia eloquent and powerful evidence of the fact that she had lost the Cold War. In fact, the bombing helped to consolidate Russia's political elite and a large part of the population in the anti-Western camp, playing directly into the hands of the communists and the nationalists.[11]

Psychologically, there was a meaningful difference between this situation and Russia's former geopolitical losses. Withdrawal from Eastern Europe and the reunification of Germany were seen as a unilateral gesture of goodwill on Russia's part – were they not? NATO's expansion, for all its alleged strategic damage for Russia, was nevertheless negotiated with Moscow, and received Russia's reluctant consent (crowned by the Russia–NATO Founding Act). But here, for the first time in the post-Cold War decade, something had been accomplished without any regard for Russia.

This was a revelation. The taboo of openly talking about Russia's defeat was lifted, with some profound psychotherapeutic effects. What followed was a two-week carnival of national ambition. It was a ritual exorcism, complete with spontaneous mass demonstrations at the US Embassy in Moscow, the sign-up of volunteers for combat in Serbia, threats of supplying arms to Milosevic and of re-targeting Russia's nuclear missiles, and a sharp increase in the domestic role of the military. This emotional outburst proved once again, as did the 1993 and 1995 parliamentary elections, that post-Cold War post-traumatic syndrome runs deep in the national consciousness. However, once the taboo subject of Russia's defeat was raised, resentment and aggression were reified in a symbolic verbal manner (popular demonstrations, declarations in the State Duma, etc.), and, thus, somewhat mitigated and healed.

Indeed, the steam of the Russian nationalist engine all went into the whistle. By mid-April 1999, nationalist fever had diminished. Admitting to the impossibility of opposing the West or halting NATO's bombing, Russia took on a rather sensible wait-and-see position, criticising NATO's action, while gradually resuming cooperation with the West along financial lines.

Meanwhile, important domestic shifts were taking place. Prime Minister Yevgeni Primakov's heavy-handed mediation in the conflict in Kosovo gave way to the more flexible and Western-minded efforts of former Prime Minister Viktor Chernomyrdin. Later, Primakov's fall from grace was confirmed as President Yeltsin sacked his communist-dominated government and Sergei Stepashin was appointed as Primakov's replacement. The shaping of the new government and its economic programme was closely coordinated with international financial institutions.

Consequently, large-scale cooperation between Russia and these institutions resumed for the first time since the financial crisis of August 1998.

Finally, President Yeltsin emerged out of the political shadow, scoring two major victories over the communist Duma: first, he defeated attempts to impeach him; second, he succeeded in having his selection for the office of prime minister, Sergei Stepashin, approved at the first attempt. The economy, thought moribund, started showing signs of revival: the rouble was strengthening, and the stock market was recovering from the shock of August 1998. Suddenly, against all odds, Russia embarked upon a 'liberal spring'.

In other words, just as Russia's political system had managed to absorb the internal shock of the August 1998 financial crisis, so it handled the external impact of the 1999 Kosovo crisis fairly well. Moreover, there had been no long-term political repercussions on the domestic scene. The consequences for Russian foreign and security policy, however, were less salubrious. Generally, in the last seven to eight years, ever since the Andrei Kozyrev line based on liberal internationalism and the abandoning of 'national interests' faded away, Russian foreign policy has oscillated between minimalist cooperation with the West and damage limitation. The Kosovo crisis once again sent Russian foreign policy into a damage limitation mode, undermining mutual trust and the fragile mechanisms of cooperation with NATO. The West's war in Kosovo unravelled the political and psychological achievement of the 1997 Paris Declaration and the NATO–Russia Founding Act. From appeasing Russia the West turned to sidelining Russia – a policy that was consistent with Russia's dwindling economic and diplomatic power, but one that sounded hardly encouraging to the country's elite.

Apart from dealing a blow to national pride, the Kosovo crisis showed that Russia remained vitally dependent on the new world order's economic environment, as represented by IMF loans, Western markets for Russian oil and gas, and a vested interest on the part of the country's elite and an increasing number of ordinary citizens in economic and political openness. Several polls conducted by Russian newspapers among anti-NATO demonstrators near the US embassy in Moscow showed that people were ready to burn American flags, but would never agree to give up the free circulation of US dollars, or the opportunity to travel to the West. Respondents also did not seem willing to support higher military outlays in the Russian budget.

The 1999 war in Kosovo was of symbolic significance to Russia. Like the August 1998 financial crash in Russia, induced by a crisis in the emerging markets and a fall in world oil prices, it clearly showed the limited role of the Russian State with regard to transnational impacts, be it NATO or the global financial markets. The 1998 crisis highlighted Russia's economic dependence, just as the 1999 Kosovo war showed Russia's geopolitical predicament. Or, put otherwise, the 1998 crisis demonstrated that Russia is irresistibly drawn into the world of geo-economics, and 'Kosovo' illustrated that Russia is invariably ejected from the world of geopolitics. Taken together, these developments mapped Russia's major drift from geopolitics to geo-economics, a move which is obviously far from complete but has already progressed far enough to keep Russia anchored in a cooperative framework at the margin of Western institutions and to guarantee against a radical revision of Russia's foreign and security policy.[12]

The crisis in Kosovo has thus had a dual effect on Russia. It created some immediate damage to Russia's relationship with the West. A more important fact, however, was that Russia proved not to be inclined to neo-imperialist temptations, and remained unlikely to slide into isolationism and confrontation with the West even under the most adverse circumstances. Russia was disturbed but not displaced. An ailing giant had been certainly irritated, but did not care to move.

Other added value appeared in the field of information and international PR. The geopolitical accident in Kosovo suddenly put Russia in the limelight. A lonely Russian reconnaissance boat travelling (at a top speed of 12 knots) into the Adriatic; Viktor Chernomyrdin's shuttle diplomacy; the Russian paratroopers' surprise spurt to Pristina airport ahead of NATO troops as KFOR was entering Kosovo in June 1999 – all of these made international headlines. Russia suddenly became 'interesting'.

After the West's initial neglect, all of a sudden the West began looking for ways to involve Russia in crisis management. Semi-isolated, Russia unexpectedly started winning points on the diplomatic front. The crisis in Kosovo created a common information field, a common context within which the dialogue with the West resumed. Indeed, one can see similarities with the debates on NATO's expansion, which also gave Russia a voice and a place at the negotiating table of European security for a good four years (1993–97). Both NATO's expansion and the war in Kosovo gave Russia an interface with the West, providing a forum where Russia could claim its national interests, which otherwise would not even be heard. In both cases, Russia seemed to have come out a loser, but these perceived losses have raised the level of global awareness about Russia, its problems and its residual strengths. One is reminded of a daily ritual phrase, a magical incantation, repeated by US and NATO leaders: 'Our goal is to keep Russia involved.' In the world ruled by mass media, it is perceptions and images that count, not the actual territorial/strategic gains or losses. In both cases, Russia's role (often hypothetical and imagined) was emphasised by the global media, evoking distant memories of its lost glory, and this partly compensated for perceived geopolitical damages.

So what was the outcome of the Huntington–Fukuyama duel? In general, Huntington's argument was not fully relevant in Kosovo, where one could see a clash of ambitions and a collision of destructive policies rather than a genuine clash of civilisations. Everyone, including NATO and the Serbs, Russia and China, played by the rules of the global civilisation. National positions seemed to make little difference. 'Kosovo' has demonstrated that Russia is drifting away from the good old world of 'grand chessboards'. After withdrawal from Afghanistan and NATO's expansion, after Chechnya and Kosovo, any talk of Russia's 'national interests' and 'grand strategies' serve mainly to make newspaper headlines and to increase the heartbeat of the realist die-hards, rather than to position Russia in the twenty-first century. Russia is being 'seduced' (in the Baudrillardian sense) rather than coerced into the global civilisation, just as are its neighbour, China, and much of the Arab world. The new world order (NWO) is a hegemony working mostly by means of seduction, promoting brands like NATO, Boeing, CNN, democracy, IMF, human rights, the Euro, Marlboro, etc. Above all, coercive actions like the one in Kosovo are needed to enhance brand recognition.

Fukuyama did not score a clear-cut victory in Kosovo either. His light-hearted neo-liberal utopia had been devised with a good deal of irony, but in Kosovo the NWO arrived in an unseemly and sinister manner. This was not the history ending 'with a whimper', but rather the re-writing of history with all its pitfalls, enmities and blood.

Behold, the new world order cometh

In 1970, the Polish director Andrzej Wajda made a film titled *Landscape After the Battle*, which won him wide international acclaim. It is a love story set in a concentration camp in Poland in late 1944, abandoned by the German troops and taken over by the allies. It begins on a euphoric note, showing prisoners in their striped robes pouring out of the barracks into the fresh snow. However, the long-awaited liberation does not bring freedom. Days go by, and as people are still kept inside the camp, the occupation authorities install a new repressive order, using the prisoners as bargaining chips in the geopolitical game of late Second World War. This is a film about the absurdity of heroic myths, a story of both hope and disillusionment, and of the anguish and torment that remain the lot of individuals under any rule.

The landscape after the battle in Kosovo is murky and dubious. Together with the return of over 800,000 ethnic Albanian refugees, almost 250,000 Serbs, Roma and others have been ethnically cleansed, or were forced to flee.[13] The UN civil administration UNMIK and NATO's KFOR cannot guard the monopoly on violence, and acts of ethnic revenge against local Serbs are occurring on a regular basis, with several hundred reported killed or missing. Various offsprings of the KLA, from militias to guerrilla groups to criminal bands, are roaming free in the province.[14] The advent of a new democratic leadership in Belgrade following the popular uprising in October 2000, and two rounds of elections in September–December 2000, have delayed the Kosovo solution even further. Ironically, the continuing rule of Milosevic had been Kosovo's best hope for independence, as the international community regarded his claim to Kosovo as illegitimate. Now, however,

Serbia is run by Vojislav Kostunica and Zoran Djindjic, legitimate leaders recognised by the West. Both are equally unwilling to let Kosovo go; and this time the West will have to give them a say in Kosovo's affairs. It is characteristic that the Kosovo Albanian leaders met this change of the guard in Belgrade with suspicion. Now, as the dream of independence is virtually slipping from their hands, in a twist unimaginable only a year ago, the next stage of the conflict could take place between the Kosovo Albanians and KFOR.[15] The future of Kosovo suddenly looks more uncertain than it was following the end of NATO's air war.

On the military side, one of the biggest bombing campaigns in history has proven far from effective. For seventy-nine days a relatively small Yugoslav contingent with weapons from the 1960s and 1970s held its own against the mightiest military machine in the world and retained its capacity to respond with anti-aircraft fire – a remarkable achievement. Until the last two weeks of the war, when the Kosovar guerrillas' *kamikaze* tactics flushed the Serbs' armour into the open and rendered it vulnerable to NATO strikes, the infamous Serb army had escaped serious injury.[16] Even though Milosevic is now toppled, Serbian resilience and NATO's incapacity to diminish it and halt the ethnic cleansing during the seventy-nine-day war have sent all kinds of wrong signals around the globe.

NATO's decision to attack was a mistake from the beginning. Once the bombing had started, the Alliance proved surprisingly obdurate and inflexible, as well as hesitant and indecisive. Despite mounting evidence of the ineffectiveness of the bombing, loss of civilian lives, and the acceleration of ethnic cleansing, NATO did not modify its strategy and opt for a wiser course, a halt to the bombing or a riskier ground operation. This lack of flexibility and political will is quite understandable, given that NATO is an alliance of nineteen nations ruled by consensus and the politicians,[17] not by orders and the military; but it is nevertheless damaging to the Alliance's credibility.

In purely technical terms, the bombing campaign has not opened a new chapter in the history of warfare, as some were claiming. It has once again demonstrated that air power alone cannot produce victory. Military supremacy and high-tech weaponry provide no substitute for political solutions; on the contrary, they tend to increase tensions and reduce the likelihood of a lasting settlement. NATO's brand of military power may still be relevant in 'traditional' inter-state wars and high-intensity conflicts; however, most future conflicts will be of medium to low intensity, involving great numbers of civilians, just as in Kosovo or in Algiers. Judging by the case of Kosovo, NATO is ill-equipped to handle such contingencies.

The 'message' which the Kosovo war sent to potential perpetrators and troublemakers around the world has been mixed. NATO has yet to prove that it has the skills, tools and political will to handle any regional conflict effectively. The absence of such proof is a truly dangerous development, with consequences reaching far beyond the Balkans. Should similar flare-ups occur simultaneously in places like Tibet, the Caucasus, Kurdistan and Eritrea, is NATO going to intervene, and, if it is, has it shown the capacity to do so rapidly and efficiently? And if NATO does not intervene, will it appear as a credible remote deterrent? While answers to these questions remain at best in the balance, NATO's operation in Kosovo served as a background (and arguably a pretext) for the start of Russia's second war in Chechnya and for a regional conflict in Kashmir – involving two nuclear powers, India and Pakistan. In general, NATO's new role of self-appointed arbiter in regional conflicts is likely to increase reliance on nuclear weapons around the globe. The post-Kosovo world is not necessarily a safer place.

Nor does NATO's recourse to moral argument as being superior to the norms that govern international law make for a safer world. Laws, like sovereignty, may be outdated, but they at least tend to be inviolate, providing for stability in the system. On the contrary, norms are always subject to interpretation. Should Russia (or, hypothetically, the CIS Tashkent Treaty on Collective Security) now decide that human rights are being violated in Tajikistan, will the West endorse Russian intervention? Or what if Iran resumes its war with Iraq on the grounds that Saddam Hussein has violated Islamic norms?

What happens next? Fidel Castro, at the EU–Latin American summit in June 1999, cited the possibility of a NATO intervention in Colombia's cocaine provinces on behalf of the 'civilized world'. Meanwhile, protesters in East Timor in 1999, prior to the entry of Australian-led peacekeepers, were carrying slogans inviting NATO to their protection. Should the Alliance have become involved? Or will NATO engage only on specific occasions that (a) provide good PR feedback; (b) have no nuclear weapons and (c) run no risk of Alliance casualties?

The problem here is not NATO. The Alliance is not driven by an individual's malicious will, nor does it, by itself, seek world domination. NATO, and the nations that comprise it, is a mere instrument of a rising discourse that is somewhat awkwardly called the new world order (inadvertently paraphrasing the 'brave new world'). The post-sovereign, post-Westphalian, world need not be endowed with greater pluralism, freedom of choice and multi-culturalism. Old national totalities are giving way to transnational ones; discourses of power are changing location but not the mode of operation. Or, rather, the discourse of power has become a-local (global) and a-topic (Utopian). It is neither good nor bad: it is the 'thin air' air of postmodernity, and it is not in our power to change the atmosphere.

However, one is always left with an option of deconstructing the new discourse of power by looking into its innate binary nature. In the story of Kosovo, the dichotomy imposed on the audience by the mass media was the false choice between the clear and present evil of Milosevic (and everything that comes with him, like violent nationalism and ethnic cleansing) and the seemingly unavoidable use of military force by NATO (complete with 'collateral damage'), a choice between ethnic cleansing and NATO bombing. Apart from the fact that a 'third way' can often be envisaged (for example, an earnest search for a political solution or the use of economic mechanisms of 'seduction', whereby instead of bombing the enemy into submission one can buy him into agreement by allocating just a fraction of the funds spent on waging war), this dichotomy is clearly simulated. It is produced and communicated within the same binary opposition, making the recipient choose between 'us' and 'them', 'inside' and 'outside', 'Europe' and 'anarchy'.

Each side in this dichotomy has power as a goal and violence as its means. But while Milosevic's violence was ruthless and straightforward, the use of power by the West has been disguised as principle. A violence of a declining, archaic kind that has no moral pretence is opposed by a violence of the future, endowed with most of the world's resources and moral authority. Choosing between them is like choosing between the atrocities of Dachau and the bombing of Dresden, between Auschwitz and Hiroshima. Are we forever confined to this binarity, to the vicious circle of violence?

The 'new' discourse on European security has so far failed to come up with an answer. Indeed, the very notion of 'security' seems to have forever chained Europe to modernity, the world of Yalta, Versailles and Kosovo Pole, to the world of power, border and the Wall. One of the greater deficits of the European project is not the lack of political resolve, or the lack of its own peacekeeping force. It is the lack of imagination, as Europe has proved to be unable to envision its own identity beyond the narrow confines of security, systemic thinking and the friend–foe paradigm. Forget the Age of the Internet: European security is still in the Age of the Brick, erecting walls and destroying bridges, disciplining and punishing in a Foucauldian prison.

Notes

This chapter originally appeared online in CTHEORY, available: http://www.ctheory.com/a74.html (accessed 5 January 2001). It draws on discussions with a group from the Osteuropa-Institut of the Free University of Berlin (Klaus Segbers, Christoph Zürcher, Graham Stack and Simone Schwanitz). Special thanks to Tuomas Forsberg and Henrikki Heikka for a lively email exchange on the problem of Kosovo.

1 E.H. Carr, *The Twenty Years' Crisis, 1919–1939: An Introduction to the Study of International Relations* (London, Macmillan, 1981 [1946]).
2 'Messy War, Messy Peace', *The Economist*, 12 June 1999.
3 The term *Ostmoderne* was first used in Christoph Zürcher, *Aus der Ostmoderne in die Postmoderne. Zum Wandel in der Früheren Sowjetunion* (Berlin, Arbeitspapiere des Osteuropa-Instituts der FU Berlin, 1998).
4 See chapter 6, by Maja Zehfuss.

5 On 28 June 1389, Serb Tsar Lazar chose to lead the Serbs into battle against hopeless odds at the Field of Blackbirds in Kosovo rather than capitulate to the Turks. Since then, Kosovo Pole has become one of the foremost symbols of Serb history and martyrdom, and a territorial anchor of national identity.
6 For comparisons between the wars in Kosovo and in Chechnya, see chapter 10, by Christoph Zürcher.
7 Jean Baudrillard, *La guerre du golfe n'a pas eu lieu* (Paris, Galilée, 1991).
8 A step in this direction was made during the Gulf War when CNN reportedly insisted in certain cases that the bombing was carried out at night. This looked more spectacular on TV, although it made the bombing less precise, increased collateral damage and carried greater risk for the US military personnel.
9 Cynthia Weber, *Faking It: US Hegemony in a 'Post-Phallic' Era* (Minneapolis, University of Minnesota Press, 1999).
10 Heikki Patomäki, 'The Tobin Tax: A New Phase in the Politics of Globalisation?', *Theory, Culture & Society*, vol. 17, no. 4 (August 2000); and Heikki Patomäki, *Democratizing Globalization. The Leverage of the Tobin Tax* (London, Zed Books, 2001).
11 According to figures cited by Viktor Chernomyrdin, the Russian envoy to the Kosovo talks in May and June 1999, before the NATO attack 57 per cent of Russian respondents had a positive attitude towards the United States, and 28 per cent a negative one. In early May 1999, the figures were 14 per cent positive and 73 per cent negative (Viktor Chernomyrdin, 'Impossible to Talk Peace with Bombs Falling', *Washington Post*, 27 May 1999).
12 See Sergei Medvedev, *Russia's Futures: Implications for the EU, the North and the Baltic Region* (Helsinki, UPI and Berlin, IEP, 2000), p. 19.
13 Tim Judah, 'Kosovo One Year On', BBC World News, 16 March 2000, available: http://news.bbc.co.uk/hi/english/world/europe/newsid_676000/676196.stm (accessed 3 January 2001).
14 Jonathan Marcus, 'NATO's Incomplete Victory', BBC World News, 14 March 2000, available: http://newsvote.bbc.co.uk/hi/english/world/europe/newsid_671000/671432.stm (accessed 3 January 2001).
15 Judah, 'Kosovo One Year On'.
16 'Messy War, Messy Peace', *The Economist*, 12 June 1999.
17 As General Michael Short, US commander of the air campaign, bluntly put it: 'It was war by lowest common denominator.' See Allan Little, 'Behind the Kosovo Crisis', BBC World News, 12 March 2000, available: http://newsvote.bbc.co.uk/hi/english/world/europe/newsid_674000/674056.stm (accessed 3 January 2001).

2 Peter van Ham

Simulating European security: Kosovo and the Balkanisation–integration nexus

Introduction: writing security

Security is among the most debated and contested concepts in the study of international relations (IR). 'Security' commands a unique metaphysical and disciplinary power which involves the drawing of imaginary lines, the consolidated resentment of difference (*vis-à-vis* the 'other'), as well as the constitution of self-reflective collectivities ('identity'). Although it has become slightly embarrassing to make yet another effort to reconceptualise 'security', I argue in this chapter that a critical approach is required, mainly because 'security' is a fundamental point of reference and an essential modifier for a state that is gradually losing its pre-eminence within Europe and the wider world. In many ways, it is 'national security' that has dominated the security debate and has established a set of elaborate practices and traditions, all of which have a rather formalised referent: the state. This conceptual hegemony has crowded out other discourses, most notably on transversal and personal security. For now there is hardly a tradition or body of literature that attempts to conceptualise 'security' in non-statal terms. The only way to read security is through the state, and in this way 'security' both *writes* and *rights* the state in its claim to sovereign authority for disciplining space and people.

In this discursive context, 'security' therefore follows the old script of political realism that defines the security problematique as the *field* and the *operations* that touch upon the survival of the political unit: the sovereign state. But, unfortunately for realists' peace of mind, the contemporary European political theatre does not follow the established script of security–sovereignty written by political realism. Offhand and ad lib performances by other (f)actors have turned this European stage in a politically surreal territory in which the ontological givens of modernity have become unrooted. Although governmental discourses about European security continue to methodically mobilise the assumptions, codes and procedures that enforce our understanding of humanity as subdivided in territorially defined statal spaces as their primary and natural habitat, it is becoming obvious that such efforts to classify, organise and frame Europe's collective consciousness along these lines are ineffective as well as doomed to failure.

This essay argues that 'security' has remained captive to orthodox statal thinking for too long. The argument is informed by the critical thinking of Cynthia Weber and Ole Wæver, and asserts that in order to come to a better understanding of contemporary Europe we should accept that the idea of 'European security' no longer follows the logic of representation (in which 'security' posits the state within legitimate boundaries), but now abides by a logic of simulation (in which there is no longer a rooted foundation but instead an unsteady chain of signifiers).[1] Jean Baudrillard's claim that '[i]t is no longer a question of a false representation of reality (ideology), but of concealing the fact that the real is no longer real'[2] is especially relevant for my argument. For Baudrillard, postmodern society has entered the era of the simulacrum, the abstract non-society that is devoid of cohesive relations, shared meaning and significant change.[3] In this void, 'truth', 'reality', as well as 'power', are devoured.

My point is that the contemporary European debate on security has transmogrified the notion of 'European security' into a simulacrum, a representation of the 'real' that is now omnipresent, so that it has become impossible to distinguish this 'real' from its original referent. 'European security' has become a complex sign, an image of the 'real' that constitutes a novel realm of experience and practice that is 'hyperreal'. In the debate about European security it has become clear that the representational relationship has been eclipsed and the traditional subject–object distance erased. Old language games are no longer appropriate, no longer based on stable meanings. Instead, the original referent (the state) is, to all intents and purposes, vanquished and assimilated by a new set of codes and models. In this new game, 'European security' does not simply become a myth or a fantasy, but tends to become hyperreal: depleted, dissipated and without power; it is hyped, feigned and faked, and perhaps therefore is more real than *the real thing*: the state itself.

In this funhouse of the hyperreal, Europe's postmodern security has become an *ersatz* experience, an image which may sometimes conceal (but usually just accentuates) that the 'original' of statal security no longer seems to exist. This essay examines the war in and over Kosovo as an example of how security is continuing to write Europe's geopolitical space and argues that 'Europe' has (mis)used Serbia and Kosovo in a classic modern exercise of identity construction by disciplining the Balkan 'other'.

'Security' as a political struggle

Like sovereignty, security is not so much an ontological given with a stable meaning as the site of a continuous political struggle in which the nature of statehood as such may be inferred from practice and experience. All efforts to define, redefine and reconstruct security therefore engage in a wider political practice in order to stabilise the concept's definition and purpose. Wæver has argued that 'security' lacks a generic concept, but that it has a clear temporal dimension derived from an established set of practices. The label of 'security', says Wæver, 'has become the indicator of a specific problematique, a specific field of practice',[4] in which the state determines the rules of the (language) game. In terms of semiotics, 'security' is therefore not a signifier (indicator) which refers back to a referent (that it is supposed to represent); rather the

> utterance *itself* is the act. By saying it, something is done (as in betting, giving a promise, naming a ship). By uttering 'security,' a state-representative moves a particular development into a specific area, and thereby claims a special right to use whatever means are necessary to block it.[5]

Security has thereby become an act; the word–concept itself has become its primary reality, affording the state special rights and privileges. By fixing the meaning of security (always in spatial and temporal dimensions), security thereby *de facto* writes the state.

Wæver identifies three major problems with the statal hegemony over the security discourse. First, it tends to imply that any response to a security problem, risk or perceived threat is to be expected first and foremost from the state. Second, the concept of security tends to reinforce the logic of nationalism and the Manichean us–them thinking grounded on the tradition of viewing threats as coming from the 'outside' (i.e. beyond the state's own borders). This also tends to encourage the militarisation of our thinking. Third, since the concept of security is basically defensive in nature, it tends to defend the *status quo* and thereby precludes alternative realities that may be preferable to that which *is*. Wæver summarises his arguments in his claim that '[w]hen a problem is "securitized," the act tends to lead to specific ways of addressing it: Threat, defense, and often statecentred solutions'.[6] The discourse of security is not a neutral academic terrain, but a continuous struggle for political power, access to resources and the authority to articulate new definitions and priorities of security. 'Security' is therefore a socially constructed concept that emerges from its discourse (or, in this case, through a 'speech act') and the discursive practices that constitute the ever-shifting boundaries and capacities of sovereign states and the interpretative communities in which they are embedded.

Clearly, in most discourses, the referent (object) of 'security' remains the state. But how should we read 'the state' in the European context? Barry Buzan has argued that states have three basic components: the idea of the state (nationalism); the physical base of the state (population, etc.); and the institutional expression of the state (political system).[7] In the political discourse, 'national security' therefore represents three circumstances: the nation, the people and the government. Traditional approaches to this problematique tend to be framed by a logic of representation in which the national community formally authorises 'its' government to express 'its' voice in the international theatre. Weber has argued, however, that this logic of representation is seriously flawed, mainly because it has become unclear what the boundaries of the 'people' are and what means (and legitimacy) the national government has to serve as the signifier (and voice) of this 'imagined community'.[8] Following Baudrillard, Weber therefore suggests that the state has become a sign without a referent and, hence, is hyperreal.

This may explain why the popular media continues to endow the state with a sanctity that is, to say the least, mystifying. The socio-spatial modern triad of security–sovereignty–territoriality is more often than not treated as if it were the nation's equivalent to virginity, with the inevitable implication that losing 'it' would be a decisive stage, at times comparable only to rape.[9] But the anthropomorphism inherent to this individual–state analogy overlooks that pre-given material bodies may not be unproblematical in terms of identity and politics.[10] State power may also be read as a gendered problematique insofar as it is 'a historical product and expression of male predominance in public life and male dominance generally'.[11] Weber argues that the sovereign state has a clearly feminine domestic side and a masculine international side, which implies that the international arena 'refers to the projection of this domestic identity into the public sphere of relations among states'.[12] By paying homage to the state's virginal identity, we therefore continue to worship the state as the optimal cultural and democratic area, whereas the postmodern state is now selling the remains of its sovereignty to the highest bidder on a daily basis. European states are clinging desperately to as much political authority, democratic legitimacy and problem-solving capacity as they possibly can, but are also prepared (and occasionally coerced) to re-read the notion of territorial sovereignty as a *quid pro quo* to remain in the 'geopolitical business' in the first place. Within the global political space, states are occasional criminal rapists as well as defenceless victims. National virginity has been lost long ago, but we continue to believe in the state's virginal conception and its capacity to deliver.

In her work, Weber identifies the concept of 'sovereignty' as the principal sign that through a swirl of discursive practices rescues and writes the state's hegemonic fantasy. But the same can be said for the code of security, a concept policy makers and diplomats like to call upon to legitimise their particular international practices, without realising that the 'security' they refer to has become a hollow shell: it lacks a nation, a people, as well as a government. 'Security' therefore now mainly has (following Baudrillard's nomenclature) an 'alibi function': it tries to assert the *realness* of the state and its components; it tries to reaffirm and discursively frame and read that which it is supposed to signify in the first place. But given the continued hollowing out of the territorial state, to do so has become increasingly difficult. Especially in Europe, the idea of 'national security' fails to pass most serious reality checks, which may explain why the anaemic notion of 'European security' is now being reinscribed with new meanings and given a new lease of life in the invigorated context of post-Cold War European integration.

European security as a *tabula rasa*

Wæver has made a persuasive argument that during the Cold War, the concept of 'European security' has functioned as a means and a mechanism to enforce cohesion within the two halves of Europe.[13] The discourse on European security was not so much on what was threatening Europe from the outside as a continued debate on how to frame Europe from *within*, which in turn limited the options of Europe's actors within confined disciplinary parameters. This reading of European security has been one of the most notable casualties of the deep geopolitical quakes of 1989–91, leaving most policy makers and academic analysts in the dark as to how to reinscribe this concept with meaning now that the reductionist categories that dominated the traditional security discourse have passed away.

This discourse has immediately raised the question of whether one can meaningfully debate European security in the absence of clear foundations? The answer seems to be less than clear-cut. It is clear that to tell stories about European security is to imply the very existence of 'Europe' as a referent object. This is the alibi function of all discourses of European security, since assuming that 'something' is (possibly) threatened is to insist upon its very existence. In this sense, 'security' functions as the alibi for 'Europe'. The European security discourse also discursively frames the diverse meanings of 'Europe', fixing its geopolitical boundaries by locating its practices and by speaking as if a stable European citizenry already existed which it could authoritatively represent – this, whereas the notion of 'Europe' is a forest of ideas, symbols and myths. 'Europe' seems to function as a mirror reflecting the image of a multitude of ideas and meanings, rather than as a prism concentrating the minds and hearts of its peoples around a central theme. What is Europe and what does it stand for? Who is European, and what does being European imply? These are questions that the discourse on European security not only fails to answer, but deliberately ignores, since efforts to 'find' answers concerning the foundational authorities would detract from the logic of simulation which underpins this debate. Policy makers and theorists try to 'solve' these questions of Europe's foundations by preventing such interrogations from being seriously undertaken in the first place.

It is this locale, this site of friction, which should be the focus of academic analysts of European security, since the meaning of 'Europe' is fixed and stabilised by the invocation of the security speech act. Security, perhaps by default, is the main tool for writing Europe, a tool for claiming its essential foundations through fixing the boundaries between inside–outside and the claim to organise, occupy and administer Europe's space. Since the European Union (EU) is the only truly European security institution functioning on the supranational level, the process of European integration has become the main platform on which European security can be constructed. From Europe's perspectivalist vision of its space, the contours of a Eurocentrically calibrated world map of security are gradually becoming clear. By adopting a 'European' security perspective, a process of distantiation of appearances and events is supposed to emerge, setting priorities and seeking to 'arrange and display the world around a sovereign center of judgement, a rational I/eye that observes and in so doing disciplines the ambiguity, contingency, and (barbarian) chaos of international affairs and the world'.[14] The European security discourse is therefore an effort on the part of all European states to set Eurocentric standards to describe, read and write the continent's geopolitical structure in an effort to colour Europe as a patriotic – and therefore 'safe' – (blue) space. This follows the argument made by Gearoid O Tuathail and John Agnew that '[t]o designate a place is not simply to define a location or setting. It is to open up a field of possible taxonomies and trigger a series of narratives, subjects and appropriate foreign policy responses.'[15]

By conceptualising European security, 'Europe' is politically spatialised to represent its own 'imagined community', its own hyperreal political stage on which its performative identity may gradually take shape. But by doing so, Europe inevitably challenges traditional statal notions of security. This makes the notion of 'European security' so problematic an abstraction, since in its textuality it is challenging, and is itself continuously challenged by, 'security' *tout court*. The discourse of 'European security' should therefore be deconstructed by problematising its limits and conditions. Rather than a genealogy of European security (which would trace historically how theorists have defined 'European security'), we need to analyse the textuality of the concept and find out how 'European security' is being produced within the various discursive networks of difference.[16] This would follow a Derridean approach by displacing the question of 'European security': it would problematise its circulating limits and conditions and investigate its conceptual meaning(s) in the reading and writing of European security as a text. We should therefore not assume that the notion of 'European security' is self-evident and non-partisan, but ask how it is charged by particular meanings and strategic uses within the existing (but ever-changing) context of power/knowledge networks. 'European security' is therefore itself a sign which marks a specific site within a wider geopolitical space/power/knowledge system, a system which produces the scripts for many actors, which affects the dramas and comedies that are being played, and which therefore never passively *is*, but is always under dynamic (de)construction.

Many tactical interventions can be made to illustrate and analyse the different aspects of the wider problem of how 'European security' is constructing Europe's political space. No doubt there is a need for more concentrated attention in order to congeal more exhaustively the meaning(s) around this concept. The remainder of this essay investigates how the marginal – and at the same time very central – question of 'Kosovo' has turned into the principal paradigmatic sign in the complex text of European security. It asks how its very marginality has emphasised the unravelling fringes and limits of the sovereign presence of what 'Europe' thinks it stands for, and how it has affected (and continues to affect) the concept of 'European security'.

Kosovo and the margins of modernity

In its efforts to write Europe's geopolitical space, the EU has adopted a Wittgensteinian approach, using the metaphor of *Familienähnlichkeiten* (i.e. 'family resemblances') to illustrate the complex networks of similarities of Europe's peoples who are nevertheless quite different in their essence. Ludwig Wittgenstein argued that in the various resemblances between the members of a family 'we see a complicated network of similarities overlapping and crisscrossing: sometimes overall similarities, sometimes similarities in detail.'[17] In its semantic politics, the EU has continually applied this metaphor of family resemblance (the 'European family') to illustrate how Europe could relate to the countries of Central and Eastern Europe (and vice versa). In doing so, the EU has rejected the framing of an undisputed definition of 'Europeanness' and has not codified the unequivocal features and characteristics of those who belong to Europe and those who do not. Apart from an internalised culture of cooperation, a deeply ingrained willingness to make compromises, no checklist of criteria that will assure entry into this 'Club Europe' has been presented.

But despite this acknowledgement (even appreciation) of difference, the EU now seems to have fallen in the traditional trap of modernity and its concomitant quest for control and planning. The EU is willing to accept difference in the pluralism of its prosaic politics (language, culture, education, etc.), but certainly not in the area of heroic politics, the reading–writing of 'big events'. In this field of heroic politics, the EU has hardly been able to make its voice heard and is competing with potent statal claims to 'security'. As happens with organisations such as NATO, the EU's 'desire for security is manifested as a collective resentment of difference – that which is not us, not certain, not predictable'.[18] The 'enemy' of Europe's volatile identity is thereby defined as the 'unknown', the 'unpredictable' and the 'unstable'. By reading Europe's 'other' in this way, the meaning of 'European security' is stabilised as efforts to limit the pluralism of the continent's centres, to limit its multiple meanings to a strict canon and a fixed site, and to solidify the current fluidity of Europe's identity.

The challenge for the EU has been to prevent a slow drift from a postmodern politics of family resemblance to a narcissistic policy of passive self-absorption and epistemic closure. It was Sigmund Freud who observed (in 1917) that 'it is precisely the minor differences in people who are otherwise alike that form the basis of feelings of strangeness and hostility between them'.[19] This 'narcissism of minor differences', as Freud labelled it, is a discursive mechanism which frames the meaning of European security. Michael Ignatieff has argued rightly that these 'differences' (be they between the sexes, between religions, races or nations) are in themselves neutral, but that a 'narcissist is incurious about others except to the extent that they reflect back on himself. What is different is rejected if it fails to confirm the narcissist in his or her self-opinion.'[20] This closure for the 'other' and the 'outside' is where prosaic politics ends and heroic security concerns begin. Narcissism thereby marks the inside–outside divide by feeding modern fears of fluidity and by (sometimes violent attempts of) keeping ambiguity at bay.

Nowhere have these margins of modernity been more clearly marked than in Kosovo (and earlier, but less distinctly, in Bosnia). Starting with the dissolution of the Federal Republic of Yugoslavia, rump-Yugoslavia (nicknamed 'Serbia') was identified as the strange and alien entity threatening European security at the end of the millennium by its ethnic and sectarian essentialism, its barbarian methods of 'ethnic cleansing', and its altogether premodern values, attitude and practices. In short: Milosevic's Serbia was not sticking to the carefully crafted script of 'European' conduct. By falling out of line, by not accepting the rationales of European integration and European security, this Serbia was posing itself as the main challenge to the emerging new European order (NEO). By ignoring the logic of NEO realism (or, as Mikkel Vedby Rasmussen calls it in chapter 9, the West's emerging 'governmentality'), Serbia brought a question to the fore, one which European policy makers and theorists have tried to ignore: on what stable foundations can 'European security' be constructed?

It is here that, from a Foucauldian perspective, the story of NATO's military intervention against Serbia (as well as its Montenegran appendix) might tell us how the West's disciplinary power has been involved in the actual construction of 'European security'. This is a story of the discursive production of an operational meaning along the lines laid out by Weber, who has argued that 'intervention is understood as the flip side of sovereignty ... And what it means to violate sovereignty is decided by theorists when they operationalise the meaning of intervention.'[21] In Europe's security discourse, 'Kosovo' therefore tends to allegorise the Balkanisation of Europe, the ultimate metaphor of chaos and disintegration which supposedly is the antithesis of the *real* Europe of peace and stability. As Wæver argued in this context: 'Balkanisation is a tool for legitimising an international order *without* a named enemy... "Security" thus becomes shorthand for the argument: We have to do everything to ensure that integration, and not fragmentation, is the outcome.'[22] To speak of Milosevic's Serbia as the ultimate threat to 'European security' is to imply the strategic relevance of the notion of security through integration. Kosovo therefore serves as a useful alibi for the stabilisation of what 'European security' actually means by operationalising it through military intervention. Thanks to these acts of stabilisation, Kosovo has written (and, to some extent, continues to write) European security.

The story of Kosovo tells us that those political actors who do not accept NEO realism, who defy the logic of integration and cooperation, *de facto* deny their Europeanness, their family resemblance to other European (family) member states, and should expect to face the serious consequences. Serbia's eruption into premodern savagery in the 'heart of Europe' has offered the rest of Europe a not-to-be-missed chance to manifest and constitute itself as the pinnacle of modern rational civilisation. Serbia's killing of Kosovo has set the parameters of the Balkanisation–integration nexus, offering 'Europe' (and the West in general) a unique opportunity to suggest itself as the strong centre that keeps the margins from running away. This may explain the comical pride of many Romanians to be situated 'north of the Danube', as if the Danube were a twenty-first-century Styx, a mythical border between life and death, between European affluence and Balkan anarchy. But by posing this nexus as the main (if not only) platform for discourse, 'European security' becomes a speech act itself: it becomes the central tool for building an integrated Europe by solidifying a socio-political order that does not (yet) exist in actuality. Here, again, hyperreality takes precedence over the 'really real'. But this time it might be (merely) a weak version of hyperreality, since the difference between Europe and its copy are all too well understood. The all-too-human observer, however, 'consciously chooses the illusion, the hyped, the fake, or the copy as somehow better, sexier, more exciting – more real'.[23]

Writing security on the Balkan screen

What happened in the Balkans during the 1990s is therefore often seen as a somewhat bizarre, and certainly counterproductive, revolt against the logic of European integration. The death of Yugoslavia in 1991 (coinciding with the birthpangs of Croatia and Slovenia after their recognition as independent states by Germany in December of that year) implied a reversal of Europe's commitment to a unitary Yugoslavia. The crumbling of a federal political entity like Yugoslavia was (and remains) a painful screenplay for the rest of Europe to witness, reminding the other (family) member states how fragile the continent's peace and calm actually are.

The Bosnian slaughterhouse has projected the horrors of war and ethnic strife with an unprecedented transparency and visibility onto the mental and TV screens of Europeans, crushing the comfortable distance between 'Europe' and its supposedly premodern Balkan antipode. Bosnia has made war a live drama with exaggerated, almost obscene, images of fear and hate. European viewers easily (and readily) forgot that the Bosnian war was in essence a *modern* war, a quest for space, territory and identity. It was a war about questions still very much alive in the rest of Europe, although most other European states had by now learned how to resolve (and/or suppress) these disputes through complex political and administrative mechanisms. It uncomfortably reminded Europeans that their efforts to deterritorialise politics remain a fragile and far from completed project whose ratchet may well break under the combined pressures of sectarianism and narcissism. 'Bosnia' and 'Kosovo' therefore function as disciplining allegories of what a forthright assault on Europe's current political project of integration may ultimately lead to, reminding *all* observers, almost on a daily basis, how the veneration of identity may undermine the multicultural ideal of Europe.

This has been the irony of the West's actions in Bosnia and Kosovo, since in its claim and efforts to promote tolerance it has been prepared to use (military) force, if necessary. But, as Stjepan Mestrovic has suggested, the 'postmodern program of promoting *organized* tolerance is fundamentally flawed, and doomed to failure'.[24] Mestrovic points out that Western tolerance 'denotes an air of contemptuous superiority on the part of those who do the tolerating. To tolerate is to put up with something or someone, not to sympathize or understand.'[25] Europe's approach to the Balkans has therefore been based upon narcissism, rather than a sense of genuine toleration based on compassion. Europe is saying to Serbia what Baudrillard has said on 'America': 'utopia has arrived. If you aren't part of it, get lost!'[26] When Serbia claims political authority over Kosovo simply because this territory is an integral part of its history, and of its cultural and religious identity, it is challenging Europe's now dominant postmodern narrative of culture as consisting of rootless, circulating fictions and signs that no longer refer to history, ethnicity and accepted myths. This explains why after having declared the 'end of history', fundamentalist ethnocentrism and Balkanisation caught the West completely off guard. It was shocked by the real blood seeping from the Balkans which gradually reached the virginal doormat of the European 'centre'.

In his fury over Europe's passive Bosnia policy, Mestrovic has depicted the West as a 'voyeuristic consumer of abstract fiction because the distinction between fact and fiction has been lost'.[27] The Balkans have become the site of a prolonged docudrama with stereotypical characters, Mestrovic argues, who stage a play full with the usual sordid images western TV audiences have by now got used to; scandalous, violent and even sexual images which may, according to Mestrovic, raise the question whether the Balkan wars are a 'prelude to a future in which audiences will have been reduced to postmodern Romans watching bloody spectacles in the electric arena comprised of televised images?'[28] Following a somewhat perverse Baudrillardian logic, this would turn the Balkans into a hyperreal site of simulation precisely because it is televised, made abstract on a screen which produces little other than violence and sensationalism. Real war and televised war therefore blend together, preventing real emotion and real compassion for the still very real victims of ethnic strife and attempted genocide. Or, as Andreas Behnke argues later on in this book:

> Only when [NATO's] verbal representation is controlled, structured and disseminated by spin-doctors and clever spokespersons, only when the visual 'evidence' is presented in the form of videogames, only when we stay within the framework of this de-ontologised version of warfare, can NATO's claims [of moral superiority] be sustained.

Bosnia has shown for the first time how the referents of Western modernity – truth, morality, justice – have now been emptied of real content, seemingly confirming Baudrillard's conjecture that social reality is composed of mere fictions mostly played out on the TV screen. 'Kosovo', on the other hand, has provided the West with an opportunity to publicly visualise these lost referents by claiming the moral highground and re-establish the rhetoric of Europe's Enlightenment ideals.

NATO's air campaign against Serbia (not to be confused with something as arcane and brutal as 'war' – see Pertti Joenniemi's chapter in this volume), started on 24 March 1999 and lasted seventy-eight days. NATO warplanes flew 37,465 sorties (an average of 480 every 24 hours), dropping more than 20,000 'smart bombs', destroying parts of Serbia's industrial and civilian infrastructure, and killing an unknown number of Yugoslav troops as well as some 500 civilians (the exact figure is still unknown). The tragedy of Kosovo finally seems to have dehypnotised the West's post-emotional stare at the Balkans and to have provoked Europe to draw its own 'line in the sand' by including Kosovo in Europe's security equation.[29] But in practice this 'line' was drawn in the air, indicating that Europe did not want to become 'engaged' on the ground but was committed to Balkan security in only a general and abstract way through an antiseptic aerial operation. The proclaimed victory of the West's airpower has confirmed these ocularcentric fantasies of technological mastery and transcendence, stimulating the deterministic logic of mediated vision and techno-imagery. NATO's air campaign and its video-supported mission briefings have made it clear that these new technologies open up the possibility of simultaneous engagement and *dis*engagement with the 'other' we encounter on our mental and our TV screens.[30] The 'line in the sand' is therefore also a protective line that keeps these images from obtruding too deeply into the European consciousness.

Technology thereby serves to isolate and insulate the viewers from the frightening immediacy of Balkanisation. Speaking of the problematique of postmodern involvement in the world, Kevin Robins has therefore claimed that the 'point now is not whether we can achieve a certain distance and detachment from the fearful principles of reality, but whether we can ever become reconnected to a world that we no longer take for real, a world whose reality has been progressively screened out'.[31]

It is here that 'European security' is being framed most clearly. The televisualisation of European politics has reduced the multiplicity of difference and abridged power and authority to an entertainmentised phenomenon. Technology has imposed a distance between the ideal of a peaceful and stable 'Europe' and the 'other': vision is mobilised and employed to avoid direct contact lest we be contaminated with the Balkanisation-bacillus. High-flying fighter-pilots are called upon to hit their targets without physical contact with the enemy, ensuring their visual sovereignty through smart bombs and surgical strikes. With each bomb, NATO and Europe have been building their own utopia, their own secure space over which they have full control, a new European order that is beyond disappointment and disillusionment, a transparent space that can be controlled from a safe distance with a sovereign Cartesian perspectivalist gaze. This is the ultimate simulation of 'European security', since the *really real* has been disciplined to fit the imagined ideal of European security. By simulating European security, Europe has been disembodied and the option of chaos and catastrophe suspended (or even annulled).

It has become tempting to assume that this technological superiority and rationality legitimises Europe's hegemony over the 'other' (and, most notably, other *cultures*). But, despite this panoptic ambition, full mastery over Europe's space will prove to be a dangerous illusion. The ontological closure that it involves does not make moral questions meaningless or irrelevant. The psychic numbing of the European audience may have detached vision/ knowledge from feeling. The telegenic war in Kosovo and Serbia may have concealed the fact that, despite surgical strikes, really real victims still scream and they do still bleed really real blood. But the world of the image and the simulation has not removed the moral obligation to remember that in the discursive construction of its security Europe has for three months intimidated an entire population, dropping cluster bombs and killing and maiming thousands of innocent people as the 'accidental collateral damage' accrued in the great cause of European peace and stability.

Kosovo: the pre-context of European security

In this 'space-between' knowledge and power in European politics, the textual nature of 'European security' becomes intelligible. Any approach emphasising textuality recognises that 'reality' is not a simple description of a lucid world of facts, but that it concerns meaning- and value-producing practices and language. It is of little use to challenge the boundaries of the battlefield of ideas concerning 'European security' without acknowledging this inevitable intertextuality. It is therefore much more important to understand how one approach and reading of 'European security' comes to stand above other readings and silences them by often arbitrarily separating them from the canonical version of 'events'. The Kosovo drama has again indicated that rationalist and technological approaches to European security have now taken on the character of simulacra which may be 'appealing and persuasive in their modelled abstraction, but metaphysical and exclusionary in their hyperreal application'.[32]

NATO's air campaign has legitimised not only NEO realism: it has made another step in legitimising the structure of meaning that circulates in the very debate on 'European security'. It goes without saying that this NEO realism implies a collective amnesia about other possible forms of meaning and the marginalization of other readings and philosophical vocabularies. This discursive formation of meaning has now resulted in a logocentric disposition which imposes the Balkanisation–integration opposition as the practical nexus on which all events and policies must be situated. By this move, 'Europe' situates itself as the coherent sovereign voice (which it isn't), making itself unproblematical (or at least less problematical), and assuming an extra-historical identity that is beyond critical interrogation. Moreover, by invoking the notion of 'security', modern discourse has tried to discipline and stabilise 'a region of historical contingency and chance that refuses to submit to the sovereign truth of reason and that calls forth the means of the state to exclude or subdue it in the name of reasoning man'.[33]

The discourse of 'European security' therefore produces a parallel paradigm of European *sovereignty*, a paradigm that faces serious challenges of local resistance (of the still-resilient state), as well as external opposition (which questions the notion of 'Europe' as a privileged space of peace and stability). It is at these unruly frontiers and borders that the concept of 'European security' is being challenged and problematised. Balkanisation testifies to the recalcitrant domain of anarchy within Europe, a domain that has to be subdued by the sovereign figure of the 'international community'. Much of this book deals with how these practical and theoretical frontiers are being shaped and what their wider implications will be for 'Europe' in general. Whereas 'Europe' should stand for the sovereign centre of domesticated territory and originary presence, 'Kosovo' stands for the continuity of 'international politics', the inside–outside divide that privileges and legitimises the domestic space of identity and continuity over the anarchic space of difference and discontinuity. It is this residual Balkan space that still seems to escape the rational truth of 'integration' and 'reasonable humanity', and must therefore be silenced and disciplined.

It is also in these locations that the new mode of NEO realism, the mode of order, is being produced, and occasionally imposed. Without the clear signs of 'war' and 'security' as the inscription of international dangers, 'there would be no notion of a well-bounded domestic social identity – a population of sovereign men who know themselves to be at one with a social totality that is imperilled'.[34] Kosovo therefore illustrates Michael Shapiro's argument that enmity and war are essential for the maintenance of a coherent society and body politic.[35] Since security is what takes politics beyond the ordinary, beyond the established rules of the game,[36] it allows (and even calls for) extraordinary measures to be taken to address the existential threat. The novelty with Kosovo is that this mode of statecraft is not practised within a statal context, but that it is in the name of 'Europe' that a new narrative of modernity is constructed to fabricate and rationalise *European* domestic society *vis-à-vis* the unruliness and backwardness of the Balkan fringe. It is in the name of 'European security' that boundaries are drawn to discipline the behaviour of those within and to distinguish 'Europe' from the 'other'. By altering the referent of security as a speech act, 'Europe' is *de facto* finding and constructing itself.

It is therefore all the more fitting that the writing of 'European security' has taken place in the only true hyperreal country in the world, since the Federal Republic of Yugoslavia (FRY) did not really exist (and has never existed *de jure* as a sovereign state).[37] Perhaps this is exactly the sort of anomaly that can find no place in the NEO realism of the twenty-first century, the sort of (what Weber calls) 'formless feminine fluids' that must provoke 'Europe' to use its 'stabilizing influence ... so [that it] may heterosexually serve masculine purposes'.[38] Kosovo stands for an understanding of 'European security' that legitimises the use of military force in order to *de*legitimise the use of military force. It is the site where people have been killed and bombs have been dropped for the sake of stability, peace and human rights. It remains the domain where the forces of integration and Balkanisation do battle, since 'the multiculturalist doctrine that is fragmenting our universities as well as our intellectual life, and the "ethnic cleansing" of the Serbs, belong to the same troubling cultural and historical moment'.[39] In Kosovo, Europe is still fighting itself in a narcissist attempt to get rid of the undesirable, of chaos and anarchy.

Kosovo is therefore both the *pre*text and the ultimate *con*text in which the contemporary reading of 'European security' is taking place. But it remains problematic to accept the 'other' as a legitimate ontological presence, mainly because doing so raises the possibility 'of accepting the Other's characteristics as a legitimate alternative and, consequently, of being taken over by the Other'.[40] The Milosevic regime has never been the opposite of the NEO, but rather its ultimate symptom, its hyperreal foundation from which a new mode of order now seems to be emerging.[41] In this sense, therefore, Baudrillard was correct when he argued that the 'real story is that the Serbs, as vehicles of ethnic cleansing, are at the forefront of the construction of Europe. For it is being constructed, the real Europe, the white Europe, a Europe whitewashed, integrated and purified, morally as much as economically or ethnically'.[42] On this reading, 'Europe' seems to have (mis)used Serbia as well as Kosovo to acquire a sense of self, to temporarily and spatially define what it is *not*. If Europe's simulated security in future is not constituted on a more substantial basis, it will remain a travesty and an apparent and transparent fake. But perhaps that's why we will like it all the better.

Notes

1 Cynthia Weber, *Simulating Sovereignty: Intervention, the State and Symbolic Exchange* (Cambridge, Cambridge University Press, 1995), pp. xi, xii.
2 Jean Baudrillard, *Simulations* (New York, Semiotext(e), 1983), p. 48.
3 Timothy Luke, 'Power and Politics in Hyperreality: The Critical Project of Jean Baudrillard', *Social Science Journal*, vol. 28, no. 3 (1991).
4 Ole Wæver, 'Securitization and Desecuritization', in Ronnie D. Lipschutz (ed.), *On Security* (New York, Columbia University Press, 1995), pp. 50–1.
5 *Ibid.*, pp. 54–5.
6 *Ibid.*, pp. 62–5.
7 Barry Buzan, *People, States and Fear: An Agenda for International Security Studies in the Post-Cold War Era* (New York, Harvester Wheatsheaf, 1991), p. 65.
8 Benedict Anderson, *Imagined Communities: Reflections on the Origin and Spread of Nationalism* (London, Verso, 1991).
9 Cynthia Weber argues that in international relations theory, 'intervention is defined as the violation of one state's sovereignty by an uninvited intruder. It is rape on an international scale.' See Weber, *Faking It: U.S. Hegemony in a 'Post-Phallic' Era* (Minneapolis, University of Minnesota Press, 1999), p. 94.
10 Judith Butler, *Bodies that Matter. On the Discursive Limits of 'Sex'* (New York, Routledge, 1993), and Robert Hanke, 'Theorizing Masculinity: With/In the Media', *Communication Theory*, vol. 8, no. 2 (May 1998).
11 Wendy Brown, 'Finding the Man in the State', *Feminist Studies*, vol. 18, no. 1 (spring 1992), p. 12.
12 Weber, *Faking It*, p. 90.
13 Wæver, 'Securitization and Desecuritization', p. 71.
14 Gearoid O Tuathail, *Critical Geopolitics: The Politics of Writing Global Space* (Minneapolis, University of Minnesota Press, 1996), p. 34.
15 Gearoid O Tuathail and John Agnew, 'Geopolitics and Discourse: Practical Geopolitical Reasoning in American Foreign Policy', *Political Geography*, vol. 11 (1992), p. 194.
16 Neil Renwick, 'Re-reading Europe's Identity's', in Jill Krause and Neil Renwick (eds), *Identities in International Relations* (London, Macmillan, 1996).
17 Ludwig Wittgenstein, *Philosophical Investigations* (Oxford, Blackwell, 1953), numbered remarks 66–7.

18 James Der Derian, 'The Value of Security: Hobbes, Marx, Nietzsche, and Baudrillard', in Lipschutz (ed.), *On Security*, p. 33.
19 Quoted in Michael Ignatieff, 'Nationalism and Toleration', in Richard Caplan and John Feffer (eds), *Europe's New Nationalism. States and Minorities in Conflict* (New York and Oxford, Oxford University Press, 1996), p. 213.
20 Ignatieff, 'Nationalism and Toleration', p. 214.
21 Weber, *Simulating Sovereignty*, p. 20.
22 Wæver, 'Securitization and Desecuritization', pp. 72–4.
23 Steven Best and Douglas Kellner, *The Postmodern Turn* (New York and London, Guilford Press, 1997), p. 103.
24 Stjepan G. Mestrovic, *The Balkanization of the West: The Confluence of Postmodernism and Postcommunism* (London and New York, Routledge, 1994), p. 10.
25 *Ibid.*, p. 11.
26 Jean Baudrillard, *America* (London, Verso, 1986), p. 111.
27 Mestrovic, *The Balkanization of the West*, p. 79.
28 *Ibid.*, p. 83.
29 Stjepan G. Mestrovic, *Postemotional Society* (London, Sage, 1997).
30 Kevin Robins, *Into the Image: Culture and Politics in the Field of Vision* (London, Routledge, 1996), pp. 6–7.
31 *Ibid.*, p. 13.
32 James Der Derian, 'The Boundaries of Knowledge and Power in International Relations', in James Der Derian and Michael J. Shapiro (eds), *International/Intertextual Relations: Postmodern Readings of World Politics* (Lexington, MA, and Toronto, Lexington Books, 1989), p. 7.
33 Richard K. Ashley, 'Living on Border Lines: Man, Poststructuralism, and War', in Der Derian and Shapiro (eds), *International/Intertextual Relations*, p. 268.
34 *Ibid.*, p. 305.
35 Michael J. Shapiro, *Violent Cartographies: Mapping Cultures of War* (Minneapolis, University of Minnesota Press, 1997).
36 Ole Wæver, 'Identity, Integration and Security', *Journal of International Affairs*, vol. 48, no. 2 (winter 1995).
37 Aleksandar Boskovic, 'Hyperreal Serbia', in CTHEORY, 2 April 1996, available: http://www.ctheory.com/e39.html (accessed 12 November 2000).
38 Weber, *Faking It*, p. 92.
39 Patrick Glynn, 'The Age of Balkanization', *Commentary*, vol. 96, no. 1 (July 1993), p. 24.
40 Ronnie D. Lipschutz, 'Negotiating the Boundaries of Difference and Security at Millennium's End', in Lipschutz (ed.), *On Security*, p. 218.
41 Slavoj Zizek, 'Against the Double Blackmail', *The Nation*, 24 May 1999, pp. 20–1.
42 Jean Baudrillard, *The Perfect Crime* (London, Verso, 1997), p. 135. See also on a similar theme, David Campbell, 'Apartheid Cartography: The Political Anthropology and Spatial Effects of International Diplomacy in Bosnia', *Political Geography*, vol. 18, no. 4 (1999).

3 *Pertti Joenniemi*

Kosovo and the end of war

Introduction: deviant voices

NATO's bombing campaign in Kosovo and the refusal of most Western leaders to regard it as war have prompted numerous questions about the nature of this episode in recent European history. How should 'Kosovo' be categorised? Can it be covered by the usual linguistic repertoire, or does 'Kosovo' testify to the fact that 'war' has become conceptually inapplicable?

For most observers the term 'war' remains good enough. In their view, war is well and alive. The bombing campaign in Kosovo may not correspond to the Clausewitzian definition of war, but war antedates the modern state by a good number of millennia, and is therefore more than the continuation of statist policies by other means. Hence, the concept's transcendental nature gives it the power to bridge even significant temporal and spatial variations. In mainstream strategic thinking, Operation Allied Force does not stand out as an exceptional case in the history of armed conflict, and 'war' has therefore been used to label it without too much hesitation. Without doubt, collective violence has been employed, which allows 'Kosovo' be referred to as a war in this basic sense. With only a few exceptions, it is therefore still claimed that the Kosovo encounter has featured too few irregular and asymmetrical aspects to undermine the contingent character of war. Deviant voices can still be silenced.

Nevertheless, doubt about this orthodox reading of 'Kosovo' is mounting. Some critics now claim that 'Kosovo' just does not fit the standard categories of armed conflict and war, and that many irregularities have to be studied. These critics refuse to adhere to orthodox vocabularies and call for new analytical conventions that go beyond the accepted mainstream. They concede that coercive elements have indeed been involved in the Kosovo campaign, including the collective use of violence, but that there are many features of 'Kosovo' that radically deviate from what we traditionally have come to understand as 'war'. The distinctions and borderlines that have over time helped to carve out the concept of war (setting it apart from non-war) now seem to be faltering. A previously well-delineated and uncontested concept, 'war' no longer seems to be its good old self, the critics claim. 'Kosovo' therefore not only sets in motion a conceptual transition by breaking essential boundaries, but it may well be indicating a full-fledged conceptual crisis which needs to be reflected in the terminology that is to be used to describe these new phenomena.

'Kosovo' therefore signals a profound ontological clash, which has turned war into an openly contested concept. War has become increasingly debatable; it has become a moving target that appears to be losing its name. For Western policy makers and analysts this is especially disconcerting, since this emerging conceptual ambivalence applies not only to remote armed conflicts on the international system's periphery, but now seems to have infected the centre of Europe as well.

My aim here is to probe this breach in the discourse on war. The emerging clash of concepts is used as a vantage-point for an inquiry into the discursive strength of the concept of war in its different articulations. I ask how and why this concept is being rendered open to doubt? What is the significance of the various efforts of re-articulation; and what efforts are being undertaken to close this uncomfortable debate prematurely? In order to place this debate in perspective, I first review the unfolding of the concept of war during recent years. Such an inquiry is necessary since some of the arguments presented in the context of 'Kosovo' feed on previous claims of 'endism', i.e. that modern war seems to be withering away. This essay therefore argues that war is dying out, as it were, and that it is this change in the transcendental nature of war which has opened up space for doubt concerning the 'established truths' about conflict in general. This shift allows previously invisible and marginalised views to come out into the open.

However, it is also possible to think that the Kosovo debate – and the uncertainty about the core terminology – actually involves a broader problem. In fact, it could point beyond 'endism' (be it the end of war, the state, or other central planks of modernity). The search for new terms further undermines the central tenets in the established discourse on war, and may well contribute to the legitimising of new ones. What is underway may not be just the faltering of traditional categories but the emergence of new ones, and these rewritten concepts are by no means neutral and descriptive in essence. These efforts are elements of a process of signification and legitimisation which may be part of the formation of a new discursive order. We should therefore ask ourselves what the Kosovo campaign was really about, and, more generally, what such a reconfiguration of war would imply for the emerging NEO? What are the discursive consequences of these new interpretative schemes, and how do they contribute to the shaping of new identities, subjectivities and social order?

These questions are posed since we need to know what kind of vocabulary we should (and can) use to describe an event like 'Kosovo'. It is of particular importance because our understanding of war has been central to the story of sovereign authority and modern statehood. The aim of this essay is therefore to map the alterations in the vocabularies used to describe 'Kosovo' by focusing on the productive aspects of war. I argue that this concept is changing rapidly and dramatically, and I try to trace the subjectivities and particular social formations that hinge on such a change.

War: a floating signifier?

Taking into account that many of the established features of the international system now tend to appear less natural, authorised and permanent, it is hardly surprising that basic questions concerning war have been problematised as well. It is recognised that war is not a permanent and unchanging principle or institution, but rather a social practice with its own history. Quincy Wright has argued that modern war 'rests upon an elaborate ideological construction maintained through education in a system of language, law, symbols and values'.[1] War is a practice with typical modes of performance; it is historically constructed and (therefore) variable. War is an essential part of an international system dominated by states whose sovereignty is (or has been) the prime constitutive principle. War's historically variable modes of performance are closely linked to the nature of the political system itself, whereas war has also been constitutive of the political framework in which the performance occurs. With this in mind, war is increasingly approached – to use a term introduced by Ernesto Laclau and Chantal Mouffe – as a 'floating signifier'.[2]

It may well be that the modern project can no longer muster the strength to anchor the concept of war and offer it a privileged, distinct place and role within the international system. During the twentieth century, modernity has defined the legitimate understanding and role of war, and has furnished it with a temporal and spatial permanence. This effort has not, primarily, been one of trying to do away with war, but can perhaps be better described as an essential aspect of modern inter-state relations. It is precisely the recognition and delineation of the sphere of war that has been conducive to a certain 'taming' of war, and, more generally, to the delineation of the unknown. As an unproblematic given, war has ratified and sanctioned the establishment of homogenous and stabilised 'insides', while deferring difference and contingency to the 'outside', i.e. the sphere of anarchy and unpredictability. By defining the 'outside' as the space of war, modernity has made the world of politics readable and instructive. The modern framing of the inside–outside dyad has been so firm and uncontested that it has become possible to consider war as an 'institution', or a 'regime', which also allows us to use such generalisations as the 'war-system'.

The distinction between the spheres of war and peace (i.e. the domestic intra-state realm) has served as the basis for border drawing in general, and allowed the establishment of divisions between order–anarchy, cosmos–chaos, we–they, self–other, inside–outside, domestic–foreign, friend–foe, and a long list of other binary oppositions.[3] Anchoring war has brought about ontological security through stable social identities. The idea of two different political spaces in the modern world of sovereign states – one within states and another between states – has also made it possible for international relations (IR) theory to comport itself as a theory of survival, while political theory and law have been reserved for questions dealing with social order, the organisation of the 'good life', as well as the notions of 'progress' and 'history' through cumulative scientific and political achievements.

However, the widening search for alternative expressions now confirms that the concept of war is in trouble. Edward Luttwak, for example, has coined the expression of 'postheroic warfare' by distinguishing between traditional and novel forms of war.[4] Chris Hables Gray uses the more general term 'postmodern war', whereas Mary Kaldor prefers the more limited notion of 'post-Clausewitzian war'.[5] Richard Mansbach and Franke Wilmer may be closer to the 'endism' debate with their notion of the 'end of the Westphalian period', a term closely related to the ideas of John Mueller and Christopher Coker on the fundamental 'obsolescence of modern war'.[6] Some concepts related to war which for a long time have been pushed to the sidelines – such as the 'just war' – now seem to be resurfacing.[7] The search for alternative vocabularies – either denoting 'endism' or attempts to provide novel labels for new kinds of (armed) conflict – confirms that conceptual destabilisation is having its effect. The central ingredient of the emerging counter-discourse on war is that war and violence are now increasingly defying the inside–outside nexus, thereby questioning the centrality of the state and the continued relevance of the story of modernity.

Apart from the challenge of 'Kosovo', war (like the notion of sovereignty) has become vulnerable to the ongoing pressures of globalisation and the complementary move of localisation. This should not come as a surprise, since the disregard for historical and cultural articulations in this connection has been accompanied by an eruption of contingency. The arrival of complex and ambiguous forms of armed conflict implies that traditional political vocabularies no longer serve as reliable points of reference. They are no longer helpful in drawing the inside–outside borders that have shaped our conventional understanding of what wars – and, more generally, international relations – are (supposed to be) all about. Kalevi J. Holsti has therefore claimed: 'War today is not the same phenomenon it was in the eighteenth century, or even in the 1930s. It has different sources and takes on significantly different characteristics.'[8]

Some critics of the traditional approaches to 'war' – including the military historian Martin van Creveld – even argue that the concept should be consigned to the dustbin of history. This claim rests on the observation that, over the last few decades, inter-state war has become improbable. Traditional 'war' has become the ultimate exception to the rule, rather than the essential (and even constitutive) component which defines the very nature of international politics. With the vanishing of (military) violence, security has become less of an issue, opening up space for other arguments and concepts – integration, for example – which are now allowed to take the initiative in organising the political scenery. The ongoing debate on the 'end of war' illustrates and supports this change. Coker argues that humankind 'may have been reprieved from the undertow of violence which marked the twentieth century'.[9] Van Creveld claims that a 'ghost is stalking the corridors of general staffs and defense departments all over the developed world – the fear of military impotence, even irrelevance'.[10] Van Creveld is supported by Michael Mandelbaum, who argues that it is 'possible that not only war – protracted struggles among great powers with revolutionary consequences for international politics – but even modern war – the use of mechanised weapons in formal battles between the professional armed forces of sovereign states – is dying out'.[11]

However, the 'endism' debate is limited to traditional inter-state war, which, as an ultimate instrument of power-politics, no longer dominates the security environment across large areas of the world. Even though 'war' continues to offer IR a unifying code and language (despite the fact that armed conflict is relatively rare and is geographically unevenly spread), it is no longer read as a structural necessity, which has opened the way for new organising principles and departures. The grand narrative of regular and instrumental major war has been replaced by a pattern of violence which is more localised and less easy to define as either 'internal' or 'external'.[12] Students of global politics are therefore faced with a choice: should they continue to label these (armed) conflicts 'wars', even in a very general meaning of the word, or should they develop new vocabularies more in tune with the determining aspects of these new kind of conflicts?

Max Singer and Aaron Wildawsky have suggested that the concept of 'war' be divided into two different spheres.[13] They argue that a certain differentiation is in order since inter-state relations are no longer imbued with anarchy and that broad 'zones of peace' exist in parallel to 'zones of turmoil'. Clearly, there is no peace in the absolute sense as the political scene is coloured by manifestations of political violence such as terrorism, civil strife, massacres and, occasionally even genocide. Today's violence is often initiated by non-statal actors, killing soldiers as well as civilians and frequently organised in non-territorial ways. Mark Duffield and Mary Kaldor have further argued that contemporary conflicts usually are not conducted in a statist manner and not limited to a clear territorial space.[14] These conflicts now tend to blur the prevalent inside–outside logic, since they appear in small pockets of conflict, crossing statal lines of demarcation. In terms of temporality, conflicts may be characterised by their longevity and protracted nature, or they may take the form of occasional clashes and outbursts with a shorter duration.

But the unravelling of modern war also includes the language itself, since we now tend to talk about 'strife', 'low level conflicts', 'private and informal wars', 'wild zones', 'kalashnikov zones', 'no-go areas', 'pathological anarchies' and 'insurgencies'. Other new terms (such as N. Theyer's 'wars without reason', Alain Minc's *zones grises* – i.e. geographical and social areas where the rule of law does not apply – and Philip Cerny's notion of 'insecurity from below'), also indicate that essential changes are taking place.[15]

It therefore appears that the concept of war, in defying the desire for categorisation and definability, does not stay within the confines and the discursive principles of modernity. The image of statal actors aiming their military forces against each other, followed by combat between their organised armed forces – an image upon which the discourse of (modern) war basically rests – has been blurred. Patterns appear to be unfolding that go beyond any narrow conceptualisation of 'war', bringing about 'noise' instead of erasing it, and failing to draw clear boundaries by means of which we are able to identify and separate identities.[16] Now that modern state-based faultlines have lost much of their importance, the concept of war seems to be both *de*bordered and *re*bordered.[17] The inside–outside delineation of states is crumbling and no longer defines distinct coherent security spaces now that armed conflict is no longer part of the standard repertoire of Western politics. Instead, violent conflicts stand out as enclaves amid an otherwise rather peaceful environment, and within such a more mixed and complicated political pattern states stand out as one category of actors among many others. With conflicts no longer confined to armed struggle between statal actors, many states have gradually lost the primacy which they were supposed to have as the monopolists of legitimate violence and the guarantors of political order.

These deviations explain why the concept of war has become insecure and why basic questions about war have re-entered the political agenda. A number of redefinitions have occurred that signal an epistemic change in the discourse on war. There is no longer one dominant form of conflict that dictates what war is about, but rather a proliferation of particularisms. Previous knowledge, which has privileged state-centred perspectives and territorially bounded violence, now seems to be unable to contribute to our understanding of contemporary events. Consequently, 'war' is treated in a less coherent and dogmatic manner, and various interventions on its nature open up perspectives which previously were difficult to explore with any credibility. At the same time, it should be acknowledged that efforts to divorce oneself from traditional understandings of war remain the exception, rather than the rule, and they tend to remain exploratory in character.

War as usual

How should we approach the Kosovo campaign against the background of war's increasingly uncertain meaning? Is 'Kosovo' to be read as 'war as usual', or do the critical voices have a more convincing story to tell on the basic nature of this event?

In general, the Kosovo campaign has only added to the problematising of our notion of what war is all about. It has certainly not encouraged a return to war as an unproblematic given, although there has been room for rather conventional interpretations as well. For quite a number of observers, 'Kosovo' *has* been 'business as usual', a conflict that should be framed in a traditional manner. In the view of (what probably is) the majority of analysts, no 'contamination' has occurred and the old register of concepts is considered both useful and sufficient. In this perspective, the concept of war is both self-evident and non-debatable; it dispels doubt and suggests that the name of the game has remained unchanged: simple and straightforward 'war'. This modern ontology of war still dominates the debate on Kosovo, where the story of the conflict is told in terms of order versus anarchy, whereby the principle of sovereignty continues to draw lines between friend and foe. In this perspective, war remains the ultimate boundary-making, and not boundary-breaking, form of political action.

One clear example of this traditional view is to be found in the recent writings of Ivo Daalder and Michael O'Hanlon, who read 'Kosovo' as a novel manifestation of the old story of 'order versus anarchy'.[18] Adopting a Realist nomenclature, they talk about 'Kosovo' in terms of 'the path to war', 'losing the war', or 'winning the war'. They uncritically assume that the discursive strength of the classical notion of war remains intact and they are not troubled by the fact that in the case of the Kosovo campaign NATO achieved its objectives without a single combat fatality (at least on its own side). They also disregard the inequality of the actors in the campaign, or the absence of the usual mutual recognition of sovereignty, which during modernity has constituted warring factions and framed the idea of what war is (or should be) all about. Daalder and O'Hanlon concede that events have unfolded in a somewhat exceptional manner, but are not convinced that the traditional reading of the 'war' concept has been undermined by these irregularities, which would necessitate the use of alternative vocabularies to describe contemporary armed conflict. Like many other proponents of the 'war-as-usual' outlook, these authors agree that war takes a variety of forms, making it occasionally difficult to recognise. However, the possibility of war remains and continues to form the liminal condition against which international politics is being conducted. This is supposed to assure the traditional register of politics and security, and to confirm and stabilise its validity and relevance.[19]

Jenny Edkins arrives at similar conclusions, although she responds primarily to the way in which tropes such as the Holocaust and Nazism have been used to articulate humanitarian concerns during the Kosovo campaign.[20] Edkins argues: 'What Kosovo represented was by no means the beginning of a new form of governance in which humanitarianism overrides state sovereignty, as liberal humanitarians argue.' She claims that 'Kosovo' has shown us a repetition of the old form of sovereign politics – a politics of exclusion, or a politics of the sovereign ban. She adds, however, that 'the sovereign power produced this time was NATO', i.e. the institutionalised entity being constituted was not a state (in opposition to other states), but a broader transatlantic community.[21] Yet, Edkins claims that this change in spatiality and the emergence of a broader community do not imply that 'war', as a concept, has now become a misnomer.

By categorising these different authors, it appears that those who concur with the Serbian reading of the Kosovo campaign often have little doubt about the essence of the event. Their verdict tends to be clear: the bombing campaign has been a classic act of aggression, albeit one disguised as a call to construct a 'global village' and formulate its new rules. It has been seen as an infringement of the sovereign rights of an independent country and as an unjustified meddling in that country's domestic affairs. In this view, 'Kosovo' has been an 'aggression' on the part of the West and an attempt to bomb Serbia into submission.[22] Clearly, these critical accounts also use the traditional conceptual repertoire of state-based sovereignty, territorial integrity and non-interference in the sphere of domestic affairs. 'Kosovo' was therefore a conflict over the preservation of Serbia's internal integrity and an attempt to keep Kosovo a part of the Yugoslav federation. In this reading of 'Kosovo', there is little doubt about what vocabulary should be employed to describe the essence of the event: it was seen as 'war as usual', whereby the notion of war is used to stabilise and fortify existing identities and political realities.

Towards a higher order?

But 'Kosovo' can be depicted differently. Michael Ignatieff, for example, has drawn attention to the conceptual deviancies and oddities of 'Kosovo', and argued that the conflict has been one of the first 'virtual wars'. He claims that many facets of 'Kosovo' have been kept hidden and that the public image of the conflict was markedly different from the 'reality' on the ground. Ignatieff is troubled by the concepts and the images that are now used, arguing that 'virtual reality is very seductive'.[23] He seems to be aware of the trappings of virtual war, with its own fables and representations based on self-righteous invulnerability: 'We see war as a surgical scalpel and not as a bloodstained sword. In so doing we misdescribe the instruments of death.'[24]

But these 'make-believe' aspects of 'Kosovo' do not seem to have carried very far, although they were certainly there. One may argue that the nineteen

NATO countries were not aiming to hide their true aspirations. Contrary to Ignatieff's suspicions, they were not trying to turn the 'real war' into something else by resorting to some linguistic subterfuge. On the contrary, they have aimed for genuine communication, but were often unable to get their message across since their line of argumentation clearly deviated from the traditional war-speak of modernity. In many ways, 'Kosovo' was all about safeguarding and enabling unhindered communication and exchange. It has stood out (here I follow Michael Shapiro's line of thinking) as a process in which war transcended its modern meaning by reaching out and expanding the domain of political action.[25] NATO countries portrayed themselves as humanitarian champions enforcing respect for human rights. Since NATO did not label its campaign a 'war', it was already indicating that something new was underway. NATO's alleged civilisational aims called for new moral and legal criteria in order to pass judgement, which would, one could argue, call for a new military logic of action as well. But NATO's military actions were not exceptional; they did not even try to go beyond politics. On the contrary, they were part and parcel of a broader package of political aims, one that under normal circumstances is advanced by less violent means. To quote a representative statement from a NATO press release:

> NATO is not waging war against Yugoslavia. We have no quarrel with the people of Yugoslavia who for too long have been isolated in Europe because of the politics of their government. Our action is directed against the repressive policy of the Yugoslav leadership. We must stop the violence and bring an end to the humanitarian catastrophe taking place in Kosovo. We have a moral duty to do so.[26]

For NATO countries, 'Kosovo' did not signal a real war. They did not believe that the discursive power of the concept was intact, or was in line with their aspirations. There was neither a declaration of war nor parades to mark its end. More importantly, for NATO, 'Kosovo' was about something quite different, since the classic Realist reasons for war fighting (the conquest of territory, oil, empire, or other 'sovereign rights') did not apply. These modern reasons for war were absent because the conflict in Kosovo centred around the pursuit of moral aims (rather than traditional politics) by other means. The vocabulary employed related more to the tradition of a just war (a notion that preceded the era of modern wars), which was firmly grounded in denationalisation and aimed to replace politics with the imperative of universal principles and virtue.

In positioning themselves in a context that was no longer premised on geopolitical logic, NATO countries argued that their political agenda was based not on power, but on values; it was grounded in the representation not of national interests, but of international responsibilities (which included the inviolability of human life). NATO found itself engaged in a new kind of cosmopolitan mission, entangled in a battle in which 'difference' was not necessarily interpreted as enmity. NATO countries took care not to define Serbia – and particularly not the Serbs as a people – as their enemy, and continued to stress that they were out to defend human rights and not to conquer the country. Their effort was not one of pursuing egoistical self-interest within a Hobbesian setting, but to fight what Ulrich Beck has labelled a 'postnational war'.[27] Beck has labelled NATO's new political approach as 'military humanism', a phrase which tries to capture the breakdown of classical notions of war and tries to grasp the novelty of NATO's efforts.[28] NATO's aim was to enforce respect for the values of a higher supranational order and community, thereby constituting NATO itself as well as its own sphere of security.

During the Kosovo campaign, the security of the Allied states themselves was not at stake, at least not directly. NATO countries were not in danger of being attacked and their borders or territorial integrity were not under threat. It therefore appears that the transatlantic community that was constituted by the Kosovo experience was based not on the presence, but rather on the absence, of the traditional argument of statal security. The entity being created was based on arguments that go beyond conventional readings of security since it was exempt from the logic of anarchy. In order to be present at all, the notion of 'security' had to adapt itself to the core constitutive themes of individual rights, exchange and openness. As Andreas Behnke has argued, the security argument was employed in a derivative and protective manner, rather than in a productive way.[29] During 'Kosovo', the notion of security was deprived of its traditional linkages to sovereignty and instead referred to the safeguarding of an emerging non-sovereign community – one represented thus far by the idea of 'Europe'. Clearly, such an abstract referent object is no longer territorially bounded. The derivative nature of security, and the functions of such an argument in terms of border drawing, also implies that the Kosovo conflict turned into a kind of non-divisive war. It has been a conflict that defies bordering and thereby also the clear-cut classification of political space along modern lines.

Dealing with a residual case

More generally, the Kosovo move was conceptualised as a method to bring a residual case in line with the general requirements of the emerging post-Cold War system. 'Kosovo' was about constructing the new Europe, the configuration of a stable political sphere which extends the European project to cover some of its resistant fringes and to fend off subversive tendencies which tend to question the legitimacy of the 'new system'. In their efforts to legitimise their action, NATO countries have resorted to new vocabularies, using words and concepts different from the ones employed in the context of 'war', be it during the Cold War or its traditional predecessors. In doing so, the often propagated idea of a 'war against war' has acquired an altogether novel meaning.

Instead of leaning on the traditional state-centred repertoire, the Kosovo campaign was defended by arguments that border on idealism. Here, a group of Western countries was claiming that it was transcending its warlike past in favour of a broader collectivity, one of international collaboration where the rules of the game were no longer predicated on sovereignty and national interest. Such interests were still present, it was argued, but they were moulded and had gone through a civilising process. Beck has tried to capture this intriguing aspect of 'Kosovo' in his reference to the new notion of 'military pacifism'.[30] The bombing took place, it was claimed, to ensure respect for what were seen as the foundations of the post-Cold War order in Europe. NATO was not fighting for the sake of preventing Serbia from joining this new order or to exclude it from this new sphere of stability and 'non-war'. Rather, NATO's campaign was being conducted in order to ensure that this still fragile post-Cold War order could flourish and could, in future, incorporate Serbia as a possible new member. It was an effort to construct a new political spatiality which would go beyond the traditional us–them dichotomy. NATO saw itself confronted with a country which, due to unfortunate circumstances and bad leadership, had been isolated from the European democratic family of nations. Serbia (as well as Serbs) was not constructed as an outsider and made 'foreign'. Instead, it was depicted as an entity that defines the boundaries of 'our' community, and treated as a challenge – even as a case that could serve as a litmus-test to verify the very existence of that community. In other words, NATO countries gave up their sovereign right to decide upon the friend–foe distinction. Without the naming of enemies, and with the efforts of denationalisation, a system reaching beyond the modern script was provided by subjectivity.

The 'other' that was being constructed in this new kind of discourse was an echo, a faint reflection of the West's own non-civic past. In a way, NATO countries were bombing a mirror-image of their old selves. In this reading of the Balkan mirror, Serbia could hardly be depicted as a straightforward opponent, or as the 'enemy'. But it was also not viewed as a fullfledged sovereign entity, or as a dignified actor which deserved NATO's respect and could be placed on the same level as 'us'. Serbia was not located on the outside in order to reify old statal identities, or to confirm the traditional state-based system of international relations. This could not be done because the new cosmopolitan construction lacked an agreed upon external border which would allow for such a move.

The discrimination and singling out of Milosevic's Serbia therefore had to be based on its moral inferiority. This categorisation, one no longer premissed on a mediation between sovereign actors, was already present during the Rambouillet talks (of February–March 1999). The end result of the Rambouillet 'negotiations' could therefore only be a Western dictate.

Serbia was nothing more than an object located within Europe's shared space; it was considered an inferior entity, a child that should be compelled to swallow a bitter medicine. Judgement on the scale of moral superiority–inferiority provided the rationale for treating Serbia as a body upon which NATO countries could actualise their self-endowed role as the guardians of a civilisation in the making. Serbia, as a problematic case, had to be 'Europeanised' without ousting it into the sphere of external 'otherness'. Instead of confirming and constructing the traditional inside–outside nexus (which would uphold the us–them distinction), the aim was primarily to achieve de-bordering and inclusion. In doing so, NATO was doing nothing less than turning 'war' into the opposite of its modern self.

In the context of 'Kosovo', the logic of enmity was not to be confirmed, but to be transcended. The friend–foe, self–other divisions were to be broken down by bringing Serbia in from the 'cold'. Serbia, as a deviant case, had to be patronised (even by rather harsh measures) into the community of 'civilized' states in Europe. Although this move was non-exclusive, it was also clearly not benign. The end result was therefore a unity and homogeneity premised on civilizational claims – one without an outside, since these claims were considered universal. In other words, the subjectivity which was being created owed nothing to the 'outside', and this absence of any kind of external debt to difference (such as the debt represented by a deviant Serbia), resulted in NATO's claims of its own inherent boundlessness.

Averting the mirror image

In their search for legitimisation, NATO countries premised their action on a new reading of 'Europe'. The American, British and French political leadership argued that NATO's aim was to prevent 'Europe' from returning to its old self – an entity fraught with *Realpolitik* and power-political conflict and war. The leadership argued that a liminal case at the fringes of the new system had to be sorted out. The difference of a stranger, which functioned as a kind of 'internal other', had to be tackled and 'normalised' in order to prevent the spread of this kind of deviant behaviour. Such behaviour had to be discouraged as it could undermine the social and political cohesion of Europe's new post-Cold War system based on human and political rights, openness and dialogue. Against this background, the concept of war was a misnomer, since the act of bombing was not a reversal to power politics, or 'war as usual'. Instead, it signalled something revolutionary: it represented (in temporal terms), a moment of becoming, overtaking the modern concept of war and substituting it for something new, unknown.

In a similar vein, the breach of old political habits was illustrated by the fact that the bombing took place without the approval of the United Nations Security Council, a body imbued with a power-political logic from which the 'New Europe' wanted to disassociate itself. International law, as interpreted by Amnesty International in its report on 'collateral damage', was equally refuted.[31] Behnke has therefore argued that

> the re-introduction of a discriminatory concept of war no longer rests on the normative and political efficacy, or are dependent upon, a legal-institutional 'legitimisation system.' Instead, the new formulation rests on the purported empirical 'facts of life' in international politics. Scientific knowledge about realities of international politics provides its legitimacy.[32]

Another way of putting it would be to say that NATO grasped the opportunity to re-engage itself with Europe's own history. Through 'Kosovo', NATO turned itself into an agent of more universal aspirations, trying to abandon traditional identities and assuming a far broader sense of 'we' than that of the various statal actors which were performing in the campaign *per se*. Instead of falling prey to history, NATO countries aimed at grasping the opportunity of making history by virtue of a set of superior civilisatory values. Such a moment of 'becoming' – instead of just concerning itself with sovereign 'being' – was made possible by Serbia's refusal to abide by such Western values. Therefore, to describe NATO's bombing as 'war' – at least from a NATO perspective – would be a misnomer and would even undermine NATO's effort to construct itself as a new transatlantic community.

'Kosovo' has helped to construct a new doctrine of international politics by trying to come to terms with the paradoxical interplay between the global and the local, and by carving out a new kind of political space which reaches beyond statal parameters. This new doctrine of humanitarian intervention is no longer 'modern' in the sense that it is not predicated on the notions of sovereignty, a clear line between inside–outside, friend–foe or self–other. Rather, it is premised on ambivalence and ambiguity, caused by the blurring and transcending of numerous political and conceptual boundaries, including those that are essential to the modern understanding of war.

Thus new terms had to be invented and applied in order to underline the difference with modern 'war'. Various neutral ones, such as 'campaign', 'operation', 'mission', 'strike', 'attack', 'intervention', 'coercive diplomacy' or 'struggle', were frequently employed; in other cases, NATO could simply resort to using technical jargon (such as Operation Allied Force.) But despite the many non-war concepts, NATO leaders found it difficult to come up with intersubjectively shared concepts that would get across their intentions and views in a credible manner. The notion of 'war' stood out as a fixed, even inflexible, term, making it difficult to ignore or overrule due to its long history and its still dominant position. This may explain why NATO spokesmen used the term 'humanitarian war', albeit somewhat reluctantly.[33] The precise difference between 'war' and 'humanitarian war' remains hard to explain, although some discrepancy was certainly evident.

Conclusion: war as a stranger

So, has war remained its 'old self', has it metamorphosed into something altogether new, or might it be even disappearing altogether? Is war still an integral part of inter-state relations, has it gained new meaning now that it is associated with the West's efforts to establish a neo-Kantian cosmopolitan community, or is it losing ground altogether through a radical change in its discursive power?

The debate on 'Kosovo' indicates that there is considerable uncertainty about war as a concept. Core actors have found 'war' an inapplicable notion and have refrained from using it publicly. A serious critique on the concept of war has surfaced, and alternative articulations are now frequently explored. The concept seems to suffer from being inherently modern in essence and hence out of tune with the emergence of a plurality of centres, altered borders, multiple meanings and fluid identities that increasingly characterise the post-Cold War European strategic landscape. War is no longer what it used to be, and there are obvious difficulties in adapting it to the new political circumstances, although it does not seem to be disappearing altogether. The concept has only limited discursive currency, although (perhaps through a process of inertia) some of it is still there. In order to trace its current position and to locate the source of some of its continued discursive strength, a triad of basic constellations may be outlined.

Firstly, one may argue that a broad sphere of non-war has now emerged. Within such a new constellation, war remains first and foremost a memory from the past. The security logic has lost its foothold, and politics no longer seems to be focused on averting war and purely military threats. Consequently, a broad repertoire of varied civil identities has surfaced which is detached from war and matters military. The unfolding of political space no longer hinges on securitisation but, as a discourse, on themes such as markets, media, technology and other arguments geared towards unifying rather than dividing peoples and communities. The realm of 'international relations' is changing in meaning since it no longer stands out as the domain of exception, as the state of emergency and the field of *Realpolitik*. Instead, it increasingly assumes the nature of 'politics as usual'. Security-related arguments appear – to the extent that they are there in the first place – in a 'soft' form and are relegated to the fringes of the system, to be tolerated only if they can be accommodated within the dominant set of border-breaking principles. The increasing use of the notion of co-operative security is a case in point.

Secondly, there is the sphere of classic war, which remains based on the modern story of states, sovereignty and territoriality. In this constellation, war is used to safeguard established identities that are cast in terms of unambiguous friend–foe relations, and is aimed at resisting subjugation to the global–local divide that threatens to dethrone war and classic security concerns as the core principles in the construction of political space. In many cases, the option of war serves the purpose of averting systemic change and avoiding the destabilisation of cherished entrenched identities. The sphere of war therefore constitutes a residual sphere with homogeneity on the inside and difference on the outside. In this sphere, threats of inter-state war remain credible and there is little need (and therefore little discussion) of introducing other referents.

Finally, there appears a sphere where old and new conceptions of war clash. It constitutes the sphere of 'uncommon' violence and new exceptional forms of war and armed conflict. In these cases, war appears to have escaped the confines of both modernity and the modern state, and is enmeshed in the dialectical interplay between local and global forces. In this sphere, the boundaries of war's discourse (in its modern meaning) are dissolving: the inside–outside divide of states no longer seems to constitute coherent and alternative security spaces. As a concept, war is being undermined, encouraging the search for alternative terms and articulations. Security no longer circumscribes spheres that are confined to blocs and states, but imagines and creates areas of overlapping entities defined by multiplicity. War and violence assume a limited and enclaved quality in the context of a broader logic that pertains to the unfolding of international politics and political space in a more general sense. War does not stand out as a normal state of affairs within a domain marked by its very presence, but occurs as an exception and a stranger. War represents a form of discontinuity of politics-as-usual, with war unfolding as something unexpected in the midst of a broader setting coloured by the general absence of securitisation. The international community is now considered to have become the norm, whereas local conflicts are increasingly depicted as exceptions conducted by 'outlaws' (or by so-called 'failed states'), and are therefore subject to West-mediated remedies and normalisation.

The pluralism of the Kosovo campaign and the variety of interpretations concerning its essence make it difficult to place 'Kosovo' into perspective and to offer it a distinct location within the three alternative spaces outlined above. 'Kosovo' is neither a constitutive part of 'war' as a new constellation nor as wearing its traditional military battle gear. It allows itself to be interpreted from a variety of standpoints, new as well as old. It may be seen as war-as-usual, staying put and untouched by the forces of change, but it may also be interpreted as signalling – due to its many peculiarities – the very demise of modern war.

And yet the third alternative appears to be the most credible sphere of analysis. 'Kosovo' seems to represent a case where the logics of the new and the old are being played out simultaneously. A strong echo of the traditional notion of war remains present, whereby the 'old' seems to be resisting the 'new' and the incoming, albeit (perhaps) not very successfully. The Kosovo campaign seems to be imbued with aspects of these two rather different logics, and in order to figure it out, one has to bridge these different strands of thinking about war. 'Kosovo' indicates that the contemporary notion of war operates in multiple registers simultaneously, based on a dialectical process of opening up and closing down, of bordering as well as de-bordering political entities and communities, old and new concepts and ideas. Clearly, both of these contending aspects are present.

In Kosovo, war has transcended its modern meaning without becoming an integral part of the new and incoming, and without altogether leaving behind the old ideas of war. Defining 'Kosovo' is not merely providing war with a new referent or using more clearly differentiated conceptualisations. Above all, it has to be furnished with an ontology that reaches beyond the modern one. War has to be envisaged without the modern baggage that the concept still carries around, and by loosening up the conceptual ties to notions like sovereignty, statehood and traditional readings of security. But such a refiguring of war obviously has implications for a number of other concepts and practices associated with war. The events in Kosovo in 1999 exemplify war in its new disguise. 'Kosovo' stands for a site where a number of conceptual tensions, inherent in the clash between the old and the new, have been forced into the open, for everyone to see and so that no one can ignore them. 'Kosovo' therefore provides an opening for rethinking war, although the renaming of 'war' still runs against the numerous conceptual limitations set by the modern project. Luckily, some departures have now been made which may allow us to explore beyond what we know already.

Notes

1 Quincy Wright, *Study of War* (Chicago, IL, Chicago University Press, 1983), p. 356.
2 Ernesto Laclau and Chantall Mouffe, *Hegemony and Socialist Strategy. Towards Radical Democratic Politics* (London, Verso, 1995).
3 For an elaboration of the 'cosmos–chaos-argument', see Ola Tunander, 'Post-Cold-War Europe: Synthesis of a Bipolar Friend–Foe Structure and a Hierarchic Cosmos–Chaos Structure', in Ola Tunander, Pavel Baev and Victoria Ingrid Einagel (eds), *Geopolitics in Post-Wall Europe: Security, Territory and Identity* (London, Sage, 1997).
4 Edward N. Luttwak, 'Towards Post-Heroic Warfare', *Foreign Affairs*, vol. 74, no. 3 (May–June 1995).
5 Chris Hables Gray, *Postmodern War: The New Politics of Conflict* (New York, Guilford Press, 1997), and Mary Kaldor, *New and Old Wars: Organized Violence in a Global Era* (Cambridge, Polity Press, 1999).
6 Richard W. Mansbach and Franke Wilmer, 'War and the Westphalian State of Mind', paper presented at the conference 'The 350th Anniversary of the Peace in Westphalia', at the University of Twente (Enschede), 16–19 July 1998; John Mueller, *Retreat From Doomsday. The Obsolescence of Modern War* (New York,

Basic Books, 1989), and Christopher Coker, *War and the Illiberal Conscience* (Boulder, CO, Westview Press, 1998).
7 Andreas Behnke, 'Democratic Peace Theory and the Renewed Turn Towards a Discriminatory Concept of War', paper presented at the ISA Annual Meeting (Los Angeles), 14–20 March 2000.
8 Kalevi J. Holsti, *The State, War, and the State of War* (Cambridge, Cambridge University Press, 1996), p. xi.
9 Christopher Coker, 'Post-Modernity and the End of the Cold War: Has War Been Disinvented?', *Review of International Studies*, vol. 18, no. 2 (July 1992).
10 Martin L. van Creveld, *The Transformation of War* (New York, Free Press, 1991).
11 Michael Mandelbaum, 'Is Major War Obsolete?', *Survival*, vol. 40, no. 4 (winter 1998).
12 Kaldor, *New and Old Wars*, pp. 69–74.
13 Max Singer and Aaron B. Wildawsky, *The Real World Order: Zones of Peace, Zones of Turmoil* (New Jersey, Chatham House Publishers, 1993).
14 Mark Duffielt, 'Post-Modern Conflict: Warlords, Post-Adjustment States and Private Protection', *Civil Wars*, vol. 1, no. 1 (spring 1998); and Mary Kaldor, 'Introduction', in Mary Kaldor, Ulrich Albrecht and Geneviève Schméder (eds), *Restructuring the Global Military Sector: The End of Military Fordism* (London, Pinter, 1998).
15 N. Theyer, 'Rebels Without a Cause', *Far Eastern Economic Review*, 27 April 1995; Alan Minc, *Le nouveau Moyen Age* (Paris, Gallimard, 1993); and Philip G. Cerny, 'Neomedievalism, Civil War and the New Security Dilemma: Globalisation as Durable Disorder', *Civil Wars*, vol. 1, no. 1 (spring 1998).
16 Mathias Albert, 'Security as a Boundary Function: Changing Identities and "Securitization" in World Politics', *International Journal of Peace Studies*, vol. 3, no. 1 (1998).
17 This point has been made by Michael Dillon and by R.B.J. Walker. Both Dillon and Walker endeavour to uncover the larger frame of international relations of which the concept of war has been an integral part during the modern era. See Michael Dillon, *The Politics of Security: Towards Political Philosophy of Continental Thought* (London, Routledge, 1997); and R.B.J. Walker, *Inside/Outside: International Relations as Political Theory* (Cambridge, Cambridge University Press, 1993).
18 Ivo H. Daalder and Michael E. O'Hanlon, *Winning Ugly: NATO's War to Save Kosovo* (Washington, DC, Brookings Institution, 2000). The concept of war also looms large in two other recent books: Stephen Schwartz, *Kosovo: Background to a War* (London, Interpress, 2000), and Tim Judah, *Kosovo: War and Revenge* (New Haven, CT, and London, Yale University Press, 2000).
19 Charles F. Doran, 'The Structural Turbulence of International Affairs', *Survival*, vol. 41, no. 2 (summer 1999).
20 Jenny Edkins, 'Sovereign Power, Zones of Indistinction, and the Camp', *Alternatives*, vol. 25, no. 1 (January–March 2000).
21 See chapter 2, by Peter van Ham, for a similar argument.
22 This is also the view which has been taken by the Federal Republic of Yugoslavia itself. See 'NATO Aggression Against the Federal Republic of Yugoslavia' (Belgrade, Federal Ministry of Foreign Affairs, May 2000).

23 Michael Ignatieff, *Virtual War: Kosovo and Beyond* (London, Chatto & Windus, 2000), p. 214.
24 *Ibid.*, p. 215.
25 Michael Shapiro, 'Sovereignty and the Exchange of Orders in Modernity', *Alternatives*, vol. 16, no. 4 (October 1991).
26 NATO, press release, 041/1999.
27 Ulrich Beck, 'Über den postnationalen Krieg', *Blätter für deutsche und internationale Politik*, vol. 44, no. 8 (July 1999), p. 985.
28 *Ibid.*, p. 987. See also Slavoj Zizek, 'Die Doppelte Erpressung', *Die Zeit*, 31 March 1999.
29 Andreas Behnke, '"Postmodernising" Security', paper presented at the ECPR Joint Sessions, Mannheim, 26–31 March 1999.
30 Beck, 'Über den postnationalen Krieg', p. 989.
31 Amnesty International, '"Collateral Damage" or Unlawful Killings?' (June 2000).
32 Behnke, '"Postmodernising" Security'.
33 Adam Roberts, 'NATO's "Humanitarian War" Over Kosovo', *Survival*, vol. 41, no. 3 (August 1999).

4 Iver B. Neumann

Kosovo and the end of the legitimate warring state

> Humanity does not gradually progress from combat to combat until it arrives at universal reciprocity, where the rule of law finally replaces warfare; humanity installs each of its violences in a system of rules and thus proceeds from domination to domination.[1]

Introduction

One of the starting-points of this volume is that the Weberian principle of the state as possessing a legitimate monopoly on violence is fading. Sovereigns no longer hold this monopoly; it now belongs to the international community. This chapter investigates the effects of this fading of legitimacy. If war is seen as the extension of politics by other means, then there are three crucial questions to be asked about its legitimacy. First, which actors are seen as legitimate wagers of war, and by whom? Second, over what kinds of issues is it legitimate to intensify politics by going to war (*ius ad bellum*)? And, third, what are the legitimate ways of waging war?

Expanding on a framework suggested by the Copenhagen School of international relations, this chapter argues that the Kosovo war is a crucial part of two on-going shifts. First, it is increasingly time that the actors going to war are states acting in alliance – and in the name of humanity. Second, war is legitimised less by reference to the safeguarding of state citizens and their well-being, and more in terms of infringements on human rights. It is further argued that one vital precondition for this shift is that, with the demise of the left–right divide which for the last 200 years structured politics, there is only one camp left in possession of the resources to legitimately represent 'humanity'. In Kosovo, the states going to war as the NATO Alliance represented themselves as 'humanity', the implication being that Serbia was cast as an enemy not only of human rights but of humanity as such. There is an irony here, as the kind of state infringement which NATO worked on Serbia by going to war over its internal politics was itself considered a *casus belli* as recently as twenty years ago. In Kosovo, it was actually Serbia that embodied traditional thinking about the legitimacy of war, and NATO the break with that tradition. Serbia appears, therefore, as a living reminder of how the nation state, which was considered normal not too long ago, used to act.

The Copenhagen School and violisation

It is unlikely that war as a form of intensified conflict between different human collectives will disappear. Sometimes such conflicts result in the use of violence, which is itself met with violence. As a consequence, war becomes a reality, and organised violence forces itself into our repertoire of social possibilities. War is a continuation of politics by other means.

Politics is, among other things, an ongoing negotiation about who 'we' are. Since a 'we' is untenable without a relationship to some group, a 'they,' the political question of who 'we' are is in fact a matter of separating 'us' from 'them'. To use Carl Schmitt's formulation, it is a question of separating friend from enemy.[2] In light of this, the question may be recast as one of how certain symbolic economies – certain packages of elements of a story of self as well as the relations between them – work to produce war as an outcome of ever more sharply defined friend–enemy relations.

Over the last decade, the Copenhagen School has concentrated on expanding the referents of security from states and individuals to *society*, and on analysing how *political* concerns come to be treated as *security* concerns. As Ole Wæver, in the published version of the 1988 paper that launched the concept of 'securitisation', put it: 'State security has sovereignty as its ultimate criterion, and societal security has identity. Both usages imply survival. A state that loses its sovereignty does not survive as a state; a society that loses its identity fears that it will no longer be able to live as itself.'[3] A major problem with this dichotomisation (which, I hasten to point out, definitely has its uses in opening up the debate on the referents of security) is that in fact it has a detrimental effect on questions of war. The declaration of war, after all, is an activity where states still play a crucial role. While societies and society-level groups may continue to be active in a number of ways, both before and after the declaration of war, interesting grey areas emerge when a state's idea of itself can no longer be easily represented.

The Copenhagen School argues that what it refers to as securitisation can be thought of as an extension of politicisation:

> [I]ssues become securitized when leaders (whether political, societal, or intellectual) begin to talk about them – and to gain the ear of the public and the state – in terms of existential threats against some valued referent object. Securitization can thus be seen as a more extreme version of politicization. It is the intersubjective establishment of an existential threat with a saliency

sufficient to have substantial political effects. In theory, any public issue can be located on the spectrum ranging from non-politicized (meaning that the state doesn't deal with it, and it is not in any other way made an issue of public debate and decision); through politicized (meaning that the issue is part of public policy, requiring government decision and resource allocation or more rarely some other form of communal governance); to securitized (meaning that the issue is presented as an existential threat requiring emergency measures, and justifying actions outside the normal bounds of political procedure). In principle, the placement of issues on this spectrum is open; depending on circumstances, any issue can end up on any part of the spectrum.[4]

Politicisation is a matter of inscribing certain differences between self and other with meaning as the defining diacritics of self and other. That is, certain differences, which until now have not been activated as part of the political, are being politicised. This makes it possible, retrospectively, to talk about them as having been 'non-politicised' before they were 'politicised'.

Securitisation, on the other hand, includes the added burden of defining what constitutes the security politics of a certain human collective in establishing political diacritics. Wæver, who subscribes to a Schmittian definition of the political as a question of separating 'friend' from 'foe' (see above), tends to think about security as existential or ontological politics – that is, the political at its most political: the questions of telling friend from enemy, the defining of who 'we' are and, functionally, the threats to who 'we' are.

The theorem proposed is thus one in which issues can be non-politicised, politicised or securitised, and for which there exist four processes, known respectively as politicisation, de-politicisation, securitisation and de-securitisation. An identity, for example, may be securitised by speech which inscribes that identity with meaning in terms of security politics, and may also be de-securitised by speech unsubscribing such a representation.

Emphasising the importance of speech to the process of securitisation, the Copenhagen School highlights the constructed intrasubjective character of the concept of security and hence also of the *modus operandi* of security politics. Using the concept of discourse in order to de-differentiate words and action, the Copenhagen School has advanced convincing work. The outbreak of war may, of course, also be conceptualised as a speech act, such as the case when the statement 'I hereby declare war' is indeed to go to war (provided one's institutional station and preparations are appropriate). The actual waging of war, however, requires more than speech declaring war: it requires the use of force, or a violisation of politics.[5] Waging war is, by definition, a question not only of speech, but of actions. A crucial role in war involves the act of killing, and, more generally, the acts of violence which literally inscribe the will of one collective onto the physical bodies making up the body politic of another human collective. There is a reason why the number of people killed, be that 317 or 1,000, almost always becomes the defining trait of what war is.[6]

Actually, there are intimations inside the Copenhagen School itself that a speech act perspective is hardly sufficient as a focus of political analysis. For example, Wæver quotes Clausewitz to the effect that '[w]ar is an act of violence pushed to its utmost bounds'.[7] When war-like activity does not include acts of violence it is referred to by modifiers, such as 'a war of position' and 'a cold war'. In order to link the work of the Copenhagen School to the outbreak of war, it may be useful to differentiate the concept of securitisation, reserving that concept for those acts of speech which perform the tasks Barry Buzan, Wæver and others have assigned to it, and subsequently adding a new category for cases where large-scale violence is actually in evidence.

We can best apply the Copenhagen School's framework to this question by defining the threshold between securitisation and violisation as the point of the outbreak of war itself (violence on a certain scale), rather than at the point where an individual dies. This is not to deny that a certain identity is already violised in situations such as when arson is being committed against a refugee asylum, resulting in death; it is simply to acknowledge that the question of scale must be addressed. It is not societal security and the identity–society nexus that are under consideration here, but identity and war, and I will argue that this question still implicates the state very directly. Thus, for this purpose, societal violence, which is not intended to impinge on the question of state borders, may be bracketed, and attention focused on cases where the issue is the representation of states. In this way, Clausewitz's formulation of war as the continuation of politics by other means can be classified, both directly and indirectly, within the Copenhagen School framework of politicisation and securitisation. If we add the category 'violised' to the three already in circulation, and introduce the two corresponding processes of 'violisation' and 'de-violisation,' we get the following extended continuum: non-politicised–politicised–securitised–violised.

An obvious case to which the proposed extended continuum could be applied is the war in Kosovo.[8] We have in this situation a number of cases where national identities became not only securitised but violised. Serb and Croatian national identities, Bosniak political identity and Muslim religious identity provide suitable examples. By contrast, Macedonian and Albanian ethnic identities were securitised but not violised (again, the use of the suggested term 'violised' applying only when violence takes place on a certain scale). It would be interesting indeed, if it could be demonstrated that the outbreaks and non-outbreaks of war are usefully analysed in terms of violisation of identity. If it turns out that the structure of identity was not a crucial factor in the outbreaks of these wars, then this would also prove insightful.

War as legitimate violisation of politics

A different aspect, indeed a crucial concern, of the war in Kosovo is the problematique of who can *legitimately* wage war. For the last 500 or so years, this function has fallen to states, and states have orchestrated a legal discourse which consecrates their going to war in certain circumstances, over certain issues. When fought by states in accordance with this *ius ad bello*, war has been a legitimate form of violisation (inside the international law discourse). In Kosovo, however, two phenomena may be observed. First, although in accordance with the discourse of international law states were still the actors to go to war, the relevance of this discourse for the work of legitimisation that was carried out by the instigators of war was not deemed to be sufficiently wide ranging for it to stand alone. Additional legitimacy was sought by stipulating that it was an *alliance* of states which went to war, and that the war itself could be seen as contributing to a *change* in the discourse of international law, and not simply as a case of following its rules. In this way, the war in Kosovo was represented as being constitutive of a new era. This change in *who* could legitimately wage war (alliances of states acting as self-proclaimed representatives of humanity) was intimately linked to the question of over what *issues* it is legitimate to go to war (alleged infringements of human rights, that is, the rights of the constituent members of humanity).

This constituted a breach with an epochal tradition. In seventeenth-century Europe, the framework of spiritual life – Protestant or Catholic – was central when defining military goals. In the eighteenth century wars evolved around disputes over inheritance and land, whereas the Napoleonic Wars added the type of regime – republican or monarchic – to the matters of contention. An illustrative example of this tendency appears in the memoirs of the Yugoslavian communist Milovan Djilas, in which he refers to a conversation with Stalin in 1945.[9] This war is not like other wars, Stalin said to Djilas; the conqueror spreads his political system as far as his men can go. It cannot be any other way. The major point here for our purposes is the *plurality* of actors involved in constituting the major conflict line at any one time in the history of the European states' system: two during the seventeenth century, many during the eighteenth and nineteenth centuries, again two during the twentieth century. Now, with the United States being the only superpower around, the so-called 'unipolar moment' has arrived – but it is also a unipolar moment when it comes to the number of systems-constituting identity projects available. There is only one: liberal globalisation – and its opponents. This is an important condition for how human rights can emerge as a key legitimising resource, and so I return to this problematique below.

The Kosovo war defines the epoch exactly because it focused on the simultaneously existing conflict lines upon which politics is constituted. Since the end of the seventeenth century political life has centred around two great themes; the economic division between classes, and the question about which community in the nation the state rests upon. There is a tension between these two considerations. The existence of classes, understood as groups of people with different relations to the means of production, gave rise to divisions within the state. Today's European party system is still, first and foremost, the result of the previously existing class struggle about the economic distribution of wealth. The right–left axis was the political framework of industrial society. Conservative, liberal and socialist ideologies spoke to a reality dominated by the agencies of social classes clear enough that one could talk about a natural categorisation of people as between 'left' and 'right'. Politics needed this type of categorisation in order to operate. Politics is both a conflict and an arrangement to facilitate the solution to that conflict; the order is etymologically bound to the Greek *polemos*, war.

However, politics can also be traced to another Greek word, *polis*. In our context the point to retain is that politics turns itself around conflict, and the existence of the city state is dependent on the ability to restrict or apply this notion to the community. Therefore it is not accidental that the emergence of industrial society had as its accompaniment the emergence of the nation. While industrial society established new social divisions, casting worker against bourgeoisie, nationalism offered both groups a new community to which they could attach themselves. This was a community that bound them together and gave them a framework within which they could quarrel about material goods without experiencing the conflict as if they were two wholly different groups.

Between socialism and nationalism a connection was thereby established, one that served a complementary purpose. As we know, this constellation of classes and nations gave rise to two programmes of modernisation: *communism*, which would solve the problem through the elimination of classes, and *nationalism*, which would solve the problem by inserting political parentheses around the classes. The Cold War was the end-point for this development, in two respects. In the West the connection between the classes and the means of production dissolved. The struggle between socialism and capitalism, between East and West, was portrayed as a struggle between classes. In the modern West, however, the proletariat no longer exists as a production community, and the Soviet State as the kernel in the proletariat's own international order has disappeared. The carpet has been taken away from under the feet of the main principle of the organisation of politics, both at the national and at the international level.

This can of course be celebrated. It is potentially liberating for politics that the principles of the old order are disappearing. But the end of the Cold War had a second less welcome consequence. As was earlier maintained, politics needs conflict in order to function: the Cold War evolved around the idea of conflict and of conflict solution. Conflicts must be arranged in circumstances and around fundamental dividing lines that can be disputed for a long time. The right–left axis served as such a mechanism, until recently, for both the national and the international order. But what happens when this axis no longer exists in the same form as before?

With the extinction of the right–left axis, nationalism once again stands alone. The historical nationalism was an ideology, which worked as the political foundation of the right–left matrix, yet nationalism is now itself about to become the matrix for political life. The political struggle, which really caused problems, was not formulated as an economic redistribution question, but as a question about who we are, and it is exactly this question that nationalism has an answer for. In this context it is not a coincidence that the Balkan wars of the 1990s in the former Yugoslavia were fought out directly between ethnic groups, whereas the previous civil conflict, in the wake of the Second World War, had been fought out between proletarian and middle-class partisans. It follows that, in order to mediate between these ethnic tensions, one needs a multi-ethnic rhetoric, and no longer a class rhetoric. Therefore, resistance to war developed first and foremost as a programme in favour of a common multi-ethnic society and against nationalism (and not, as it did fifty years ago in the case of the communist partisans, as a class rhetoric).

This same pattern can be identified in the international context. The drama being enacted in the Maghreb can be portrayed as a struggle between land and town, between proletariat and town elites, but it is formed in principle as a struggle between the local and the global. To quote a well-known book title, it is a case of '*Jihad vs. McWorld*'.[10] And these two political powers work together, like all constellations, in order for politics to function. The so-called fundamentalist Islamic opposition in the Maghreb, and the politicians who mobilise ethnicity in the former Yugoslavia, are reacting to, among other things, increasing globalisation. And these reactions take, above all, a national identity. The *Jihad*, at its starting-point, was inextricably connected to the idea of a universal religion, in itself a form of essentialism, which has evolved historically to take on key nationalist traits. Globalisation has evolved as a threat to this nationalism, a nationalism that is now arming itself to fight against 'post-nationalism'. Here we have the new main axis, one which will order our political lives in the future.

Reactions against globalisation of course vary. What they have in common, however, is a local support for the local nation, which you find within many groups. Nation states in Europe were similar – and the bearers of that designation thought of themselves as being of a kind – because they all adhered to a common idea, namely that those who shared a cultural community should also share a political community. They had a project in common, even if they did not have a common project. The same may be said about today's opposition to integration and globalisation in the name of the classical nation state. Furthermore, in Europe, given that the European Union is a reality, the structural similarity between the traditional platforms from which the EU is being composed make for a structural conflict almost everywhere. Those who welcome globalisation also, as a rule, welcome integration, whereas those who oppose the one generally oppose the other as well.

If national–post-national as the main political axis has replaced the right–left axis, then we will see immediate negative consequences influencing the potential for constructing a consensus. As long as the right–left axis predominated, the main concern within politics was with economic distribution. Distribution could be ordered by a medium eminently divisible: money. Therefore, the so-called class compromises could be operationalised by the redistribution of money. Furthermore, it was possible to operate with a far-reaching social mobility. The adherence to the notion of class could also serve as a mechanism for manipulation. For example, one could change the factors determining one's class: position, language, address, etc. Ethnic belonging, however, is not so easy to change. The markers that define ethnic identity can be difficult to manipulate. How is it possible to change one's skin colour, for example? The colour of skin cannot be changed.[11] It can only be acknowledged as more or less politically relevant.

If nationalism is determining politics, and if nationalism manifests itself in such a way that people with a certain colour cannot be a member of that nation, then the outlook for social mobility is extremely marginal. And yet, at the same time, there is no obvious medium to be used so as to reach compromises between different ethnic groups, the same way that money could be used between classes. Money can change one's job, language and address, but not one's skin colour. Classes used to be socially complementary: where purges took place within certain classes, as in the Soviet Union, the whole society deteriorated as a result. Ethnic groups are not complementary in themselves. Ethnic cleansing can be carried out without the society immediately collapsing functionally. (As the Czech example shows, however, ethnic cleansing can produce long-term morally destructive effects: one is still troubled long after the purge of the Sudeten-Germans.)

To sum up: liberal globalisation is left as the only political programme with a worldwide appeal. It feeds opposition, but that opposition takes local forms, and has so far taken the shape of negations of globalisation (ethnic and religious revivalism, nationalism, etc.) What shape globalisation will take, and how effectively it will spread, are not issues here. The claim I wish to posit is that globalisation constitutes a major precondition for how, in the Kosovo war, NATO could so easily represent itself as the guardian of human rights and, by extension, pose even as the representative of humanity as such. There simply was no major force around to issue a credible counter-claim.

The ontologification of war

War is a matter of *who* we are and *how* we are supposed to continue to exist. These aspects of war can be more or less central, possessing a radically different meaning for each of the two sides participating in a conflict.

The stronger one side feels towards the fact that 'we' can no longer be 'ourselves' if 'we' lose the war, the more fundamental a conflict is perceived. We have, from ancient Greece, several examples of how defeat in war meant that women and children were taken as slaves and the men executed. The rationale for some wars is thereby still the physical existence of one of the combatants. It is rarely so radical, but the American tradition to demand the enemy's 'unconditional surrender', is a reminder that such absolutism is still strongly evident in the thinking of our time. One can imagine a spectrum running from Hegel's approach to war – as a situation where right stands against right – to the (mainly) Catholic tradition of 'just war', in which it is perceived that one side is fighting for the good, while the other is cast as evil.[12]

Developments in the 1990s indicate that we are moving towards this latter understanding of war. The notion of a 'just war' was once again raised as part of the discussion. This perspective has certain advantages to it, mainly because it offers us an opportunity to talk about war in such a way that moral aspects are emphasised. The danger of this perspective, however, is that one can easily be led to demonise the enemy. Just war becomes 'holy' war. Not least where the legal discourse is concerned, Kosovo may point in the direction of an undermining of the adversarial head of state's legitimate position. Previously, one looked upon the opposing head of state as symbolic of the adversary. This was the person who, if the surrender was not unconditional, was to become an important negotiating partner. Whereas today, referring to the international order, it is possible to issue a warrant for an arrest if the head of state does not seem sympathetic. War becomes more a question of good versus bad, and less of a way to settle disputes between two contradictory laws. Kosovo demonstrated this trend.

One could say a lot of good things about moral commitment to a just war and to the evolution of humanitarian law concerning war crimes. After Auschwitz, the GULag and Srebrenica, it is difficult to defend a point of view saying that there is no evil in politics. There are situations in which it is legitimate to talk about an evil opponent. But, although it is tempting to succumb to the passing of such a judgement, the act must be postponed as long as possible. Even when such a judgement has been passed one must never cease to question whether the judgement is right, and how many individual members of the collective enemy it is legitimate to include. The moralising that takes place does not necessarily take these circumstances into consideration, and induces great expense. What follows is an intensification of what is at stake. As a consequence of moralisation, for both parties, war becomes a question of who we are. It is less concerned with specific war goals such as redistribution of material resources among different groups in the society or the securing of strategically important resources. It is more difficult to negotiate with an opponent about who 'we' are than it is about specific resources, for the simple reason that resources can be divided into smaller pieces, about which one can reach a compromise. In contrast, one cannot divide identities in the same way.

If war is going to be a case study in how humanity itself is emerging as a political community, then this is an instance of good fighting evil, and it is of little point to ask how the war goals are perceived by the opponent, because he has already been cast in the subject position of evil itself. The thought behind a 'just war' has the disadvantage that one is not continuously evaluating the way in which the other side looks at the world. One knows the nature of the evil, and one knows that it is impossible to influence evil intent by arguments, but only by means of resolute action such as war.

The other side

A discourse that has no subject position for others than 'humanity' is a totalising discourse. It is always worth asking where the other is, and how she perceives the relationship. The case of Yugoslavia can be no exception. When one is to defend the old order, such a defence manifests itself in the purest form. Milosevic's Yugoslavia illustrates for us the ultimate consequences of a national doctrine that rejects everything and anyone which and who does not belong to that nation. However, before we reject this as unfamiliar, we should remember that this was a creative part of the European political order for 200 years. It is *pathos* in the war in Kosovo. The old has no possibility of victory. As Karl Otto Hondrich stated in *Die Zeit*: the Serb military are not permitted to fight on equal terms, and therefore it is only by not retreating that they can win the respect and dignity that fighting embodies.[13]

Sergei Medvedev notes in the first chapter of this book that 'Milosevic is a classic sovereign'. Indeed, the notions of sovereignty, the right of self-determination and the right to determine one's own internal affairs, dominate the Serbian discourse. Milosevic could hardly be expected to enjoy the fading of that pivotal principle of the classical European state system: the immunity of sovereigns. In the Serbian discourse, the fading of that principle, from the aftermath of the Second World War at the tribunals of Tokyo and Nuremberg via the formation of a body of humanitarian law to the founding of the International Criminal Court and beyond, has been determinedly discounted. NATO's policy is portrayed as that of an aggressor, culminating in an intrusion into other people's affairs. The main pillar in the Serbian national policy is the nation state, which they want to protect against interference and aggression from the outside. There is, of course, the problem of where to draw the borders for this nation state: for many Serbs, the Serbian 'we' is connected to Greater Serbia. But, aggression against areas outside Greater Serbia has never been on the agenda. The often drawn parallel with Hitler therefore has a fatal weakness, namely that it has never been a question of Serbia attacking the great powers of Europe or of instituting a new regime type throughout Europe. On the contrary, Milosevic and most of the Serbs argue from a set of fundamental conceptions that has been common in Europe for more than a century, namely that political division in the world runs between the 'we' in one's own nation state, on the one side, and all the others outside, on the other.

As recently as twenty years ago, Vietnam intervened in the internal affairs of Cambodia, overthrowing Pol Pot and his regime and establishing its own man in his place. It did not matter that Pol Pot as ruling head had several million human lives on his consciousness; the united West condemned Vietnam's conduct. The murder of his own citizens was therefore not accorded special political weight. This occurrence in Cambodia in 1979 serves as an example of the paucity of humanitarian intervention over the past century. Obviously, the situation has now changed. The new NATO has appeared as the flag bearer, restricting violence and defining order in the world. This new order is post-national, and must be understood as such. In opposition stands the old national state order, Milosevic and the old order proponents. One can perhaps even talk about this in a social context, Yugoslavia standing for the old order and NATO and the West for the new. All over Central and Eastern Europe people and states have to decide whether they want to submit to the post-national order, global capitalism and multi-ethnic politics, or whether they will remain within the old nation state. Perhaps one of the reasons why Milosevic had so long enjoyed the support of the Serbs was the fact that the lifestyle resulting from the Western hegemony did not necessarily appeal to the majority of the Serbs.

Legitimising weapons, targets and victims

If the subject who wages war is 'humanity', then a representation of the opponent as non-human lies close at hand. At least, it invites a dehumanising gaze at the enemy. If the enemy is defined by such a dehumanising gaze, it may have consequences for what one considers to be the legitimate means in fighting that enemy. The less human the enemy, the fewer the holds barred in picking your weapons and your strategy.

After Kosovo, the means employed in warfare have become an important issue. A so-called 'revolution in military affairs', or rather a revolution in American military affairs, is taking place. New sorts of weapons have emerged; new constellations are presented for the organisation of military personnel. This debate has taken place in a field where every weapons system and every organisational model has its acronym. Therefore, there are few people who have the opportunity of including this development in their comprehension of the world. This concerns not least the politicians, who during the Cold War used to leave the military aspects of politics to the military, and so felt no urgent need to be updated in what was happening in the defence laboratories. But, as Kosovo shows, developments in areas such as aviation power came to play a crucial role in how the war developed. From the White House one could send a message to the Pentagon saying that one was going to bomb without losing either personnel or planes. The military simulated several war operations to estimate the minimum height for planes in order not to be shot down by Serbian air defence. An altitude of 15,000 feet was estimated to be the minimum, an appraisal that turned out to be technically correct given the mission: although one plane had been shot down, not a single soldier had lost his life.

During the Gulf War, in which aviation power also dominated, the French philosopher Jean Baudrillard wrote a set of controversial articles about the conflict, saying that the war had already taken place, or alternatively, that it did not take place at all.[14] This was a familiar French provocation. Few people, particularly outside of the Left Bank, made an attempt to try to understand what he meant by this. After Kosovo it may be easier to comprehend. One aspect of war that is noteworthy nowadays is that it takes place in advance, as simulated exercises. There is, of course, nothing new about practising war. However, the planning in detail and the simulation of operations in advance – which is made possible by new communication technology – are new. This new technology can easily lead to a planning hubris, the thought that the future can be predicted in detail. Even the air raids on Kosovo became simply a routine repetition of something that originally had been done in a closed computer system in the Pentagon. It was in Washington, and not in the air above Kosovo, that it was decided which sorts of bombs should be dropped where and when.

Consequently, one could argue that the war in Kosovo had already taken place – inside the Pentagon. It becomes really problematical, however, when one also can claim that the war between Yugoslavia and NATO in Kosovo never took place. This must be understood in the sense of one antagonist using his superior technology to win a victory without getting involved in live warfare. The actions and battles which were fought did not happen between NATO and Yugoslavia, but between Yugoslavia and a third party. What was happening on the ground and in the air were, of course, closely connected. They were probably connected in the sense that the killings would not have been possible in such a form and to such a degree, had it not been for the success of the air war. And yet, they were two quite different phenomena.

The fact that the Americans had access to technology of such superiority that they did not have to conduct war in the sense of real fighting is problematical in a number of ways. In the first place, it breaks with our conception of the kinds of weapons that are legitimate in war. In the history of Europe, there have been several conceptions of the means which are legitimate in particular circumstances. For example, in the late Middle Ages, it was good Latin that one could use squared bullets against infidels, whereas against a Christian enemy one should use a round bullet.[15] In this area, international law (as *ius in bello*) has played a crucial role. We have had a debate on the legitimate bombing targets. We have, not least in connection with the Vietnam War, had earlier debates on the legitimate bombs. We need another such debate. The point is not to abolish bombing as such, but to restrict the kinds of bombs one should be able to use. This needs to be done in order that the Air Force officers, and those of us who find ourselves on the bombing side, can look at ourselves in the mirror the next day.

Bombs are technology, and an approach to the problem that considers which kinds of technology the fighters should be using is a necessary part of our conversation on war. There is, however, another aspect to the way in which the war was conducted, one that gives rise to even greater anxiety. It is the question of military decisions taken by the politicians. In the Kosovo war, it was asserted by Alliance politicians collectively that a loss of personnel could not be tolerated by public opinion. As a consequence, aircraft flew higher than the military would have preferred. The consequence of flying higher was that the bombing was less precise, and, as a result, the number of civilian casualities was higher than it would have been at lesser altitude. This tendency to an ever-increasing distance between, in this case, the pilot and the target, and the multiplication of standard procedures, has reached new heights. How should one comprehend this? Is it possible to find a proportion, so that one of 'our' pilots, for instance, should be worth 5,000 civilian lives? That would be a way of thinking which would totally break with our fundamental conception about human worth. If one assumes, however, that politicians are elected and are responsible to an electorate which demands that war be conducted without loss, this logic is sequential.

The free exchange of views in our societies makes it, at least in this case, more difficult to reduce violence, not easier. When civilians present the case so that it seems as if it is the pilot's own will (or lack thereof) to sacrifice his life in operations, they grasp an important part of the problem. People who have chosen to become officers have chosen a kind of lifestyle in which something – it can be a number of things – is more important for them than this extra risk they take by choosing the military way of life. The responsibility of politicians to their own officers and other volunteers is thereby associated with formulating clearly defined goals for military action, and making it possible for the officers to execute these in a way which they see as professionally justifiable. It is not the responsibility of politicians to entirely exempt them from the possibility of dying. When politicians insist that their own personnel are not going to die, this cannot be understood as some kind of concern for these people. Rather, it must be perceived as an attempt to avoid the political problems induced by a critical public opinion.

A no-own-losses war has indeed increased the civilian casualties which it was seeking to prevent. The political reality is that the expense of suffering losses has become so high that the temptation to let other people die instead is almost irresistible. In this case we face two concrete questions: first, whether it was immoral to start a war at all; and, second, whether it was immoral to start a war in the way it was started, namely without a ground invasion, i.e. in a way that showed no intention to accept own losses. Conducting a war without a willingness to sacrifice life seems especially problematic. And yet nothing is easier to understand politically than politicians wanting to do everything to reduce damage to themselves among their own electorate.

We have here an especially difficult case of a general problem, namely how to balance our own citizen's rights against the rights of other parts of humanity. The old thinking used to hold that the nation state's sovereignty made it relatively easy to put aside the rights of the rest of the world. In Kosovo, we faced the paradoxical situation in which bombing was legitimised by breaking this logic. What happened did not involve Yugoslavia's internal affairs, but above all human affairs. By choosing bombing, however, we opted to save lives on 'our' side by killing even more of 'them'. What has emerged is thereby a bargaining game about how war should be comprehended after Kosovo. We do not agree with ourselves at this juncture. If we want to achieve a way of conducting war in which the use of violence is mostly restricted, the war in Kosovo does not seem to be much of an ideal.

Those who revel in the fact that not a single American life was lost in Kosovo contribute to the assertion that war simply is a form of politics, along with other instruments like economic aid. Air war becomes a policy option, to which one can have recourse whenever one fancies, sometimes before all of the other alternatives have been tried. If this is to become the place of war in the political arena, it is very unfortunate. Niccolò Machiavelli argued in his *Discourses* that in war there is always a tendency to build quickly.[16] He suggested that the bare existence of fortresses could fool the Prince to use this technology to keep the population in check. In the same way, one can today issue a specific warning to Western politicians and the military not to build too many of these advanced fighting planes, because the mere existence of these superb machines tempts those in power to use them as ordinary political instruments. The wise Prince restricts violence by choosing more indirect tools for ruling.

Conclusion

The three questions put in the beginning – which actors are seen as legitimate wagers of war, over which issues it is legitimate to go to war and what are the legitimate ways of waging war? – have a certain common denominator. That is, 'humanity' may exist as a political notion, and increasingly as a legal concept, but it is not (yet?) strong enough to carry the burden placed upon it by NATO countries of legitimising the waging of war in Kosovo. As Jean-François Lyotard has argued:

> The 'reason to die' always forms the bond of the we. The paradox of the order to die is that the name of its addressee, if he or she obeys the order, can never again figure upon the addressor instance of subsequence, direct phrases, and in particular of normative phrases like '*I decree as a norm that . . .*'.[17]

States could pose as the legitimate wagers of war so long as that right had been conferred upon them by the community of states acting in unison, as legislators and guarantors of international law. The question, therefore, is whether it was humanity acting through the security community of NATO that was waging war, or whether it was NATO member states acting together as an alliance. A related problem is the dogged unwillingness of the entities involved actually to suffer losses in the process. 'Humanity' may be invoked as a legitimising speech act inside the discourse of the international law, but it spectacularly fails to legitimise the violence which follows its invocation. Serbia's attempts to legitimise its stance as a warring state defending the idea of state sovereignty was represented as an anachronism. Indeed, in Kosovo, the end of the legitimate warring state was at stake. Where is the political entity that may legitimately speak in the name of humanity?

Notes

1 Michel Foucault, 'On the Genealogy of Ethics', in Paul Rabinow (ed.), *The Foucault Reader* (New York, Pantheon, 1984), p. 236.
2 Carl Schmitt, *Der Begriff des Politischen: Text von 1932 mit einem Vorwort und drei Collarien* (Berlin, Duncker & Humblot, 1963).
3 In his piece, Ole Wæver also noted that 'Balkanization is a tool for legitimizing an international order *without* a named enemy': Ole Wæver 'Securitization and Desecuritization', in Ronnie D. Lipschutz (ed.), *On Security* (New York, Columbia University Press, 1995), p. 67. If so, then the Kosovo war de-Balkanised the Balkans and the world order. For a general discussion, compare with Barry Buzan, 'Rethinking Security after the Cold War', *Cooperation and Conflict*, vol. 32, no. 1 (March 1997).
4 Buzan, 'Rethinking Security', p. 14.
5 Iver B. Neumann, 'Identity and the Outbreak of War', in Ho-Won Jeung (ed.), *The New Agenda for Peace Research* (Aldershot, Ashgate, 1999), and Lene Hansen, 'The Little Mermaid's Silent Security Dilemma and the Absence of Gender in the Copenhagen School', *Millennium*, vol. 29, no. 2 (2000), pp. 285–306.
6 Richardson suggests 317, the Correlate of Wars project suggests 1,000 dead; for a discussion of the numerical criteria see Håkan Wiberg, *Konfliktteori och fredsforskning* (Stockholm, Scandinavian University Books, 1976).
7 Quoted in Wæver, 'Securitization and Desecuritization', p. 53.
8 Compare with the discussion of Bosnia in Espen Barth Eide, '"Conflict entrepreneurship": A Few Post-Yugoslav Reflections on the "Art" of Waging Civil War',

in *Engaging the Challenges of Tomorrow: Adjusting Humanitarian Interventions to the Character of Future Conflict* (Oslo, Norwegian Institute of International Affairs, 1997).
9 Milovan Djilas, *Memoirs of a Revolutionary* (New York, Harcourt, Brace, Jovanovich, 1973).
10 Benjamin R. Barber, *Jihad vs. McWorld. How Globalism and Tribalism are Reshaping the World* (New York, Ballantine, 1996).
11 This holds, at least for the time being; Michael Jackson may at some later point turn out to have been a trendsetter.
12 Michael Walzer, *Just and Unjust Wars: A Moral Argument with Historical Examples* (London, Penguin, 1980).
13 *Die Zeit*, 27 May 1999; also see Behnke's chapter in this volume.
14 Reprinted in Jean Baudrillard, *La guerre du golfe n'a pas eu lieu* (Paris, Galilée, 1991). Baudrillard waged his campaign not only on the stratospheric level of philosophy, but at the level of the actual: '*Les Presses de la Cité* invited me to go to the Gulf and cover the war. They were going to give me everything: money, documents, flights, etc. I live in the virtual. Send me into the real, and I don't know what to do. And, anyway, what more would I have seen? Those who went there saw nothing, only odds and ends.' Baudrillard in Mike Gane (ed.), *Baudrillard Live: Selected Interviews* (London, Routledge, 1991), p. 188.
15 R.J. Vincent, *Human Rights and International Relations* (Cambridge, Cambridge University Press, 1986).
16 Niccolò Machiavelli, *The Discourses* (London, Penguin, 1970).
17 Jean-François Lyotard, *The Differend: Phrases in Dispute* (Minneapolis, University of Minnesota Press, 1988), p. 100, note 156; compare pp. 152–5.

5 *Heikki Patomäki*

Kosovo and the end of the United Nations?

Introduction

Kosovo is not a security issue for Europe only: it must be seen in the context of global political processes. In this chapter, I argue that Kosovo was an episode in the long-term process of the domestication and marginalisation of the United Nations (UN) by the United States. These relations of domination are underpinned by Manichean dichotomous myths of good and evil and by rituals of enemy construction. Yugoslavia (Serbia) assumed the role of evil enemy, allegedly committing grave human rights' violations and, in Kosovo, even genocide. The complicity of Kofi Annan's UN appears to give the US the sovereign right to decide about global friends and enemies, in the name of a universal morality that it legislates, interprets and implements.

Although the systematic domestication of the UN began in the Reagan era, following the defeat of radical Third World calls for reforms, I start by reconstructing the 1990s' conflict between the United States and Boutros-Ghali's UN. This opens a window to an understanding both of the meaning of earlier actions and of the course of later developments in global politics, including Kosovo. What happened between the United States and the Boutros-Ghali-led UN in 1992–96? I treat Boutros-Ghali's book *Unvanquished. A U.S.–U.N. Saga*,[1] a story about his five-year term as UN secretary-general (1992–96), as a crucial new piece of evidence.[2]

On the basis of Boutros-Ghali's testimony, and with the help of theoretical and explanatory literature, I formulate four principles of the US foreign policy of the 1990s, and show how Boutros-Ghali seemed to offend all of them. These offences explain why the US wanted to get rid of Boutros-Ghali. In addition to drawing on explanatory theories, I supplement this evidence by an analysis of published UN documents, that is, press releases, speeches, reports and agendas. I also utilise a number of second-hand sources that make reference to US policy statements and opinions expressed by the UN.

Having completed an analysis of the reasons for Boutros-Ghali's expulsion, I discuss the functioning of the US-domesticated UN, led by the new secretary-general Kofi Annan. As it will turn out, recent developments, including the Kosovo episode, seem to confirm both the reconstruction of the deep grammar of US foreign policy and my analysis of global relations of domination.

This chapter is first and foremost a contribution to discussions about the prospects and consequences of US hegemony. These discussions originated in the debate about the hegemonic stability theory that took place in the late 1970s and for much of the 1980s.[3] Following the end of the Cold War, the same assumptions, themes and tenets reappeared in the revisions of the Cold War's history[4] and in the topical security policy discourse about unipolarity and US hegemony.[5] In contrast to neo-realism, my focus is on social meanings and practices, relations of domination, and their political economy underpinnings.[6] From this angle, I analyse the global consequences of the tendency on the part of the US towards an 'ever-harder will' and increasingly 'narrow power'. My rather strong conclusion will be that the US – currently driven, torpedo-like, by a predestined and potentially destructive programme – tends to be dangerous both to itself and to the world as a whole.

The UN has had a useful role in alleviating and transforming conflicts in global politics. Kosovo indicates that the domestication and marginalisation of the UN has already seriously impaired its role and capabilities. In addition, the UN has also had a lot of potential in the governance of processes known as globalisation. Yet, there seems to be very little room to rejuvenate, empower or democratise the UN. Therefore, it is my further argument that the time may have come to build foundations for a new, universal, global political organisation, at first perhaps in spite of the will of the US (and its closest ally, the United Kingdom).

Principles of US foreign policy in the 1990s

First principle: *The US is the world leader and others should follow it*

In his book *Unvanquished. A U.S.–U.N. Saga*, Boutros-Ghali depicts himself as a Western-minded scholar and politician. In the mid-1950s, when Nasser nationalised the Suez Canal, Boutros-Ghali, already active in Egyptian politics, was labelled 'pro-American' and was not permitted to travel abroad.[7] In the UN office of secretary-general, more than thirty years later, he recognised 'America [as] the only superpower' and argued that 'the first priority of a Secretary-General has to be the relationship between the United States and the United Nations'.[8] However, he also asked for relative autonomy, for instance in a meeting with Secretary of State Warren Christopher and the US Ambassador to the UN Madeleine Albright:

'I know that I must have the US support to succeed. But,' I said, 'please allow me from time to time to differ publicly from US policy. This would help the UN reinforce its own personality and maintain its integrity. It would help dispel the image among many member states that the UN is just the tool of the US'... I was sure that Christopher and Albright would understand my point of view. I was completely wrong. My words appeared to shock them... They didn't speak... It would be some time before I fully realised that the United States sees little need for diplomacy; power is enough. Only the weak rely on diplomacy... But the Roman Empire had no need for diplomacy. Nor does the United States. Diplomacy is perceived by an imperial power as a waste of time and prestige and a sign of weakness.[9]

When it became clear in 1996 that the US was 'not in favour' of his re-election for a second term as secretary-general, Boutros-Ghali made inquiries about the reasons for this opposition to him. He found the response hard to believe: 'Boutros-Ghali has been too independent.'[10] One US official even explained that 'he would not do what we wanted him to do as quickly as we wanted him to do'.[11]

Was Boutros-Ghali 'too independent'? There are reasons to believe that he was. During his five-year term, Boutros-Ghali had many substantial disagreements with the US. He did not approve of the standard Western anti-Serb interpretation of the events in Bosnia. Furthermore, he accused the Clinton administration of prolonging the conflict by its vacillating policies and myopic and one-sided criticism of the Vance–Owen plan: 'The United States wanted to reduce the 43 per cent of the territory that the Vance–Owen plan gave the Serbs. It would take two and a half more years of bloody war and war crimes before the United States, at Dayton, would give the Serbs 49 per cent.'[12]

As for Somalia, 'Clinton's inclination was to blame the United Nations for what had been entirely an American disaster'.[13] In the cases of Libya and Iraq, Boutros-Ghali claimed that the Western powers were acting against international law.[14] Clearly, for the US all this constituted too much independent thinking. Even worse for Boutros-Ghali, he considered himself a man of principle. Irrespective of the context, he could not accept the anti-diplomatic rudeness of the US foreign policy makers. Although he was ready to make compromises towards meeting the US demands for full and absolute sovereignty, reverence for its power and respect for its national interest, he could not accept the total denial of the principle of the equality of states.[15] Nor could he accept the way the US chose to violate international law as it wished.

At the very end of his term, in autumn 1996, Boutros-Ghali wrote *An Agenda for Democratisation*, a follow-up to his *An Agenda for Peace* and *An Agenda for Development*.[16] The latter half of this text, which he wrote himself – even against the advice of many members of his staff – is entirely dedicated to the democratisation of international relations. This is the most radical and frank of all of the texts he wrote as secretary-general, and it stemmed directly from his personal experiences both as an African and as secretary-general. As he explains in his *A U.S.–U.N. Saga*:

> The U.S. veto was a rejection of democracy. That America would argue for democracy within every state but reject it in the world's organisation of states was a theme heard over and over in the Arab and third-world press. It seemed strange to me too, because the key theme to my term as secretary-general was democratisation. The fact that a single vote – that of the United States – could dictate the outcome at the United Nations threatened hopes for increasing democratisation on the international scene.[17]

The *Agenda for Democratisation* emphasises that although 'interrupted by the Cold War', democratisation in accordance with the spirit of the UN Charter is also about 'the project of democratic international organisations.'[18] 'A supportive international environment for democracy' requires, in the post-Cold War situation and the context of globalisation, 'democratisation at the international level, so that democratisation within States can take root, so that problems brought on by globalisation which affect all States may be more effectively solved and so that a new, stable and equitable international system can be constructed'.[19]

Second principle: *US foreign policy is constituted by Manichean myths and rituals of enemy construction*

Boutros-Ghali is very explicit about the first principle, but in explicating the second we need some external help. My theory-informed claim is that the US foreign policy discourse is based on the Manichean dichotomy between good and evil. This claim, although able to explain a number of Boutros-Ghali's concerns, has both a methodological and a normative problem. Methodologically, it is problematical because it is so strong and simple that it tends to eradicate nuances and complications. Normatively, it is problematical because it lapses so easily itself into a form of Manicheanism.

So let me explicate this claim.[20] The claim is that there has been a *tendency* in post-Second World War US foreign policy discourse, first of all, to imagine a morally pure ideal: 'free market, human rights and democracy'.[21] Second, the actuality of the real world is counterpoised to the ideal. There is totalitarianism, tyranny, un-freedom, violation of fundamental human rights and violence. Less radically, there is also the corrupted and sinful world that leans towards state-centrism, collectivism and socialism, although this partially deviant element may respect, for instance, human rights and the principles of liberal democracy (think about the 'corrupt' and often criticised and ridiculed case of the 'Third Way' of Sweden[22]).

As in many other cultures, in the US there is a widely felt need for something that would give meaning to life and world history. Because of its artificial nature and abstract individuality, this need may, indeed, be particularly strong in the United States. Purpose also gives legitimisation to a state and its decision making. Hence the struggle to make the world accord with the morally pure ideal.

The most common way of finding purpose and legitimacy is by way of constructing enemies. First, the enemies are named or labelled. Second, this naming has to be legitimised in public. Third, myths demonstrating the necessity or inevitability of 'X' being an evil-doer are told and circulated. Fourth, these labels, legitimisations and myths, are sedimented into the deep structures of discourses, from where they can be drawn – also for strategic purposes. Fifth, rituals of 'realism' and crudeness performed against the evil-doers serve as 'vivid re-enactments of the myths' essential themes'.[23]

Boutros-Ghali's problem was that although he accepted the basic tenets of the moral ideal of the capitalist market economy, of human rights and democracy, he was an outsider both to the USAmerican myths and practices of constructing enemies. Let's consider again the substantial disagreements between the Clinton administration and Boutros-Ghali. The case of Bosnia is perhaps the most telling of them all:

> One week later, Carrington and I met on the thirty-eighth floor of the United Nations. 'If I may update you on Bosnia-Herzegovina,' he said, 'most people see it as poor Muslims being put upon, wicked Serbs, and neutral Croats. In fact, the Serbs *are* wicked, but so are the others.' I was inclined to agree with him. The West seemed to regard the Serbs as the only wrongdoers, whereas I felt that no party in Bosnia was free of at least some of the blame for the cruel conflict.[24]

But, if this is true, why were the Serbs chosen as the enemy? The Slovenians and the Croats are supposedly Western, in contrast to Muslims and Serbs. But why Serbs, not the Muslims? My hypothesis is that it was because the Serbs were willing – unlike the other nations of Yugoslavia – to continue the identity of Yugoslavia and its unifying Socialist Party. Thence, the others could be seen as legitimate liberation movements fighting against the corrupted evil-doers, namely the Serbs still inclined to bad socialism.[25] Of course, as Peter Viggo Jakobsen has pointed out, the Croats and the Bosnians were busy constructing this image of the Serbs in the US. They hired public relations firms to give them a better image in the US; moreover, the Croats and the Muslims had powerful friends in Washington – something that the Serbs did not have.[26] Furthermore, in the course of the war, this image was reinforced by Serb dominance in the battlefield and the related atrocities. Whatever the true explanation, clearly Boutros-Ghali offended the USAmerican myths and the US sovereign right to determine the identities of the evil enemies.

This was repeated with regard to the Middle Eastern enemies Iraq and Libya. By thinking and arguing that it was the West, and not the Arab usual suspects, that was violating international law, Boutros-Ghali intervened in Western myth making and its rituals of enemy construction. Quite innocently, his judgement may have been made in his capacity as a legal scholar (between 1949 and 1977, Boutros-Ghali was professor of international law and international relations at Cairo University) and an international civil servant aiming at impartiality, but that excuse was unavailable to the US and the UK.

Third principle: *US foreign policy should maximise the instant support of public opinion*

Media and public opinion figure everywhere in Boutros-Ghali's book. In many cases, the media are described as a strategic instrument for politicians. Strategic actions were conducted by way of leaking information – and, at least as often, misinformation – to the media. The US foreign policy makers used this tactic also against Boutros-Ghali.[27] Many analysts agree: cases such as the (second) Gulf War and Haiti show how the US government has been using the media in support of its preferred policies.[28]

For Boutros-Ghali, even when the media were apparently representing actualities ('news about recent developments'), they seem to have, rather, constituted those actualities, often on the basis of systematic distortion and misrepresentation. Commercial media seem to operate outside the scientific principles of source criticism and public verifiability, and the democratic principles of accountability. The result tends to be a set of very specific social practices resembling Baudrillard's infamous self-referential system of simulation, in which all sense of truth and origin is lost in the play of endlessly replicating systems of commodified signs and images.[29]

Sometimes, in Boutros-Ghali's story, the function of the commercial media is simply to draw attention away from real world issues.[30] People were, for instance, busy watching the Olympic Games in Atlanta and nobody paid any attention to the 'diplomatic embarrassments to the Clinton administration delivered in Yaoundé, Beijing and Moscow'.[31] Moreover, it has been argued that with the increased privatisation and commercialisation of the globalising media, there is a real tendency for 'info-tainment' and 'titty-tainment' – with strong tendencies to reduce everything to entertaining simulation – to substitute debates and documentaries for in-depth public affairs analyses.[32] Again, this tends to detach media representations from external reality and create instead a system of self-referential commodified signs.

Yet, the media are powerful in structuring political actions. Among politicians and analysts alike, there is a sense of the increased importance of real-time television in particular. Also, in Boutros-Ghali's story, the media appear constantly to have been setting the stage for public politics. Somalia is a case in point:

Television news programs, which earlier had aroused a groundswell of public sympathy for the victims of famine imposed by Somali gunmen, now broadcast, over and over again, distressing scenes of the captured American helicopter pilot and the footage of the dead US Ranger being dragged through Mogadishu streets. Congressman Charles Rangel, an old friend, told me that the American public was particularly outraged by this event because those who were dragging the body of the American soldier were black.[33]

Consequently, the public opinion of newspaper editors and congressmen 'surged strongly against the US presence in Somalia', although, according to Boutros-Ghali, in reality 'the October 3 raid had in fact dealt an almost devastating blow to Aidid's position'.[34] But the media seemed to be interested only in the dramatic sensations of the killings of the USAmerican soldiers.[35]

Boutros-Ghali also provides further structural criticism of the commercial media (in the US, in particular). An important theme of the book is the alleged short-termism of the media and its fatal consequences to the UN. Only sudden violence and dramatic failures seemed to be gaining attention; all success stories were silenced because there is nothing dramatic about them.[36] Let me try to analyse the role of the media in US foreign policy in greater depth.

Firstly, the US foreign policy makers seem to have been guided by the rule of instant maximisation of favourable public opinion, which is constituted by two interrelated things: media coverage and framing; and weekly or monthly opinion poll results.

Secondly, only the USAmerican opinions count, since only the citizens of the US can vote in elections or lobby effectively in Washington. Even that audience is unrepresentative: around only 40 per cent of Americans vote, and lobbying requires money and contacts. Moreover, although the US media corporations have been globalising since the 1970s, this globalisation is asymmetrical: the US is a huge exporter and a very modest importer of movies, popular music, TV programmes, news, books, magazines, advertisements, and associated lifestyles and values.[37] Most USAmericans are never exposed to foreign news, documents or entertainment, not even foreign material in English. And even when their interest is aroused they are usually ignorant of the very basics of the countries, regions and organisations concerned. Consequently, given also the tendency of the media towards mere simulation, it is possible to mislead and manipulate US citizens, particularly by ritually re-enacting the fundamental myths and their essential themes referred to earlier.

Thirdly, USAmerican public opinion follows the commercial logic of the media, for which sex and violence (including death/war) are topics warranting by far the most intensive coverage.[38] This seems to be due to the commercial exploitation of fundamental fears and desires of the human condition; and due also to their strong contrast to the boring reproduction of everyday necessities and tightly regulated behaviour at work. Sensationalised spectacles of love/sex and violence/death are captivating – but only for a while.

Fourthly, there are two rules of operation that public opinion seems to follow in relation to foreign policy: (a) a successful and limited war tends to unite the nation behind the president and his administration; but (b) there is only limited toleration for media representations of dead US soldiers, a legacy of the Vietnam experience.[39] Hence, a limited and low-risk use of military force in particular can serve to increase the support of public opinion; even higher risks may be tolerated if vital values and interests are presumed to be at stake. The real risk is, of course, that there will be casualties and an escalation of hostilities from which there is no exit, i.e. a full-scale war.

Finally, although these globalising media presuppose some kind of crude global ethics – 'The evil-doers are killing them/us, and something has to be done!' – it follows the logic of *selective sensationalism*. How does the system of selection function? There seems to be a hierarchy in the value of human beings. On the one hand, USAmericans are irreplaceable and the most valuable; West Europeans come a close second; and at very bottom are black Africans, while others fall somewhere in-between. On the other hand, a capability to pay yields disproportional coverage (also because the advertisers are more interested in paying customers). Indeed, it can also be asked: how is it possible to get covered if you are not rich? 'Maybe you have to die in large numbers in one spot at one time.'[40] So the rules behind the selection of topics come down to sensationalising dramatic situations and selecting the people in terms of their geographical location and wealth. Sensationalism is what really matters: even poor and less valuable people can be covered *if* they die in large numbers in one spot at one time.

The implication of enemy construction is that the 'evil-doers' are denied their humanity. They can be killed.[41] Given that an evil-doer can be located, it is often good politics for US foreign policy makers to attack foreign, mostly unfamiliar, places by military means – but with the condition that there is no real or significant (perceived) risk to US soldiers. Technologically advanced 'air campaigns' and particularly attacks by cruise missiles are the optimal military facilities for these purposes.

Afghanistan, Iraq, Sudan and Yugoslavia have been very good targets, because very few USAmericans have more than a very superficial knowledge of these countries anyway. They are good targets also because human life in those countries is considered much less valuable (particularly the lives of the evil-doers, whether presumed terrorists, fundamentalists, ethnic cleansers, supporters or soldiers of a tyrant, etc.) than are the lives of USAmericans. At the level of legitimisation, these kinds of military actions constitute rituals of 'realism' and crudeness against the evil-doers.

However, while the architecture of the new world order may consist of simulations, its impact will be all too real for those actors that are targeted militarily, punished economically, or otherwise threatened.[42] In the 1990s, the US has intervened dozens of times in different countries in all continents, and has imposed new unilateral economic sanctions, or threatened legislation to do so, 60 times on 35 countries which together represent 40 per cent of the world's population.[43] Sheer economic interests apart, these sanctions have typically stemmed from the (simulatory) process of identifying evil-doers and punishing them.

Fourth principle: *The US stands for the absolute, global freedom of corporate capitalism (except sometimes in the US)*

Boutros-Ghali's *An Agenda for Development* begins with the premiss that the motor of development is economic growth. The book assumes that a vibrant private sector and participation in an open world economy are the conditions for achieving this aim. Yet, Boutros-Ghali did not satisfy the orthodox economic political aspirations of the US foreign policy makers. After all, from 1974 to 1977, Boutros-Ghali was a member of the Central Committee and Political Bureau of the Arab Socialist Union, and until assuming the office of secretary-general of the UN he was also vice-president of the Socialist International. Also, in the 1990s, despite his 'modern' outlook, Boutros-Ghali was too much of a social democrat to accept USAmerican free-market fundamentalism.

What was the principle that Boutros-Ghali offended? It seems that the US stands for the absolute global freedom of corporate capitalism. Suffice it to point out here that the origins of this preference lie in the rise of the group of USAmerican statesmen, capitalists and labour leaders in the 1930s and 1940s. This group identified Americanism with liberalism.[44] The turn to neo-liberalism in the 1970s meant, ideologically, that this group was reconstituted along more *orthodox* lines. Consequently, the US started to assert its visions and interests unilaterally. Since the early 1980s, the US has acquired an increasingly strong grip on the systems of global governance, and has advocated the absolute global freedom of corporate capitalism everywhere, having indulged in partial state regulation of the market since the 1930s. Relations of domination also play a role in multilateral negotiations and arrangements. The initiatives for further liberalisation and corporate privileges have come from Washington, with the ever-loyal support of the UK. Since the US has had the largest resources, routinely used as leverage in negotiations, with the best-informed and best-equipped staff to take care of its national interests, such multilateral arrangements have constantly reflected the vision of the absolute freedom of corporate capitalism, and have also protected the areas vital to the 'national interest' of the US.[45]

US policies *may* have benefited the USAmerican national economy, but the rest of the world has been doing much less well since the Bretton Woods era. Besides economic indicators showing worsening global conditions, the poor of the world are now absolutely poorer than they have been since the beginning of the nineteenth century. Except for some improvements in health care and literacy, absolute and relative poverty have increased not only in Africa, but in Asia, the CIS countries, Eastern Europe and Latin America. In 1998–99, with the world gross output per capita growing at the rate of 1.5–1.8 per cent[46] more than eighty countries have lower per capita incomes than a decade or more ago, and at least fifty-five countries have consistently declining per capita incomes. The income gap between the 20 per cent of the world's people living in the richest countries and the 20 per cent in the poorest was 74 to 1 in 1997, up from 60 to 1 in 1990 and 30 to 1 in 1960. Income inequalities have also risen sharply within the rich countries – particularly in the US and the UK – and the global poor are now as poor or poorer than they were in 1820.[47]

It is in this context that Boutros-Ghali's social democratic tenets offended US foreign policy makers:

> The rich countries feared the rise of another movement from the poor regions of the world demanding redistribution. They were inclined to dismiss the entire subject with the assertion that development was a concept whose time had gone; any country nowadays, they said, could emulate the 'Asian tigers' if it could just summon the will to adopt the market economy. Yet this was patently impossible for the poorest of the poor, particularly Africa. They lacked the human resources, the capital, and the infrastructure to take advantage of the new global economy. And soon the Asian economy itself would falter.[48]

As if to foment the fears of the US and the UK, Boutros-Ghali himself argued that 'the gap between rich and poor was becoming morally insupportable and economically irrational, even for the wealthiest nations of the world'.[49] To grasp the extent and substance of these disagreements, let us have a quick look at his *Agenda for Development*. In it, there is a strong emphasis on the need for active governmental intervention.[50] Against the strictly universalist principles of structural adjustment programmes like the International Monetary Fund and those of the World Bank, the *Agenda* underlines the crucial differences between contexts of development. 'As conditions, circumstances and capacities differ, so too must the mechanisms for generating growth.'[51] The *Agenda* is also explicitly in favour of 'land reform and other measures of social justice', and there is also a commitment to full employment, poverty reduction, and improved patterns of income distribution through greater equality of opportunity.'[52] All of this amounts to too much independent thinking.

The limits of US domination in the UN

The US had its way: Kofi Annan became the new secretary-general as of 1 January 1997. UN developments, decisions and actions after Boutros-Ghali have certainly not helped to dispel the image that the UN is merely a tool of the US. Since the early 1980s, the US has, step by step, secured a stronger hold over the UN, also by means of financial conditioning. In 1985, the US Congress passed legislation that posed a serious threat to the financial situation and organisational principles of the UN. The Kassebaum Amendment provided that the US could pay no more than 20 per cent of the annual budgets of any part of the UN system without weighted voting on budgetary matters. A more implicit condition was to make the discourses and policies of the UN more pro-American (and pro-Israel). Also US budget cuts led to American withholdings from the UN budget.[53] Yet, simultaneously, the US rejected the proposal to reduce the USAmerican contribution of 25 per cent of the UN budget.[54]

The result has been a constant financial crisis for the UN (many countries have followed the example of the US in not paying their dues in time), and an annual struggle over the US arrears. In effect, the Clinton administration has continued the agenda that was set by Reagan: the stated object is to 'reform' the UN, but a failure to 'reform' according to US guidelines may lead to the withdrawal of the United States.[55]

The outcome of these financial and political pressures has been a gradually increasingly USAmericanised United Nations. Boutros-Ghali allowed for an over-representation of USAmericans in top UN jobs (also in the name of efficiency and a merit-based system[56]) – and when he occasionally struggled against it, the US got its way anyway.[57] On top of the overall change in the UN system after Boutros-Ghali, the thirty-eighth floor *is* also controlled by USAmericans. Half of Kofi Annan's speechwriters are USAmericans, and in effect the speechwriters act as the secretary-general's *censors*.[58] Yet, this strengthening of the US grip over the UN system has not changed the financial stand of the US.

Although the US can, to a large extent, control the bureaucratic system of the UN – and even censor discussions and research reports – and although the US can use its superpower status, ties of alliance, consent, loyalty and gratitude, as well as its financial and diplomatic resources, as leverage in persuading and inducing other states to agree with it, it can never control the UN system totally. No matter what the US does, there are other permanent members in the Security Council who can, at any time, choose to vote differently. Even the disempowered General Assembly has the power to deny the vote of the US because of its illegal arrears (a threat that has been repeated annually).

Also, from within the UN system – either spontaneously from the less obedient UN agencies or from the transnational civil society that is being incorporated into the functioning of the UN – ideas and initiatives can and do come up that are not in accordance with the principles of US foreign policy. Hence, for the US, the UN is a constant nuisance. So no matter how USAmerican the UN in fact becomes, it can still refuse to grant authorisation for US actions, or can even come up with initiatives that go against the will of the US. And although UN authorisation and the UN logo have often been useful, there are thus sufficient reasons for the continued US hostility towards, and impatience with, the UN.

The UN after Boutros-Ghali: implementing the will of the US in Kosovo and elsewhere

There are thus two major tendencies: the USAmericanisation of the UN; and the marginalisation of the UN. Along these lines, there have been substantial changes since Boutros-Ghali. Let us consider his *An Agenda for Peace*.[59] Despite disagreements between Boutros-Ghali and the US (and other Western countries) on a number of crisis situations, the concepts introduced in *An Agenda for Peace* have turned out to be the least controversial. In fact, they have been path-setting and widely accepted. Concepts such as 'peace making' and 'peace enforcement' are now part of the mainstream Western security discourse. Rupasinghe has suggested that 'the world's military establishments have seized upon these military elements in *An Agenda for Peace* and have been keen to interpret the United Nations' enhanced profile in terms of greater role for their own interests'.[60]

However, the pluralistic nature of the UN and its Security Council has been a major problem for the US (and the Western Alliance). The authority of the UN has given, and may give, legitimacy to peace making and military operations, but within the UN it has also been possible to legitimately contest US moral, legal and factual interpretations – in effect, the claims to unproblematic leadership; the autonomous rituals of enemy construction; and the domestically driven or interest-based imperatives to act 'decisively' in certain, selected cases.

From this perspective, the undeclared NATO war against Yugoslavia also can be seen as a Western liberation from the constraints of the UN – with the approval of its new secretary-general.[61] For years, as long as the situation – and the struggle against Serb repression – remained non-violent, the US and the West did not pay much attention. Once more systematic violence was started by the Kosovo Liberation Army (KLA), the situation deteriorated quickly. The Serb police started fighting back by crude means familiar from other anti-guerrilla wars. Quickly, Kosovo became an issue, and thereafter increasingly made the headlines and TV news. As the media demanded in early 1998, 'something had to be done'.

At first, the UN authorised the actions. UN Security Council Resolution 1160 of 31 March 1998 condemned the violence of both sides and advocated autonomy for Kosovo within Yugoslavia. After the fighting of the summer of 1998 and the consequent flood of mostly Kosovar Albanian refugees, Security Council Resolution 1199 of 23 September 1998 was directed more clearly at the Serbian security forces. Since Bosnia, it has been self-evident that Serbia is the principal evil-doer, not least for Mrs Albright. However, mainly because of the resistance of Russia and China, the new resolution stopped short of authorising the use of force. Next day, although the use of force was not authorised by the UN, the NATO Council asked the member states to make commitments to participation in air strikes against Yugoslavia. Finally, UN Security Council Resolution 1203 of 24 October 1998 confirmed and validated the tentative treaties on armistice and its surveillance. The task of supervision was given to the Organisation for Security and Cooperation in Europe (OSCE).

Despite the armistice, new violent incidents had occurred already before Christmas 1998. On 21 December, a Serbian policeman was shot dead in Podujevo, and three days later the KLA declared the armistice void. In early January 1999, both sides committed further acts of violence. On 15 January, in Racak, following a Serbian police operation, the bodies of forty-five Kosovar Albanians were shown to the OSCE and, most importantly, the Western media. On the basis of Ambassador William Walker's offhand and rather one-sided interpretation, this incident was broadcast widely as a cold-blooded massacre by the Serbs – naturally accompanied by graphic pictures of the bodies.[62] It led to further outraged demands 'to do something'. Moreover, Kofi Annan accused the Serbs of 'disproportionate use of violence'.

A new threat of air strikes by NATO followed. A 21-day limit was set for both parties. This brought them to the negotiation table in Rambouillet, France. In effect, at the Rambouillet negotiations NATO put forward an ultimatum to Yugoslavia: 'Either you accept our peace plan, or we will bomb you until you will do so!'[63] After a confused period of hesitation and resistance, the KLA accepted the plan on 18 March 1999 (in any case, the Kosovar Albanians would not have been bombed), but the Serbian authorities did not.[64] Why? The public picture of the negotiations remains unclear. Nonetheless, there appears to have been an agreement about the basics of autonomy and the political organisation of Kosovo.[65] There may have been some remaining disagreements about the authority and entitlements of the KLA, but it seems that the main reason was that Yugoslavia did not accept the contested Appendix B: Status of Multi-National Military Implementation Force of the agreement.

Mrs Albright gave this new text to the parties only eighteen hours before the end of talks. Yugoslavia would have accepted the OSCE presence, and was ready to negotiate the composition of 'international presence', but could not accept foreign military troops – and the NATO troops in particular – and their far-reaching rights to operate freely and with immunity *anywhere in Yugoslavia*. In a resolution of the Serbian Parliament just before the bombing, when that body rejected the presence of NATO troops in Kosovo, support was given to the idea of UN forces to monitor a political settlement there.[66] For these reasons, a widespread suspicion emerged that Appendix B was merely an excuse for the war against the 'evil-doer, Serbia', and that the real reasons for the war lay, in part, somewhere else.[67] The war may have been an attempt to draw attention away from the Monica Lewinsky affair in the US; and/or to reinforce the US leadership in NATO; and/or to extend the mandate of NATO and give it an independent and central position in the management of global security.

Because Yugoslavia did not want NATO troops on its territory, it got war with NATO. Directly, the NATO bombings caused the death of, perhaps, 2,000 people, many of them civilians (roughly as many casualties as in the Kosovo crisis before the war). The infrastructure and economy of Yugoslavia was badly damaged, and the cost of reconstruction alone will be at least US$40 billion. No one has even tried to measure the loss of output and the decrease in the living standards of the citizens of Yugoslavia. The NATO countries spent some US$50 billion on the war, more than their annual official development assistance budget. Indirectly, the bombings precipitated the war between the KLA and the Serbian authorities in Kosovo, with a consequent death toll of 5,000–10,000 people. The bombings, the war and the related Serbian criminal terror campaign led also to a huge refugee problem: most Kosovo Albanians fled from their homes for one reason or another. Last but not least, the war also led to increases in NATO military expenditure and triggered a further development of European defence capabilities.[68]

Kofi Annan made the UN complicit with the US and the UK in NATO's bombing. Even though it was widely accepted that the NATO bombings verged on a breach of international law, particularly the UN Charter but also NATO's own founding document, the 1949 North Atlantic Treaty, Kofi Annan did not, at this point, raise any criticisms of NATO (though he has subsequently raised some critical questions).[69] Instead, he repeatedly gave his support to the Western interpretations, actions and peace plan. Before the bombings, he criticised Serb actions in Kosovo for breaching humanitarian law.[70] After the bombings had started, he 'urged the leaders of the North Atlantic Alliance to suspend immediately the air bombardments,' *on the condition* that the Yugoslav authorities accept *all the conditions* that NATO had put forward.[71] A few weeks later, he appears to be giving a moral justification for his compliant position in terms of the rights of Kosovo Albanians:

> No government has the right to hide behind national sovereignty in order to violate the human rights or fundamental freedoms of its peoples. Whether a person belongs to the minority or the majority, that person's human rights and fundamental freedoms are sacred. Emerging slowly, but I believe surely, is an international norm against the violent repression of minorities that will take precedence over concerns of state sovereignty.[72]

In the absence of condemnation of the violation of existing international law, and in the absence of any mention of the procedures according to

which new international law should be legislated and violations of universal morality determined, Kofi Annan's compliance at the time of crisis seems to have far-reaching consequences. What is particularly important in this context is that it seems to give the US (and the US-led NATO) what it wants:
(a) unquestioned leadership;
(b) the sovereign right to determine global friends and enemies, in the name of the universal morality that it legislates, interprets and implements;
(c) sovereign right for the US government to act in accordance with its domestically driven public opinion imperatives, and its economically or militarily driven national interests, given that those interests are compatible with universal morality.

The UN's compliance is guaranteed even when UN procedures are disregarded.

Parallel to these three consequences is that Kofi Annan's compliance has authorised the further marginalisation of the UN in global peace, security and human rights matters. His attempts to defend the principles of the UN Charter appear weak.[73] It is also telling that US officials appear to be blaming the UN for the post-war situation in Kosovo, a situation that was brought about by NATO.[74] Besides marginalising the UN, and making it a scapegoat for NATO's failures, the Kosovo episode has also contributed to an obscuring of the everyday violence and suffering that exists in the global political economy. More than ever, political attention and funding are concentrated on short-term crises.[75]

Conclusion: the dangers of hard will and narrow power

In a book written almost forty years ago, *The Nerves of Government*, Karl Deutsch maintained that will is related to power.[76] An actor or an organisation may try to act 'in character', that is, by refusing to learn and by remaining unchanged. This is what Deutsch calls 'hard will'. He explained that 'by the power of an individual or organisation, we then mean the extent to which they can continue successfully to act out of their character'. Power is therefore also the ability of organisations 'to impose extrapolations or projections of their *inner structure* upon their environment'. He argued that 'power in this narrow sense is the priority of output over intake, *the ability to talk instead of listen*'. In this sense, the US is more powerful than ever. Yet it has also become more dangerous than ever, for such 'narrow power becomes blind, and the person or the organisation becomes insensitive to the present, and is driven, like bullet or torpedo, wholly by its past'.

Will – like character – is constituted by one's understanding of the world, of genuine identity, of the right conduct of action, as well as by one's historically constructed interests and preferences. In the absence of resistance and conflicts, narrow power can continue to resemble Richard Ashley's understanding of hegemony as 'an ensemble of normalised knowledgeable practices, identified with a particular state and domestic society, that is regarded as a practical paradigm of political subjectivity and conduct'.[77] However, the more there are differences, organised resistance and systematic conflicts, the more the attempt to act in character will become violently Weberian. Indeed, some already argue for stronger and more decisive US actions, on the grounds that the chief threat to the unipolar system is US failure to do enough (perhaps also because of the constraints of domestic public opinion and international law).[78] An actor's fate can also be self-destructively wilful if the actions upon that will turn out to be counterproductive. As Deutsch argues:

> Will and power may easily lead to self-destructive learning, for they may imply the overvaluation of the past against the present and the future, the overvaluation of the experiences acquired in a limited environment against the vastness of the universe around us; and the overvaluation of the present expectations against all possibilities of surprise, discovery and change.[79]

At the moment, the tendencies to simply reinforce the hard will and narrow power of the US seem strongest: the relative success of the privileged US economy within the largely stagnant and very unstable global economy; and the apparently unquestioned success of the US in imposing its will upon the world. At play is also the traditional Hegelian fallacy of identifying success with being right. Moreover, it is its political success that gradually destroys the possibility of the US elite hearing anything different. The domestication of the UN is a case in point. Kosovo is merely an indication of this more general tendency. Perhaps only a major economic collapse of the US would enable it – in particular, its foreign policy-makers – to learn something new and, in particular, to learn to listen to others. But perhaps even the now long-overdue stock market crash will not be enough.

The UN's General Assembly has been the only truly global public political forum for which all states are equal. It has provided a framework for decolonisation and the pursuit of the reform of international institutions. The UN Charter has provided seeds for a claim made on behalf of an alternative organising principle of world affairs, namely for a democratic community of states, with equal voting rights in the General Assembly of nation states, openly and collectively regulating international life in accordance with the UN Charter and human rights conventions.[80] Despite its many practical shortcomings and problematic state-centrism, the UN has thus provided a forum, constituted by legal procedures and rules, where differences have encountered each other in a peaceful manner and where, sometimes, common policies on a number of issues have been worked out.

The domestication of the UN by the US has severely damaged both the moral basis of UN pluralism and the legal procedures and rules on which the UN has been based. After the events of the last fifteen years, very little of the spirit of the UN Charter is left; and NATO is seriously aspiring to the role of *the* global security organisation. There are also very few signs to indicate that the US would allow a rejuvenation or a democratisation of the UN, or even grant more autonomy to the present UN. Nor is it easy to organise resistance against US hegemony in the struggle for transformations within the UN without becoming just another enemy for the US, given its economic privileges and interests, its Manichean tendencies, and the entanglement of its public politics with the functioning of the short-sighted, self-referential and simulatory commercial media. It is likely that the consequent confrontation would quickly bring any progress made to a halt.

Hence, the UN can only survive and succeed in transforming itself with the help of organised, non-confrontational, external support. The best way seems to be to tackle an essential aspect of globalisation, at first without the consent of the US, by organising an arrangement that will also yield revenues to the global community. In effect, this means global taxation, but first on a non-universal basis. A means of feeding part of the revenues into the UN system should be found.[81] In this way the UN could be emancipated from the financial stranglehold of the US. Even this may be difficult to achieve. It is telling that, in January 1999, the 1996 Helms–Dole Bill was re-introduced in the US House of Representatives (Prohibition on United Nations Taxation Act of 1999). This bill prohibits US 'voluntary and assessed contributions to the UN if the UN imposes any tax or fee on US persons or continues to develop or promote proposals for such taxes or fees'.[82] Even remote association with attempts to seize control over globalisation by means of introducing global taxes or fees may thus turn out to be detrimental to the UN.

However, the idea could be to develop a system of taxation outside the UN framework and then to feed part of the revenues into the UN system. By selectively allocating the funds to those activities that have been governed on a more democratic basis, the systematic bias of the present UN system could be dissolved. This should also open up a public political space for differences. But even then there is no guarantee. After all, the special veto power accorded to the permanent members of the UN Security Council may eternally prevent all changes.

David Held has observed that 'the titanic struggles of the First and Second World Wars led to a growing acknowledgement that the nature and process of international governance would have to change'.[83] Perhaps the choice, then, is either to wait passively for the next titanic catastrophe which is likely to come in one form or another, or to begin building a parallel and more efficient and democratic global system than the UN. In the latter case, we can at least hope for an opportunity to transform that parallel system into a new universal political organisation, which perhaps will help prevent that catastrophe from ever occurring.

Notes

I am most grateful to Hilkka Pietilä for the original (even if indirect and unintentional) impetus to write this chapter; to Pauline Eadie for research assistance; to Hayward R. Alker, Stephen Chan, Tuomas Forsberg and Anna Leander for their comments on an earlier draft; and to Peter Viggo Jakobsen who commented on a later draft and, along with Tonny Brems Knudsen, provided important material on the role of the media, on humanitarian intervention and Kosovo. Last but not least, I would like to thank Katarina for many discussions on the fate of the UN, as well as for reading the last version of the manuscript very carefully and making a number of valuable suggestions for improvements.

1 Boutros Boutros-Ghali, *Unvanquished. A U.S.–U.N. Saga* (London, I.B. Tauris, 1999).
2 Because of classification, relevant primary source materials for US foreign policy and UN-related meetings and negotiations in the 1990s are scarce. I do not presuppose the truth of Boutros-Ghali's interpretations. However, I take Boutros-Ghali's explanation of his disagreements with the US to be a substantially true account of his position and an accurate reproduction of others' comments and statements. Should any evidence to the contrary emerge, at least some aspects of the following reconstruction will have to be revised. Obviously, an analysis of different interpretations of the same events and episodes would provide a methodologically more full and reliable account.
3 For seminal statements of this theory, see Robert Gilpin, *War and Change in World Politics* (Cambridge, Cambridge University Press, 1981); Robert O. Keohane, 'The Theory of Hegemonic Stability and Changes in International Economic Regimes 1967–1977', in Ole R. Holsti *et al.* (eds), *Change in the International System* (Boulder, CO, Westview Press, 1980); and Charles P. Kindleberger, 'Dominance and Leadership in the International Economy: Exploitation, Public Goods and Free Riders', *International Studies Quarterly*, vol. 25, no. 2 (June 1981). For an important 1980s' critique, see Susan Strange, 'The Persistent Myth of Lost Hegemony', *International Organization*, vol. 41, no. 3 (summer 1987). Isabelle Grunberg has shown that the appeal of the theory stemmed from its myth-like narrative structure. The day-to-day quandaries of the US foreign policy makers were mixed with USAmerican ethnocentrism, assumptions about the benevolence of the US and claims that the 'small exploit the rich'. These were the basic elements of a story told in terms of ancient mythical narrative structures. See Isabelle Grunberg, 'Exploring the "Myth" of Hegemonic Stability', *International Organization*, vol. 44, no. 4 (autumn 1990).
4 In his revision of the Cold War's history, Robert S. Snyder argues that ultimately the breakdown between the US and the Third World revolutionary states was prompted by the revolutionary states, and that consequently US policies in the Third World were not mistakenly aggressive. Quite the contrary: Snyder implies that US interventions were well justified. See Robert S. Snyder, 'The U.S. and Third World Revolutionary States: Understanding the Breakdown in Relations', *International Studies Quarterly*, vol. 43, no. 2 (June 1999). David N. Gibbs, an associate professor of political science at the University of Arizona, has disputed Snyder's claims and raised some important questions, most prominently: does

international relations scholarship suffer from biases, or blinders, that favour official US policy? Is it influenced too much by the post-Cold War triumphalism of political culture in the United States? In a sense, my paper follows this line of inquiry. See Greg Nowell, 'Prof. Gibbs vs. ISQ', *Chronicle of Higher Education*, no. 6 (1999).

5 Recently, William C. Wohlforth has argued that unipolarity fosters peace and stability, and that the post-Cold War hegemony of the US is unprecedently strong. He claims also that US interventions are 'demand-driven' and that they should be, in the future, even more decisive. In other words, Wohlforth assumes that US interventions, and more generally, US power projection is good for the world as a whole. See William C. Wohlforth, 'The Stability of a Unipolar World', *International Security*, vol. 24, no. 1 (summer 1999). For earlier discussions, see e.g. Charles Krauthammer, 'The Unipolar Moment', *Foreign Affairs*, vol. 70, no. 1 (winter 1990–91); and Michael Mastanduno, 'Preserving the Unipolar Moment: Realist Theories and U.S. Grand Strategy after the Cold War', *International Security*, vol. 21, no. 4 (spring 1997).

6 For a critique of neo-realism's methodological fundamentals and its inability even to correctly identify the end of the Cold War, see Heikki Patomäki, 'What Is it That Changed With the End of the Cold War? An Analysis of the Problem of Identifying and Explaining Change', in Pierre Allan and Kjell Goldmann (eds), *The End of the Cold War. Evaluating Theories of International Relations* (Dordrecht, Martinus Nijhoff, 1992). For the basics of the critical realist alternative, see Heikki Patomäki, 'How to Tell Better Stories About World Politics', *European Journal of International Relations*, vol. 2, no. 1 (1996); and Heikki Patomäki and Colin Wight, 'After Post-Positivism: The Promise of Critical Realism', *International Studies Quarterly*, vol. 44, no. 2 (June 2000).

7 Boutros-Ghali, *Unvanquished*, p. 303.
8 *Ibid.*, p. 6.
9 *Ibid.*, p. 198.
10 *Ibid.*, p. 290.
11 *Ibid.*, p. 291.
12 *Ibid.*, p. 71.
13 *Ibid.*, p. 105.
14 *Ibid.*, pp. 186, 296.
15 *Ibid.*, see for example on pp. 115–16.
16 Boutros Boutros-Ghali, *An Agenda for Peace. Second Edition with the New Supplement and Related UN Documents* (New York, United Nations, 1995 [1992]); 'An Agenda for Development. Report of the Secretary-General', A/48/935, 6 May 1994; and Boutros-Ghali, *An Agenda for Democratization* (New York, United Nations, 1996).
17 Boutros-Ghali, *Unvanquished*, p. 319.
18 Boutros-Ghali, *An Agenda for Democratization*, article 32.
19 *Ibid.*, articles 58 and 60, respectively.
20 Conceptually, I am following James A. Aho, 'Heroism, the Construction of Evil, and Violence', in Vilho Harle (ed.), *European Values in International Relations* (London, Pinter, 1990).
21 My argument should thus be distinguished from David Campbell's post-structuralist claim that identity necessarily (logically) gives rise to an evil 'other'.

See David Campbell, *Writing Security. United States Foreign Policy and the Politics of Identity* (Minneapolis, University of Minnesota Press, 1992).
22 For a political economist analysis of the Nordic model as a moral and political ideal, its relative decline and its future prospects, redefined in globalist terms, see Heikki Patomäki, 'Beyond Nordic Nostalgia: Envisaging a Social/Democratic System of Global Governance', *Cooperation and Conflict*, vol. 35, no. 2 (June 2000).
23 See Aho, *Heroism*, pp. 19–24.
24 Boutros-Ghali, *Unvanquished*, p. 42.
25 It is noteworthy that 'Interim Agreement for Peace and Self-Government in Kosovo' (23 February 1999) declares that 'the economy of Kosovo shall function in accordance with free market principles'.
26 Peter V. Jakobsen, 'Focus on the CNN Effect Misses the Point: The Real Media Impact on Conflict Management is Invisible and Indirect', *Journal of Peace Research*, vol. 37, no. 2 (March 2000), p. 140.
27 Boutros-Ghali, *Unvanquished*, see e.g. pp. 5 and 271.
28 Jakobsen, 'Focus on the CNN Effect', p. 134.
29 Jean Baudrillard, 'The Evil Demon of Images and the Precession of Simulacra', in Thomas Docherty (ed.), *Postmodernism: A Reader* (New York, Harvester Wheatsheaf, 1993), p. 194.
30 For an interesting account of ideology as unknowing, i.e. as processes and systematic absences that make something unknown, not understood, hidden, undiscussed and/or distorted, see N.J. Thrift, 'On the Determination of Social Action in Space and Time', *Environment and Planning D: Society and Space*, vol. 1, no. 1 (1983), p. 45.
31 Boutros-Ghali, *Unvanquished*, p. 286.
32 About 'info-tainments', see Edward S. Herman and Robert W. McChesney, *The Global Media. The New Missionaries of Corporate Capitalism* (London, Cassell, 1997), pp. 153–4. About 'titty-tainment' (a term introduced originally by Zbigniew Brzezinski), see Hans-Peter Martin and Harald Schumann, *The Global Trap. Globalization and the Assault on Democracy and Prosperity* (London, Zed Books, 1997), pp. 12 and 52.
33 Boutros-Ghali, *Unvanquished*, p. 107.
34 *Ibid.*, p. 106.
35 Jakobsen, 'Focus on the CNN Effect' (p. 134) agrees that these pictures mattered, but claims that they affected only the timing of the US withdrawal: 'The Clinton administration had already begun contemplating a withdrawal when the 18 soldiers were killed on 3 October 1993' (p.136). But this only serves to prove the point. Because of the potential media effect on public opinion, casualties are not tolerated.
36 Boutros-Ghali, *Unvanquished*. See for example p. 172.
37 Herman and McChesney, *The Global Media*, p. 152.
38 This is also recognised by the US entertainment industry, for instance in the films: *Bob Roberts. Vote First, Ask Questions Later*, where the principal character is a part-time entertainer (a right-wing version of Bob Dylan) who resorts to imaginary violence against himself in the face of major revelations about his connections to financial scandals and drug trafficking; *Primary Colors*, which is a (serious) parody of Clinton's first presidential campaign; and *Wag the Dog*, which

is a story of a presidential sex-scandal giving rise to an imagined war in Albania. See James Der Derian's interesting points about the dispersion of facts and fiction in his *Anti-Diplomacy. Spies, Terror, Speed, and War* (Cambridge, Blackwell, 1991).

39 In an article that tries to demonstrate that the American public is 'pretty prudent' and able to discriminate against cynical manipulation of the 'rally round the flag' effect, by econometrically analysing opinion polls over 1949–84, Lian and O'Neal argue nonetheless (p. 294) that 'a favorable response by the general public to a use of force is more likely when the US is involved in a severe crisis and the president's actions are prominently reported [in the media]; in addition, a president's popularity is more apt to be boosted when the country is not at war or fatigued by war, when his popularity is low initially, and when there is a bipartisan support for his actions'. Bradley Lian and John R. O'Neal, 'Presidents, the Use of Military Force, and Public Opinion', *Journal of Conflict Resolution*, vol. 37, no. 2 (June 1993). These tests do not capture the CNN effect or the world historical context of the late 1980s and 1990s. The CNN – real time global TV – effect is a relatively new phenomenon. Moreover, since the late 1980s, the US 'has not been at war or fatigued by war', but has rather been euphoric about, and reassured by, the end of the Cold War and the revival of its hegemony. There is every reason to believe that the manipulation effect has become stronger since the mid-1980s.

40 As it was succinctly put by P. Sainath in 'Dead Reckoning', *The Guardian*, 7 August 1999.

41 Aho, *Heroism*; see also Johan Galtung, 'Cultural Violence', *Journal of Peace Research*, vol. 27, no. 3 (August 1990).

42 Der Derian, *Anti-Diplomacy*, p. 197.

43 Charles William Maynes, 'US Unilateralism and its Dangers', *Review of International Studies*, vol. 25, no. 3 (July 1999), p. 517.

44 Mark Rupert, *Producing Hegemony. The Politics of Mass Production and American Global Power* (Cambridge, Cambridge University Press, 1995).

45 Multilateral negotiations and arrangements are outcomes of interactions where the positioning and transformative capacities of actors differ. Multilateral practices (and regime theories) are subjected to a critical power analysis in Heikki Patomäki, 'Republican Public Sphere and the Governance of Globalising Political Economy', in Maria Lensu and Jan-Stefan Fritz (eds), *Value Pluralism, Normative Theory and International Relations* (London, MacMillan, 2000). The unilateralism and aggressive reciprocity of US trade policy is discussed in P. Martin, 'The Politics of International Structural Change: Aggressive Unilateralism in American Trade Policy', in Richard Stubbs and Geoffrey R.D. Underhill (eds), *Political Economy and the Changing Global Order* (London, MacMillan, 1994).

46 The growth rate is estimated on the basis of the World Bank's *Human Development Report 1998*, 1998.

47 UNDP, *Human Development Report 1999* (New York and Oxford, Oxford University Press, 1999), particularly 'Overview', pp. 1–13, and pp. 38–9.

48 Boutros-Ghali, *Unvanquished*, p. 160.

49 *Ibid.*, p. 158.

50 *Agenda for Development*, articles 47–50, 65, 82.

51 *Ibid.*, article 67; see also articles 64, 94–5, 141.
52 *Ibid.*, articles 23 and 43.
53 Tapio Kanninen, *Leadership and Reform. The Secretary-General and the UN Financial Crisis of the Late 1980s* (The Hague, Kluwer, 1995), pp. 41–4.
54 *Ibid.*, p. 73.
55 Judith Miller, 'As US Relations with UN Languish at a Low Point, Is Clinton or Congress to Blame?' (*New York Times*, 5 August, 1999), writes: 'The U.N. official said American resentment was stronger under the Clinton administration than it was even during the presidency of Ronald Reagan, who made no secret of his low opinion of the United Nations. "At least with Reagan we knew where we stood and the United States more or less paid its bills on time," the official said. "But Clinton has made so many unfulfilled promises, then he stabs us in the back and tells us that he feels our pain."'
56 'Merits' mean degrees from Harvard, Yale and other US 'ivy league' universities.
57 Boutros-Ghali, *Unvanquished*, pp. 230–1.
58 In Latin, the term *censor* means an assessor or a critic, someone who is entitled to give an opinion or an appraisal. A systematic bias in censoring also means, of course, censorship in the modern sense of the term. It is very questionable whether there is any freedom of speech in the UN.
59 See http://www.un.org/Docs/SG/agpeace.html (accessed 5 January 2001).
60 K. Rupasinghe, 'Coping with Internal Conflicts: Teaching the Elephant to Dance', in Chadwick F. Alger (ed.), *The Future of the United Nations System: Potential for the Twenty-First Century* (Tokyo, United Nations University Press, 1998), p. 166.
61 Although I have not been able to confirm this, it seems that Kofi Annan was, in fact, at least in his personal capacity, very angry with the US on the evening of the first crisis meeting of the Security Council. If this really was the case, then it is likely that Kofi Annan's press statements of the time were censored and re-written by his speechwriters. After the crisis, Kofi Annan has indeed raised some critical questions. See his article 'Two Concepts of Sovereignty' in *The Economist*, 18 September 1999: 'To those for whom the Kosovo action heralded a new era when states and groups of states can take military action outside the established mechanisms for enforcing international law, one might equally ask: Is there not a danger of such interventions undermining the imperfect, yet resilient, security system created after the second world war, and of setting dangerous precedents for future interventions without a clear criterion to decide who might invoke these precedents and in what circumstances? Nothing in the UN Charter precludes a recognition that there are rights beyond borders. What the Charter does say is that 'armed force shall not be used, save in the common interest.' But what is that common interest? Who shall define it? Who shall defend it? Under whose authority? And with what means of intervention?'
62 In fact, on the basis of the later reports of the Strategic Issues Research Institute, the OSCE and the EU Expert Forensic Team, it seems that the Serbian police operation, following killings of Serbian police in the area, was pre-announced to the OSCE observers and the media, who were allowed to attest the scene. A battle between the KLA and the Serbs broke out. Some fifteen KLA fighters were killed. After the defeat of the KLA in Racak, the Serbian police arrested and probably also shot some twenty civilians (apparently, some of them had

tried to escape, and a few succeeded). The murder of these people was as illegal and immoral as it was unnecessary; but it hardly constitutes a case of 'systematic cold-blooded massacre of civilians', not to speak of 'genocide' or 'ethnic cleansing'. Rather it should be seen as a hot-blooded revenge for the KLA actions. See Pekka Visuri, *Kosovon sota* (Helsinki, Gaudeamus, 2000), pp. 88–94.

63 *The Economist* ('Kosovo on Hold'), 27 February–5 March 1999, writes: 'OR ELSE. That is what the West told the Serbs and ethnic Albanians gathered in the French chateau of Rambouillet for an extended fortnight of negotiations this month: agree to the West's plan for NATO-policed autonomy for Serbia's southern province of Kosovo, or else. Or else what? Well if the Serbs say no, we'll bomb them. And if the Kosovars say no? Er, well, they won't.'

64 Nothing short of full independence, with practically no regard to the Serbian population, would have been enough for the Kosovo Albanians. See R. Jeffrey Smith, 'Rebels' Intransigence Stymied Accord', *Washington Post*, 24 February 1999. It is possible that the Kosovo Albanians accepted the agreement only because they were assured that this would lead to air strikes against Yugoslavia. See Visuri, *Kosovon sota*, p. 99.

65 The relevant information is publicly available on the internet: 'Full text of Kosovo Agreement', BBC World News, 23 February 1999, available online: http://news.bbc.co.uk/hi/english/world/europe/newsid_285000/285097.stm (accessed 5 January 2001). BBC World News reproduced the text of the final conclusions released in a statement issued at the end of the Rambouillet Kosovo peace conference. Conclusion 3 reads: 'These have been complex and difficult negotiations, as we expected. The important efforts of the parties and the unstinting commitment of our negotiators Ambassadors Hill, Petritsch and Mayorsky, have led to a consensus on substantial autonomy for Kosovo, including on mechanisms for free and fair elections to democratic institutions for the governance of Kosovo, for the protection of human rights and the rights of members of national communities; and for the establishment of a fair judicial system'. The next day BBC World News summarised the negotiations. There was an agreement for substantial autonomy for Kosovo; a military conference was set for March 15; and the principle of a peace deal. There was no agreement on NATO presence in Kosovo; technical details of autonomy; and signing a formal peace deal. ('Warring Sides Play Down Kosovo Deal', BBC World News, http://news.bbc.co.uk/hi/english/world/europe/newsid_285000/285082.stm [accessed 5 January 2001]). See also P. de la Gorce, 'Négociations en trompe-l'oeil', *Le Monde Diplomatique*, June 1999. The full text of the Rambouillet 'Interim Agreement for Peace and Settlement in Kosovo', 23 February 1999, can be found for instance at http://www.monde-diplomatique.fr/dossiers/kosovo/rambouillet.html (accessed 5 January 2001).

66 The full paragraph from Steven Erlanger ('Milosevic's New Version of Reality Will Be Harder for NATO to Dismiss', *New York Times*, 8 April 1999) goes as follows: 'Those questions were summarized today by President Clinton: 'It is not enough now for Mr. Milosevic to say that his forces will cease-fire on a Kosovo denied of its freedom and devoid of its people. He must withdraw his forces, let the refugees return, permit the deployment of an international security force. Nothing less will bring peace with security to the people of Kosovo.' The reference to an international force instead of a NATO force [in Clinton's speech] was a

small but significant shift. In a resolution of the Serbian Parliament just before the bombing, when that body rejected NATO troops in Kosovo, it also supported the idea of United Nations forces to monitor a political settlement there.'
67 See Visuri, *Kosovon sota*, pp. 98–101.
68 *Ibid.*, pp. 163–84.
69 *The Economist* ('Law and Right. When They Don't Fit Together', 3–9 April 1999) argued that most legal experts say the bombings are against international law, although they may be morally justified. On the other hand, Martti Koskenniemi, in his keynote address on 'Challenges to International Law, Organisation and World Order' at the IPRA conference in Tampere, Finland, 6 August 2000, argued that it is always possible to find international legal reasons for bombings, for instance by extending the meaning of 'self' in the notion of self-defence, or by arguing that the oppression of Albanians is against the UN Charter, and therefore there must be means to address the problem. Although in abstract that may be the case, in concrete contexts these argumentative possibilities may not be plausible. Indeed, I find it highly implausible to identify the self of Kosovo Albanians (and the KLA in particular) with the self of NATO. Moreover, if 'self' is interpreted as an empty signifier, the notion of self-defence would become a totally open justification for any kind of military aggression by any party in any conflict situation with any mutual violence (and the UN Charter forbids, in general, the use of violence). And even if the UN Charter established a need for 'doing something' about human rights' violations, that 'something' does not imply military aggression. It could imply a military intervention only if it could be shown that there is no alternative to the use of violence. Ultimately, the legal and moral arguments for the NATO war against Yugoslavia come down to this TINA (there-is-no-alternative) view. If I am right that the remaining unacceptable issue at the end of the Rambouillet negotiations was *Appendix B* of the agreement, the TINA claim is not only false; it is ridiculous. Also, see note 62 above.
70 'Secretary-General Gravely Concerned at Escalation of Violence in Kosovo', press release SG/SM/6936, 22 March 1999. See also the first statement after the war started, 'Secretary-General Profoundly Outraged by Reports of "Ethnic Cleansing" Conducted by Serbian Forces in Kosovo', press release SG/SM/6942.
71 'Secretary-General Offers Conditions to End Hostilities in Kosovo', press release SG/SM/6952, 9 April 1999.
72 '"Our Differences Can and Must Be Outweighed by Our Common Humanity" Stresses Secretary-General in Commencement Address to University of Michigan', press release SG/SM/6977, 30 April 1999.
73 See Kofi Annan's earlier article 'Walking the International Tightrope', *The New York Times*, 19 January 1999; see also note 64.
74 'But from that same moment it was clear that part of the US strategy was to set up the UN (already denied adequate resources, personnel and authority) as the fall guy for the not-so-peaceful conclusion of the Yugoslavia war. The US rejected any UN role in decision making about military action. But now Washington holds the UN accountable for the messy and violent aftermath of the US-NATO war.' P. Bennis, 'The Law of Empire: The US Sets Up the UN to Take the Blame in Kosovo', *Baltimore Sun*, 19 August 1999.
75 As was forcefully pointed out by Koskenniemi; see note 70 above.

76 Karl W. Deutsch, *The Nerves of Government. Models of Political Communication and Control* (London, The Free Press of Glencoe, 1963), p. 111. The following citations are from the same page.
77 Richard Ashley, 'Imposing International Purpose: Notes on a Problematic of Governance', in Ernst-Otto Czempiel and James N. Rosenau (eds), *Global Changes and Theoretical Challenges. Approaches to World Politics for the 1990s* (Lexington, MA, Lexington Books, 1989), p. 269.
78 William C. Wohlforth, 'The Stability of a Unipolar World', *International Security*, vol. 24, no. 1 (summer 1999), p. 8.
79 Deutsch, *The Nerves of Government*, p. 248.
80 David Held, *Democracy and the Global Order. From the Modern State to Cosmopolitan Governance* (Cambridge, Polity, 1995), pp. 85–9.
81 For an argument that the Tobin Tax (currency transactions tax) can be realised in two phases, first on a non-universal basis, then globally, and that the organisation governing it should assume a democratic structure and a policy of selectively supporting the UN, see Heikki Patomäki, 'The Tobin Tax: A New Phase in the Politics of Globalisation?', *Theory, Culture & Society*, vol. 17, no. 4 (August 2000); and, much more thoroughly, Patomäki, *Democratising Globalisation. The Leverage of the Tobin Tax* (London, Zed Books, 2001).
82 The Bill was introduced in reaction to Boutros-Ghali's proposal of a modest levy on international air fares, which provoked very angry reactions in Washington. See Boutros Boutros-Ghali, 'Global Leadership After the Cold War', *Foreign Affairs*, vol. 75, no. 2 (March–April 1996). Other proposals include currency transactions tax (the Tobin Tax); arms sales tax; proceeds from mining the seabed; a pollution tax; a tax on international trade; a tax for parking geo-stationary satellites and for using electro-magnetic spectrum; charges on maritime ocean transport; on fishing rights in high seas; on maritime dumping of wastes; and on advertising via TV channels that span the globe. About these proposals, see South Centre, *For a Strong and Democratic United Nations. A South Perspective on UN Reform* (London, Zed Books, 1997), pp. 89–90.
83 Held, *Democracy and the Global Order*, p. 83.

6 Maja Zehfuss

Kosov@ and the politics of representation

On 24 March 1999, NATO started a bombing campaign against targets on the territory of the Federal Republic of Yugoslavia in order to stop, or so it was claimed, alleged human rights' violations by armed forces in what, in Serbia, is called 'Kosovo'. The Federal Republic of Germany (FRG), with a coalition of parties in government, which had previously been opposed to any use of force beyond its borders, especially in the absence of a UN mandate, deployed forces to participate in this operation. Federal Chancellor Gerhard Schröder insisted that there was no alternative.[1] Foreign Minister Joschka Fischer asserted that only the last resort of violence was open.[2] NATO's actions were, in other words, made inescapable by reality.

This reality was, in NATO's portrayal of the situation, one of a 'deepening humanitarian tragedy unfolding in Kosovo as Yugoslav military and security forces continue and intensify their attacks on their own people'.[3] The Milosevic regime, however, claimed this to be untrue and spoke of NATO aggression against Yugoslavia.[4] Milosevic insisted that the French and British people 'should be ashamed of themselves because of the threats of NATO-thugs against a small people'.[5] The debate over what exactly had happened 'on the ground' in Kosovo before and during NATO's intervention carried on even after the bombing raids were over and international troops had been sent to the area. The scale of human rights' violations (hence the number of victims), for instance, was considered crucial in terms of justifying NATO's actions as imperative on humanitarian grounds.[6] In relation to this, a debate ensued over whether the estimated figure of about 10,000 Albanians killed by Serb forces could be corroborated on the basis of the number of bodies found.[7]

This is a contest over the accuracy of representations. Hence, the point of the debate is to prove or disprove one or other version of reality through the use of evidence. Fact-finding missions in Kosovo after the bombing campaign and their use in this kind of debate are part of this conception of the world.[8] In this view, linguistic representations may communicate material realities but the representations are in some way separate from these realities. More crudely put, they are names for objects. While this notion of the relationship between what we call *reality* and *language* may, as any look at the reporting of Kosovo shows, be in tune with what passes for common sense, the idea that language simply names objects has long been challenged.

This chapter considers a different conceptualisation of reality and representation in relation to the Kosovo conflict. The first section looks at Ferdinand de Saussure's arguments in order to offer some thoughts on the role of naming in relation to the Kosovo conflict. Naming concerns the relationship of language and reality. Using Jacques Derrida's thought, the second section argues that the idea of the existence of a reality, which constrains our actions, is itself a representation, which has political implications. The third section explores how NATO's Kosovo operation and the FRG's participation were represented as demanded by reality and, building on Derrida's arguments, highlights the problematic nature of these statements. The conclusion stresses how the representation of the situation in Kosovo as an inescapable reality places it beyond our responsibility and thereby, at the very moment of its representation, it undermines the claim that the military operation was necessary in the name of a common humanity. Grasping the conflict as an ethico-political matter requires, or so I argue, a rethinking of the limits which we hold to be those of reality.

Naming: reality and representation

When we refer to a political situation, we invariably name who and what is involved. We name, for instance, 'Kosovo' as the territory or political entity where specific events are unfolding; 'the Serbs' and 'the Kosovo Albanians' as those involved; and, say, 'human rights' violations' as what is going on. This may seem innocent enough, a process of identifying something which is already there. We simply match a list of terms to things. The idea that the words we use in language stand for 'objects' and thus reflect an independent reality has, however, been challenged by some thinkers who have contributed to a 'linguistic turn' in philosophy.[9] Ferdinand de Saussure who is engaged in linguistics and whose work has been crucial for poststructuralist thought has also fundamentally questioned it.

Saussure rejects the idea that language consists of a list of terms, which corresponds to a list of things. He particularly objects to the assumptions that ideas exist prior to and independently of words and that the link between a thing and a name is unproblematic. Rather Saussure asserts that a linguistic sign is a link not between a thing and a name but between a concept and a sound pattern.[10] Crucially, the sign functions on the basis of differences in relation to other terms of language, and it is arbitrary, or rather unmotivated, because the link between the signifier and the signified is arbitrary.[11] The sign is, however, pre-given to the individual.[12] Language as a system always already exists and the speaker must operate within it. It is important that words do not represent independently existing concepts but are part of a system of language. Saussure draws attention to the arbitrariness of signs by pointing out that the same objects are called different names in different languages.[13] Hence, names are not natural or necessary in linguistic terms. However, their relation to the linguistic context, and hence arguably to the political context, is not arbitrary at all.

Throughout the 'Kosovo' crisis, naming played a crucial role. Both the territory and a political entity were consistently identified by Western governments as 'Kosovo', a Serbian term, whereas Albanians refer to 'Kosova'. Both mean 'blackbird'. The problem is, whether the place in question rightfully belongs to Serbia as the birthplace of the Serb nation in the 1398 battle on the 'Kosovo' field,[14] or whether autonomy or even independence should be granted to 'Kosova' on the grounds that its population today, which is largely Albanian, is seeking self-determination. In this context, the persistent usage of either of two equally arbitrary signs should be of concern, not merely to the sensitive scholar but to much wider audiences. In fact, this problem was one mentioned in the press.[15]

The usage of Kosovo rather than Kosova implied that independence was not on the cards. What was at issue was a 'troubled province' of the Federal Republic of Yugoslavia rather than a newly or future independent state.[16] Hence, despite their explicit support of the Albanians as victims of Serb atrocities, in using the Serb name Western governments already construed the situation in a way that favoured the Serb, rather than the Albanian, view. Obviously, this is not to say that they really supported the Serbs rather than the Albanians, but that naming already implied taking a position. The inevitability of this positioning is reflected in the need felt by those writing on Kosovo to protest that their usage of the Serb term is merely a matter of practicality and not, as Tim Judah puts it, 'a secret signal of support for one side'.[17] However, the German Green Party attempted to avoid altogether a political decision inherent in the naming, and proposed to write Kosov@, which was supposed to capture both the *a*- and *o*-endings. Predictably, this move was considered somewhat ridiculous, especially as it is impossible to actually pronounce Kosov@.[18] A recent visit to the website of the Green Party showed that it now also uses the term which dominated the discourse: Kosovo.[19]

The use of Kosov@ and even the sensitivity to either 'Kosovo' or 'Kosova' are based on a prior process of naming. 'The Albanians' and their concerns are separated from 'the Serbs' through the use of language. Two clearly identifiable groups of people are constituted and created as subjects in this move.[20] Bizarrely, the victims of Serb atrocities were often identified as 'Kosovo Albanians,' combining the Serb term for the territory with the notion that those being named are essentially Albanians.[21] If 'the Albanians' have identifiable common ideas about their political future, they should be referred to as Kosova Albanians.

As the debate about Kosov@, and the explicit justifications of the usage of Kosovo, show, it was sometimes acknowledged that naming was a political act, as it implied taking a position. However, the issue seems to me to be more fundamental. Following Saussure, naming is not a simple act of linking a name to an existing object, which might be called one or other thing. Rather it is a productive practice.[22] Judith Butler, referring to Louis Althusser, points out that being called a name is 'one of the conditions by which a subject is constituted in language'.[23] According to Althusser, hailing, or 'interpellation', is the process whereby individuals are recruited into subjects by an ideology as they realise that it is they who are being hailed.[24] This draws attention to naming as a twofold political process of making subjects and positioning them at the same time. Firstly, our name is not merely a label attached to us as *a priori* existing individuals. It establishes us in our relationship to the social world, i.e. in our subjectivity, while at the same time serving as an act of objectification. Prosecution, for instance, must first identify the victim as an object through its name.

Secondly, although names are arbitrary in their sound pattern, they are not random in the linguistic and political context. If being called by a name turns us into subjects (and indeed objects) within an ideology, then naming is related to the assigning of power positions. For example, 'Albanians' in 'Kosovo' are unlikely to be as powerful as they are in 'Kosova' because the names already imply that the best they can hope for is autonomy, rather than independence. Tim Judah argues that there has been a transition from 'Kosovo' to 'Kosova', leading to a situation where the 'Albanian Kosovars' have taken over, thus excluding the Serbs and other minorities.[25]

The assertion that naming is part of subjectification draws attention to the issue of how we conceptualise reality and our relationship to it. Saussure's critique of the idea that linguistic concepts are reflections of independently existing objects opens up the opportunity to question representations of reality. It does not, however, offer any views on the status of representation and of reality as such, or on that of the power relations involved. This view is open to the reply that the atrocities and bloodshed on the ground in Kosovo (or Kosova) are more real than their representation; and that it is that situation 'on the ground', rather than the secondary issue of how it should be properly called, which deserves our attention. This valuing of the supposedly real over representation, based on the possibility of differentiating between the two, is problematical. Engaging with Jacques Derrida's thought enables us to explore why.

Derrida: reality as representation

If language is not merely a reflection of an independent reality, the relation between representation and reality is in question. Derrida's critique of what he calls logocentrism, 'the determination of the being of the entity as presence',[26] revolves around the claim that Western thought is based on the value of presence. In logocentric thought representation and reality are not merely divorced, but valued differently. Representation is always inferior to that which is supposedly present and therefore seen as 'real'.

Taking presence as a secure foundation for our thought assumes presence to be given, pure and absolute. However, according to Derrida, presence is an effect of differences, and the mutual exclusiveness of presence and absence is impossible. Referring to Saussure's claim that 'arbitrary' and 'differential' are correlated characteristics,[27] Derrida introduces the notion of *différance*. On the one hand, it refers to something being not identical, discernible. On the other hand, it refers to a 'temporal or temporizing mediation or a detour that suspends the accomplishment or fulfilment of "desire" or "will," and equally effects this suspension in a mode that annuls or tempers its owns effect'.[28] Derrida suggests that *différance*

> is a structure and a movement no longer conceivable on the basis of the opposition presence/absence. *Différance* is the systematic play of differences, of the traces of differences, of the *spacing* by means of which elements are related to each other. This spacing is the simultaneously active and passive ... production of the intervals without which the 'full' terms would not signify, would not function.[29]

This claim implies that when we cannot show the thing itself, 'we go through the detour of the sign'.[30] Hence, the sign is deferred presence: '[S]ignified presence is always reconstituted by deferral, *nachträglich*, belatedly, *supplementarily*'.[31] The sign, as supplement, is always dangerous because it necessarily contains two contradictory dimensions. On the one hand, the supplement adds itself, enriches another plenitude and thus functions as a surplus.[32] 'But the supplement supplements. It adds only to replace. It intervenes or insinuates itself *in-the-place-of*; if it fills, it is as if one fills a void.'[33] Thus, while the supplement enriches the presence, at the same time the sign endangers presence by replacing it. As the 'sign is always the supplement of the thing itself',[34] it 'takes its place' in both meanings of the term: it stands for it in its absence but at the same time already replaces it.

If the sign is not a stand-in for pure presence, there is nothing beyond signification. In other words, there '*is nothing outside of the text*'.[35] This claim has created much indignation in those who understand it to imply that the 'real world' does not exist. What Derrida is driving at is that 'all reality has the structure of a differential trace, and that one cannot refer to this "real" except in an interpretive experience'.[36] Derrida explains his point using the logic of supplementarity in relation to Jean-Jacques Rousseau's *Confessions*:

> *There is nothing outside of the text* [there is no outside-text; *il n'y a pas de hors-texte*] ... What we have tried to show by following the guiding line of the

'dangerous supplement,' is that what one calls the real life of these existences 'of flesh and bone,' beyond and behind what one believes can be circumscribed as Rousseau's text, there has never been anything but writing; there have never been anything but supplements, substitutive significations which could only come forth in a chain of differential references, the 'real' supervening, and being added only while taking on meaning from a trace and from an invocation of the supplement, etc.[37]

This is particularly important in view of what is at issue here. The claim that 'there is nothing outside of the text', as the imprecise translation puts it,[38] is likely to arouse emotions insofar as it can easily be construed as questioning the reality of the bloodshed and the suffering of 'real people in real places'. Discussing the status of reality in relation to Rousseau's *Confessions*, as Derrida does, is one thing; doing so in relation to massacre and rape in Kosovo is quite another. It could be seen to ignore, if not ridicule, the suffering of the victims. However, Derrida's thought does not imply that the real world with its bloodshed does not exist. Rather, because we conceive what we think of as life on the model of a text, the seemingly clear distinction between inside and outside is blurred. 'One wishes to go back *from the supplement to the source*: one must recognise that there is *a supplement at the source*.'[39] Hence, that which we call 'real life' turns out to be 'constituted by the logic of supplementarity'.[40] As a consequence, the positive value attached to the real as opposed to the represented, the signified, the supplement, is not natural, but is indeed political. Derrida's arguments lead us to radically reconsider the notion of representation. It is not merely that several, and as Saussure might point out, arbitrary, representations of reality are possible. What we call 'reality' is itself a representation, and what comes to be represented as 'reality' is political.

The reality of Kosovo

Serb atrocities against the 'Kosovo Albanians' were identified as the salient feature of the reality which for NATO made it imperative to act. It was estimated that about 1,500 Kosovo Albanians had been killed in the Serb offensive in the summer of 1998 and about 300,000 had fled their homes to hide in the surrounding area. Despite negotiations and a partial withdrawal of Serb security forces, the situation continued to deteriorate. The UN High Commissioner for Refugees estimated that on 23 March 1999, when it had to suspend its operation in Kosovo, about 360,000 people had become refugees, either within the region or beyond.[41] After the OSCE observers had left Kosovo, reports of the Kosovar refugees had now become the only source of information.[42] As they were considered to have a stake in exaggerating the Serb atrocities to which NATO's actions were claimed to be a reaction, verification was both difficult and vital. One of the verification mechanisms relied on corroboration of reports by several groups of refugees. The refugees' reports detailed mass expulsion, rapes and killings.[43]

As Chancellor Schröder explained, the 'Alliance was forced into this step, in order to stop further grave and systematic violations of human rights in Kosovo and to prevent a humanitarian catastrophe there'.[44] NATO Secretary General Javier Solana and the German Army Inspector Helmut Willmann also used the description 'humanitarian catastrophe'.[45] The German Defence Minister Rudolf Scharping argued that no further time was to be lost in the face of the misery of the refugees.[46] For US President Bill Clinton it was a case of the civilised world fighting against ethnic violence and brutal crimes.[47] According to one commentator, NATO was forced to act in order not to become complicit in the death of thousands.[48] Thus two salient features of reality were identified: firstly, the human rights' violations and the resulting human suffering in Kosovo; and, secondly, the necessity of NATO military action as an immediate consequence of this suffering.

This representation of reality is hard to escape. To argue that what we call reality is itself a representation seems simply an act of disrespect towards the victims of physical violence, if only from a position which sees itself as able to separate the real and the represented. While one may be quite prepared to accept that, as Derrida claims, we cannot refer to the real except in an interpretive experience,[49] the real is typically considered to provide some form of limitation to this insight. In this view, whether torture is good or bad is a matter of fact, not of opinion or interpretation.[50]

The emotive power of human suffering had been important in German debates about military involvement abroad prior to the Kosovo operation. It is interesting to explore these earlier discussions in order to contextualise the German reaction to the Kosovo war. The problem the FRG was experiencing with post-Cold War international military operations, starting with the 1991 Gulf War, is often portrayed as a tension between commitment both to anti-fascism and to pacifism.[51] This debate concerned the Greens in particular, if by no means exclusively, because they had portrayed themselves as a pacifistic party. The 'heirs of the peace movement' had been overwhelmingly opposed to Bundeswehr participation in the Gulf War.[52] Yet Bosnia, and subsequently Kosovo, posed a completely different problem. Because of the atrocities committed, and the Holocaust imagery related to them, Bosnia came to be seen as a fundamental challenge to a pacifistic position.

In the summer of 1995, Joschka Fischer, then a leading politician of Alliance 90/German Greens, and from October 1998 Foreign Minister, argued that accepting a policy of war and murder in Bosnia would have far-reaching consequences for Europe. The key question he posed to his own party was: 'Can pacifists, can especially a position of non-violence accept the victory of brute, naked violence in Bosnia?'[53] He likened the position of the West in the 1990s to the appeasement in the 1930s and expressed his worry that the German Left would lose its moral soul if it ducked the issue of standing up to the new violent politics with 'whatever argumentative escape it may be'.[54] His rhetorical question was whether the Greens could 'put principles higher than human lives'.[55]

Fischer backed the idea of a military intervention in Bosnia, even though he stopped short of explicitly saying so. He thereby questioned a fundamental tenet of Green politics, the principle of non-violence, and predictably generated outrage and debate among his party colleagues.[56] What is of interest here are the reasons why Fischer apparently felt compelled to do so. He claimed it was the terrifying reality of the cruelty and barbarity that had led him to rethink the principle of non-violence. In the face of real violence the unavoidable interpretative experience comes to be seen as somehow unnecessary, an 'argumentative escape', a luxury enjoyed by those safe at home in their living rooms, merely watching the bloodshed on television.

Less than four years later, Fischer had become Germany's foreign minister, and his government authorised, with parliamentary consent, the Bundeswehr's participation in Operation Allied Force. An ashen-faced Fischer insisted that he had done everything humanly possible for a diplomatic solution. He admitted that he simply could not figure out what else to do.[57] The German weekly *Der Spiegel* commented that the German leadership, all good pacifists or at least card-carrying 'civilians' in the past, looked honestly distressed at the prospect of going to war.[58] When, for 'the first time, the western defensive alliance started out of area into a war of aggression against a sovereign country, and that on a questionable basis in terms of international law without a UN mandate',[59] when 'German fighter planes were flying bomb raids on another state for the first time since the end of the Second World War',[60] those in charge in the FRG were not exactly the usual suspects. They had grown up as participants in sit-ins at NATO's missile bases, in human chains and at 'peace workshops',[61] and looked distinctly uncomfortable in their current role of commanding the military in a real war. The irony of their position was not lost on them. At one point Fischer publicly admitted that he sometimes thought he had lost his way.[62]

While human chains may, to their way of thinking, have been a credible response to the threat of nuclear weapons, which is construed as potential rather than fully real, such non-violent protest rings hollow in the face of the atrocities in Kosovo.[63] Defence Minister Scharping used a particular vocabulary to describe them: genocide, slaughterhouse, ethnic cleansing, selection, concentration camps.[64] These terms suggested that what was at stake was not the crude materiality of what was going on, but its position in a wider interpretative context, within which the West, and the FRG in particular, were conceptualised. However, this point could be seen as unimportant because of the arguably indisputable reality of death. Derrida questions the underlying assumption of such talk about death which 'takes the form of an "it is self-explanatory": everybody knows what one is talking about when one names death'.[65] While Derrida recognises death as a limit, it is not a self-evident, natural limit. Rather, as Drucilla Cornell explains, it is the 'limit of any system of meaning [that] is, for Derrida, graphically represented to us in death'.[66]

The deaths of the Kosovars certainly were interpreted and related to systems of meaning. They mattered greatly in their symbolism with respect to the history of the Holocaust. They mattered quite clearly in relation to the lives of the Serb civilians. As Gordana Milanovic, a Serb woman living in FRG, put it: 'Now Herr Fischer should explain to me how he wants to protect thousands in Kosovo by bombing millions'.[67] Yet they mattered rather less in another context. The German commander for the Kosovo operation, General Helmut Harff, supported the deployment of ground troops, a move rejected by the government. He asked whether the argument against this course of action was supposed to mean that the 'life of a raped, massacred woman is worth less than that of a soldier who is trained to defend himself'.[68] Harff's question about the refusal to commit ground troops suggests that death and its significance were a matter of interpretation. Thus, it seems that the 'reality' of a situation, even if it is one involving death, depends on how it is contextualised. One could therefore assert that there is nothing beyond the text of our representations of reality which could tell us how exactly bloodshed matters or whose life should be protected.

The different valuation of lives, which is apparent in the refusal to commit ground troops, also exposed a tension in the position of the German government. Harff's contextualisation implied that the failure to commit ground troops to the operation contradicted the government's stated objective of helping the Kosovars.[69] It is interesting to note in this context that the massacres in Kosovo were seen to legitimise the FRG's war operation but not asylum for the Kosovar refugees in the FRG.[70]

In fact, the German government seemed very eager to confirm its willingness to participate in NATO's operation. As early as June 1998, then Defence Minister Volker Rühe had already stated that the Bundeswehr would participate in a NATO operation.[71] In the period of transition to a new government in the autumn of the same year the continued willingness to do so was carefully established and articulated.[72] Rühe's successor, Scharping, confirmed on the eve of the first air raid that German soldiers would be part of the operation from the start.[73] After the bombing had started, a SAT-1 television reporter rather proudly claimed that Bundeswehr Tornados were flying 'in pole position'.[74] When the Russian Prime Minister Yevgeni Primakov visited Bonn to mediate between the West and Belgrade, the FRG leadership was reportedly concerned, above all, to avoid a 'second Rapallo' which would undermine the West's trust in Germany.[75] It had to be clear that, as Fischer had declared like so many others before him, there would be 'no German *Sonderweg*', no German special path.[76] According to Fischer,

Germany stood 'on the right side for the first time this century'.[77] Kosovo, despite all the agonising about the death of pacifism, provided a welcome opportunity to demonstrate the end of German abnormality.[78]

The supplement: identity, credibility, cohesion

The end of German abnormality was articulated within a Western identity, which was thought to be enacted in Operation Allied Force. According to Chancellor Schröder, the Kosovo operation demonstrated that NATO is an alliance based on common values, especially human rights.[79] The Kosovo operation had enabled the Alliance to show that it is a community of values above and beyond being a defensive alliance.[80] The Operation thus provided an opportunity to endorse NATO's proclaimed new post-Cold War identity. In tune with NATO's human rights' identity, the air raids were meant to limit the Serbs' ability to inflict harm on the KLA and the civilian population in Kosovo.[81]

However, NATO's credibility was an issue throughout.[82] At times this issue seemed more central than the goal of protecting the Kosovars. When President Clinton outlined the three aims of the operation, he mentioned demonstrating the strength and resolve of the Western Alliance ahead of preventing Yugoslavia's President Milosevic from further use of violence and restricting his military capabilities.[83] NATO Secretary-General Solana stressed 'NATO solidarity, unity and resolve' with respect to the operation.[84] And Chancellor Schröder simply said: 'If only for the sake of its credibility as a community of values NATO was forced to act against mass expulsion and mass murder in Kosovo.'[85] Considering the argument that Operation Allied Force was all about protecting the lives of innocent Kosovar civilians, and the idea of human rights more broadly, this focus on NATO's credibility seems inappropriate.[86] Indeed, the very name of the operation seems to indicate NATO's conception of self.

The point is not that NATO was more interested in its own unity than it was in the declared aims of Operation Allied Force, as if these were unrelated issues. One could argue that the maintenance of the NATO coalition was necessary to carry out the military operation that was to protect both the Kosovar civilians and the ideal of human rights. Hence, maintaining the consensus among the NATO states, as well as the credibility of the Alliance, might not have been the aim as such, but they were necessary to the overall goal. Strengthening NATO's credibility and its post-Cold War cohesiveness are, then, welcome side-effects of the operation as well as its preconditions. This brings us back to Derrida's argument, as one could say that NATO's unity was only a supplement to the defence of human rights in Kosovo. The cohesiveness of the Alliance was not supposed to be the primary goal of the West, but was something added, a surplus. However, as Derrida warns, 'the supplement supplements. It enriches only to replace.'[87] While NATO's solidarity may have been intended to help and protect the Kosovars, such solidarity, following Derrida's argument, at the same time endangered this objective by replacing it.

The debate over the sending of ground troops to Kosovo offers another illustration of this mechanism. Although the deployment option was seen to have been almost unavoidable in terms of military logic, it was rejected by all key powers except the United Kingdom.[88] The fear of large-scale casualties, and the expected loss of domestic support in NATO countries as a result, were seen to be the reasons.[89] In contrast, an air war with smart weapons was attractive because the threat to the lives of NATO soldiers and civilians was considered low.[90] 'Real' war, involving ground troops and thus probably a higher level of casualties, was to be avoided in order to prevent a break-up of NATO's unity. This option was thus evaluated not primarily in terms of what was supposed to be the main goal of the operation, the protection of the Kosovars, but in terms of the supplementary consideration of NATO's solidarity.

The point, however, is not a simple overturning of the means–end relationship.[91] Whether NATO 'really' wanted to protect the Kosovars, or to reinvent itself and sustain its new identity, is in many ways the wrong question to ask. Operation Allied Force can be construed both as protecting the Kosovars and as contributing to their expulsion and slaughter.[92] More pertinently, it can be seen as a practice, one which produced the Kosovo Albanians as subjects in a particular political context. The NATO operation, however much intended to help and however much it did achieve what were presented as its aims, could not but reproduce the identity of 'Kosovo Albanians' as victims of the present state system in which they cannot practise self-determination. Therefore, it also produced them as a danger to the 'text' of which NATO is a part.

Conclusion

This chapter has argued that what we hold to be reality is itself a representation. We produce reality and its subjects whenever we represent them, and representing them is an inherent part of our political practices. Portrayals of the Kosovo conflict have tended to suppress the productive effect of Western practices. The crisis was conceptualised as a 'no-choice' situation. Typically, when we have no choice, we are thought not to be responsible for our actions, for example when someone holds a gun to our head or when we cut off a fellow climber from the rope below us in order to save ourselves. While moral philosophers might have protracted debates about what exactly is happening in such situations, the idea that we are not responsible when the only alternative is death holds some persuasive power.[93]

Germany's Chancellor Schröder argued that there had been no choice for the West in relation to the Kosovo operation.[94] As a result, the responsibility for the air raids rested exclusively with Milosevic.[95] Western governments emphasised, time and again, that it was in Milosevic's power to immediately end NATO's operation by acceding to the Alliance's demands.[96] As Defence Minister Scharping explained: 'Everyone in the government had scruples. In order to prevent a humanitarian catastrophe in Kosovo, we had, however, no other choice. The responsibility for the air raids rests exclusively with President Slobodan Milosevic, who leads a war against his own people in Kosovo with incredible brutality.'[97] The West was forced to act in the way it did both by Milosevic and by the reality of which Milosevic was a part. Therefore, Milosevic and that reality were to blame for any adverse consequences of NATO action.

The claim that something is demanded by reality is problematical because it conceptualises 'reality' as outside language. Jenny Edkins and Véronique Pin-Fat claim that we 'seek to convince ourselves of the existence of "reality" by trying to trace the outline of objects over and over again. As Wittgenstein points out, this is a trick of language.'[98] Derrida similarly argues that 'the truth is precisely limited, *finite*, and confined within its borders',[99] but that we fail to recognise the limit for what it is. The problem is that if we understand the boundary, which we believe we experience, as the necessary interference of an independent materiality rather than a limit to our conceptualisations, we consider our choices limited by a mysterious outside power that we cannot ever directly experience. As a result, because we have no choice, and because this is the way things are, we limit our responsibility. This conceptualisation is deeply political. In other words, the assertion of the existence of an independent reality, which in itself cannot be proved and seems to demand no proof, works to support particular political positions and to exclude others from consideration.

Facing up to the reality of not being able to do anything other than use armed force in order to protect innocent civilians from physical violence was portrayed as the responsible thing to do in the Kosovo crisis. Clearly, the assertion that reality *is* a certain way, rather than another, limits the range of options that one might reasonably contemplate. In this context, the idea of refusing the choice between 'Kosovo' and 'Kosova' can be seen not as a silly move, as some political commentators regarded it, but as an effort to disturb an established field of signification by refusing to be committed to either side of the dichotomy. In this sense, writing about Kosov@ constitutes a political intervention, an act of resistance. For the point is not to face up to a tough reality but to engage the 'limits *declared* to be insurmountable',[100] and to explore ways of thinking beyond the limits which are thought to be those of reality.

No one failed to be touched by the human suffering to which NATO's air campaign was a response, nor by the misery that followed in its wake and which was, to some extent, a consequence of it. Equally, no one is likely to be satisfied with that response, nor would they have been had the operation not happened. Clearly, it was not only the response that was unsatisfactory, but the way in which the issue was approached, discussed and conceptualised. What is interesting is not so much that the West's response fell short of what one might have hoped for. Rather it is that something seemed amiss in the ethical discourse surrounding 'Kosovo'. The way we are accustomed to speak about such crises revolves around the issues of human rights, sovereignty and war; and that way of speaking (re)produces the exclusion it seeks to remedy.

NATO and Western governments claimed to be acting out of responsibility for fellow humans. However, their conceptualisation of the events in Kosov@ and their practices produced those for whom they were claiming to take responsibility as 'other', as neatly identifiable 'Kosovo Albanians', as outside the accepted state system, and consequently as a danger to it. Having conceptually excluded this 'other' in the representation of reality, and having then recognised its humanness, the question was how to bring the 'other' back in. Military intervention, which at the same time reproduced the exclusion (for instance, by making even more Kosovars refugees), was the answer. This is a peculiar way of accepting one's responsibility for the 'other', based as it is on thinking which starts from exclusion and therefore reproduces exclusion even as it aims to overcome it. Our inability to address the Kosov@ crisis in a satisfactory manner points to our failure to investigate the role of language in producing subjects, and with them what we call reality. The question, then, is how to think differently, and that seems to require thinking beyond the limits we consider to be those of reality.

Notes

I would like to thank Stuart Elden and Michael Shapiro for commenting on earlier versions of this chapter, which was presented at the ISA convention in Los Angeles in March 2000.

1 Quoted in Josef Joffe, 'Wir haben keine andere Wahl', *Süddeutsche Zeitung*, 24 March 1999 (all translations from German sources in this chapter are my own). See also 'Nato ordnet Angriffe auf Serbien an', *Süddeutsche Zeitung*, 24 March 1999.
2 'Nato greift Ziele in Serbien an', *Süddeutsche Zeitung*, 25 March 1999.
3 General Wesley Clark, in press conference called by Secretary-General Javier Solana and SACEUR General Wesley Clark, 25 March 1999. Transcript available online: http://www.nato.int/kosovo/press/p990325a.htm (accessed 18 December 2000).
4 'Nato ordnet Angriffe auf Serbien an', *Süddeutsche Zeitung*, 24 March 1999. Russia's President Boris Yeltsin supported this interpretation. See 'Nato greift Ziele in Serbien an', *Süddeutsche Zeitung*, 25 March 1999.

5 Quoted in 'Nato nimmt weitere Ziele ins Visier', *Süddeutsche Zeitung*, 23 March 1999.
6 Gabriel Partos, 'Q & A: Counting Kosovo's Dead', BBC World News, http://newsvote.bbc.co.uk/hi/english/world/europe/newsid_517000/517168.stm (accessed 18 December 2000).
7 By November 1999, 2,108 bodies had been exhumed. Some questioned whether this number of bodies could confirm the estimated total number of Albanians killed. See, for example, Chris Bird, 'Graves Put Kosovo Death Toll in Doubt', *The Guardian*, 11 November 1999. Others disagreed: see Peter Hain, 'Kosovo's Grim Statistics', *The Guardian*, 13 November 1999, and Ian Williams, 'The Kosovo Numbers Game', in Institute for War & Peace Reporting, *Balkans Crisis Reports*, no. 92 (12 November 1999), available online: http://www.iwpr.net/index.pl5?archive/bcr/bcr_19991112_2_eng.txt (accessed 5 January 2001). On the problem of establishing the number of the dead, see also Michael Ignatieff, 'Counting Bodies in Kosovo', *New York Times*, 21 November 1999; 'UN Gives Figure for Kosovo Dead', BBC World News, 10 November 1999, available online: http://newsvote.bbc.co.uk/hi/english/world/europe/newsid_514000/514828.stm (accessed 5 January 2001); and Partos, 'Q & A: Counting Kosovo's Dead'.
8 See, for example, Julian Borger and Owen Bowcott, 'Troops Covered Up Massacres', *The Guardian*, 17 June 1999.
9 For example, Ludwig Wittgenstein, *Philosophical Investigations*, trans. G.E.M. Anscombe (Oxford, Basil Blackwell, 1974): and J.L. Austin, *How to Do Things With Words. The William James Lectures Delivered at Harvard University in 1955* (Oxford, Clarendon Press, 1975). See also Jim George, *Discourses of Global Politics. A Critical (Re)Introduction to International Relations* (Boulder, CO, Lynne Rienner Publishers, 1994), pp. 142–5.
10 Ferdinand de Saussure, *Course in General Linguistics*, trans. Wade Baskin (Glasgow, Fontana/Collins, 1974), pp. 65f.
11 *Ibid.*, Part II, pp. 67f., 113 and esp. p. 120.
12 *Ibid.*, pp. 67–9 and 71.
13 *Ibid.*, pp. 66f.
14 See, however, Ismail Kadare, *Three Elegies for Kosovo*, translated from the Albanian by Peter Constantine (London, Harvill Press, 2000).
15 See, for example, 'Wilder Klammeraffe', *Der Spiegel*, 17 May 1999.
16 Renate Flottau, Olaf Ihlau, Siegesmund von Ilsemann, Dirk Koch, Jörg Mettke and Roland Schleicher, 'Alle Serben im Krieg', *Der Spiegel*, 29 March 1999. See also 'UCK läßt "endgültigen Bescheid" offen', *Süddeutsche Zeitung*, 15 March 1999; 'Luftschläge der Nato werden immer wahrscheinlicher', *Süddeutsche Zeitung*, 18 March 1999; Klaus-Dieter Frankenberger, 'Europäische Aufbruchstimmung hier, balkanische Düsternis da', *Frankfurter Allgemeine Zeitung*, 22 March 1999. See also United Nations Security Council Resolution 1244, adopted by the Security Council at its 4,011th meeting on 10 June 1999, reprinted in Tim Judah, *Kosovo. War and Revenge* (New Haven, CT, and London, Yale University Press, 2000), pp. 314–21; and Statement by the North Atlantic Council on Kosovo, press release (99)12, 30 January 1999, section 7.
17 Judah, *Kosovo*, p. xi. See also Organisation for Security and Co-operation in Europe, 'Kosovo/Kosova. As Seen, As Told', analysis of the human rights findings of the OSCE Kosovo Verification Mission, October 1998–June 1999

(Warsaw, OSCE Office for Democratic Institutions and Human Rights, 1999), available online: http://www.osce.org/kosovo/reports/hr/part1 (accessed 18 December 2000); and Julie Mertus, *How Myths and Truths Started a War* (Berkeley, Los Angeles and London, University of California Press, 1999), p. xix. Interestingly, Judah made much of the transformation of Kosovo into Kosova after NATO's bombing campaign. See Judah, *Kosovo*, p. 297.
18 'Wilder Klammeraffe', *Der Spiegel*, 17 May 1999.
19 See http://www.gruene.de (accessed 18 December 2000).
20 On similar issues in relation to Bosnia, see David Campbell, *National Deconstruction. Violence, Identity, and Justice in Bosnia* (Minneapolis and London, University of Minnesota Press, 1998).
21 'Luftschläge der Nato werden immer wahrscheinlicher', *Süddeutsche Zeitung*, 18 March 1999; 'Serbische Offensive löst neue Fluchtwelle aus', *Süddeutsche Zeitung*, 22 March 1999. See also Judah, *Kosovo*, p. xi; Mertus, *Myths and Truths*, p. xix.
22 This issue is addressed in Michael J. Shapiro, *The Politics of Representation. Writing Practices in Biography, Photography, and Policy Analysis* (Madison, WI, University of Wisconsin Press, 1988), p. 91, and Roxanne Lynn Doty, *Imperial Encounters. The Politics of Representation in North–South Relations* (Minneapolis and London, University of Minnesota Press, 1996), pp. 175f.
23 Judith Butler, *Excitable Speech. A Politics of the Performative* (New York and London, Routledge, 1997), p. 2.
24 Louis Althusser, 'Ideology and Ideological State Apparatuses (Notes towards an Investigation)', in Louis Althusser, *Lenin and Philosophy and Other Essays*, trans. Ben Brewster (Old Woking, Gesham Press, 1971), pp. 162f.
25 Judah, *Kosovo*, p. 297.
26 Jacques Derrida, *Of Grammatology*, trans. Gayatri Chakravorty Spivak (Baltimore, MD, and London, Johns Hopkins University Press, 1976), p. 12.
27 Jacques Derrida, *Margins of Philosophy*, translated with additional notes by Alan Bass (Chicago, IL, University of Chicago Press, 1982), p. 10.
28 Derrida, *Margins*, p. 8.
29 Jacques Derrida, *Positions*, translated and annotated by Alan Bass (London, Athlone Press, 1987), p. 27.
30 Derrida, *Margins*, p. 9.
31 Jacques Derrida, *Writing and Difference*, translated with an Introduction and additional notes by Alan Bass (London, Routledge,1978), pp. 211f. (italics in original).
32 Derrida, *Of Grammatology*, p. 144.
33 *Ibid.*, p. 145.
34 *Ibid.*, p. 145.
35 *Ibid.*, p. 158.
36 Jacques Derrida, *Limited Inc.* (Evanston, IL, Northwestern University Press, 1988), p. 148.
37 Derrida, *Of Grammatology*, pp. 158f.
38 For the original passage, see Jacques Derrida, *De la Grammatologie* (Paris: Éditions de Minuit, 1967), pp. 227f.
39 Derrida, *Of Grammatology*, p. 304.
40 Jonathan Culler, *On Deconstruction. Theory and Criticism after Structuralism* (London, Routledge, 1983), p. 105.

41 Adam Roberts, 'NATO's "Humanitarian War" Over Kosovo', *Survival*, vol. 41, no. 3 (1999), pp. 112f.
42 'Serbische Offensive löst neue Fluchtwelle aus', *Süddeutsche Zeitung*, 22 March 1999. See also Partos, 'Q & A: Counting Kosovo's Dead'. I use 'Kosovar' as it can mean both 'Kosovo Albanians' and 'people from Kosovo'. This reflects the ambiguity of the situation.
43 See, for example, OSCE, 'Kosovo/Kosova. As Seen, As Told'.
44 Gerhard Schröder (federal chancellor), in Deutscher Bundestag, *Plenarprotokoll*, 26 March 1999, p. 2571.
45 'Luftschläge der Nato gegen Jugoslawien', *Frankfurter Allgemeine Zeitung*, 25 March 1999; 'Nato ordnet Luftangriffe auf Serbien an', *Süddeutsche Zeitung*, 24 March 1999; 'Bei Sanitätern und Logistik wird es eng', Interview with Army Inspector Helmut Willmann, *Süddeutsche Zeitung*, 3 March 1999. See also Statement by the North Atlantic Council on Kosovo, press release (99)12, 30 January 1999, section 5, and 'The Situation in and Around Kosovo', Statement Issued at the Extraordinary Ministerial Meeting of the North Atlantic Council held at NATO Headquarters, Brussels, on 12 April 1999, press release M-NAC-1(99)51, 12 April 1999, section 2.
46 'Nato nimmt weitere Ziele ins Visier', *Süddeutsche Zeitung*, 23 March 1999.
47 Flottau *et al.*, 'Alle Serben im Krieg'.
48 Peter Münch, 'Zum Handeln gezwungen', *Süddeutsche Zeitung*, 22 March 1999.
49 Derrida, *Limited Inc.*, p. 148.
50 Ken Booth, for instance, approvingly cites Geoffrey Warnock's claim that it is a fact that torture is bad in the context of a discussion of human rights in international relations. See Ken Booth, 'Human Wrongs and International Relations', *International Affairs*, vol. 71, no. 1 (1995), p. 107.
51 Alice H. Cooper, 'When Just Causes Conflict With Acceptable Means: The German Peace Movement and Military Intervention in Bosnia', *German Politics and Society*, no. 15 (1997), p. 103. The FRG also had a problem with this practice due to constitutional restrictions. That issue is not explored here. Arguably, the legal constraints were a problem precisely because of the tension between anti-fascism and pacifism.
52 'Nur noch Gewalt', *Der Spiegel*, 5 June 1995. See, however, 'Leithammel Deutschland', *Der Spiegel*, 3 September 1990.
53 Joschka Fischer, 'Die Katastrophe in Bosnien und die Konsequenzen für unsere Partei', reprinted in *Blätter für deutsche und internationale Politik*, vol. 40 (1995), p. 1148.
54 *Ibid.*
55 *Ibid.*
56 'Gefeiert oder gefoltert', *Der Spiegel*, 7 August 1995.
57 'Ich darf nicht wackeln', *Der Spiegel*, 15 April 1999; Manfred Ertel, Rüdiger Falksohn, Renate Flottau, Olaf Ihlau, Siegesmund von Ilsemann, Dirk Koch and Helene Zuber, 'Das Gespenst von Vietnam', *Der Spiegel*, 5 April 1999.
58 Winfried Didzoleit, Jürgen Hogrefe, Lutz Krusche, Jürgen Leinemann, Reinhand Mohn and Rainer Pörtner, 'Ernstfall für Schröder', *Der Spiegel*, 29 March 1999.
59 Flottau *et al.*, 'Alle Serben im Krieg'.
60 Didzoleit *et al.*, 'Ernstfall für Schröder'. See also William Drozdiak, 'Europe Comes Together To Back NATO Bombs', *International Herald Tribune*, 5 April 1999.

61 Didzoleit *et al.*, 'Ernstfall für Schröder'. See also Drozdiak, 'Europe Comes Together'.
62 'Ich darf nicht wackeln', *Der Spiegel*, 5 April 1999.
63 See, for example, Josef Joffe, 'Verfehltes Reifezeugnis', *Süddeutsche Zeitung*, 10 March 1998.
64 'Ich darf nicht wackeln'.
65 Jacques Derrida, *Aporias*, trans. Thomas Dutoit (Stanford, CA, Stanford University Press, 1993), p. 25.
66 Drucilla Cornell, *The Philosophy of the Limit* (New York and London, Routledge, 1992), p. 1.
67 Quoted in Birk Meinhardt and Evelyn Roll, 'Deutschland, Feindesland?', *Süddeutsche Zeitung*, 27–28 March 1999.
68 Quoted in '"Möglichst gut rauskommen"', *Der Spiegel*, 6 September 1999.
69 See Gerhard Schröder (chancellor), in Deutscher Bundestag, *Plenarprotokoll*, 14/31, 26 March 1999, pp. 2571f.
70 Refugees from Kosovo were treated as victims of a civil war, which means a lesser status in terms of protection. Heribert Prantl, 'Das deutsche Asylrecht – blind für den Kosovo', *Süddeutsche Zeitung*, 1–2 April 1999. Note also the under-preparedness of the UNHCR, which was blamed on NATO assertions that air strikes would solve rather than exacerbate the refugee problem. See Peter Capella, 'UN Agency Failed to Meet Refugee Crisis, Says Report', *The Guardian*, 12 February 2000.
71 'NATO droht Jugoslawien mit Luftangriffen', *Süddeutsche Zeitung*, 12 June 1998.
72 'Geschlossen auf unterschiedlichen Positionen', *Süddeutsche Zeitung*, 9 October 1998; Udo Bergdoll, 'Nichts ohne den neuen Kanzler', *Süddeutsche Zeitung*, 9 October 1998.
73 'Nato ordnet Angriffe auf Serbien an', *Süddeutsche Zeitung*, 24 March 1999.
74 Quoted in Flottau *et al.*, 'Alle Serben im Krieg'.
75 'Ich darf nicht wackeln'. Rapallo was where Germany and Soviet Russia concluded a treaty in 1922, arguably undermining Western trust in Germany.
76 Quoted in 'Kabinett entscheidet über Tornado-Einsatz', *Süddeutsche Zeitung*, 30 September 1998 (italics added).
77 Quoted in 'Ich darf nicht wackeln'.
78 I have explored the issue of German (ab)normality in relation to the FRG's (un)willingness to use force since the end of the Cold War in more detail in 'Militarising Germany and the Politics of the Past', paper presented at the 1999 BISA conference in Manchester.
79 Gerhard Schröder, Statement by the Federal Government on the occasion of the 50th anniversary of the North Atlantic Treaty Organisation on 22 April 1999, in Presse- und Informationsamt der Bundesregierung, *Bulletin*, no. 19, 23 April 1999, p. 193.
80 'The Alliance's New Strategic Concept', agreed at the North Atlantic Council in Rome, 7–8 November 1991, section 15, available online: http://www.nato.int/docu/comm/c911107a.htm (accessed 18 December 2000); 'London Declaration on a Transformed North Atlantic Alliance', North Atlantic Council, 5–6 July 1990, section 2, available online: http://www.nato.int/docu/comm/49–95/c900706a.htm (accessed 18 December 2000).

81 Kurt Kister, 'Angst vor einem Kampf nach Guerilla-Manier', *Süddeutsche Zeitung*, 25 March 1999; Statement on Kosovo, Issued by the Heads of State and Government participating in the meeting of the North Atlantic Council in Washington, DC, on 23 and 24 April 1999, press release S-1(99)62, 23 April 1999, esp. section 1; press conference called by Secretary-General Javier Solana and SACEUR General Wesley Clark, 25 March 1999. Transcript available online: http://www.nato.int/kosovo/press/p990325a.htm (accessed 18 December 2000).

82 See, for example, 'Zweimal total verkalkuliert', *Der Spiegel*, 12 April 1999.

83 'Luftschläge der Nato gegen Jugoslawien', *Frankfurter Allgemeine Zeitung*, 25 March 1999.

84 Press conference called by Secretary-General Javier Solana and SACEUR General Wesley Clark, 25 March 1999.

85 Gerhard Schröder, Statement by the Federal Government on the occasion of the 50th anniversary of the North Atlantic Treaty Organisation on 22 April 1999, p. 193.

86 The independent evaluation of the UNHCR's response to the refugee crisis mentions that the interests of key donor states were related to 'the NATO military campaign and not necessarily to universal standards of refugee protection': United Nations High Commissioner for Refugees Evaluation and Policy Analysis Unit, *The Kosovo Refugee Crisis. An Independent Evaluation of UNHCR's Emergency Preparedness and Response*, pre-publication edition (Geneva, February 2000), chapter 6, section 438.

87 Derrida, *Of Grammatology*, p. 145.

88 See Christoph Schwennicke, 'Wenn die Bomben ihre Wirkung verfehlen', *Süddeutsche Zeitung*, 30 March 1999; Peter Blechschmidt, 'Durch schnelles Eingreifen Leben retten', *Süddeutsche Zeitung*, 1-2 April 1999; Manfred Ertel *et al.*, 'Das Gespenst von Vietnam'. Prime Minister Tony Blair openly pressed for considering the deployment of ground troops from late April 1999. See 'Blair Pushes for Ground Assault', *The Guardian*, 21 April 1999, and Judah, *Kosovo*, pp. 269–71.

89 See, for example, Jürgen Hogrefe, Jürgen Leinemann, Paul Lersch, Rainer Pörtner, Alexander Szandar, 'Aus freier Überzeugung', *Der Spiegel*, 19 April 1999.

90 Olaf Ihlau, Siegesmund von Ilsemann, Uwe Klussmann, Dirk Koch and Roland Schleicher, 'Ziellos und traumatisiert', *Der Spiegel*, 19 April 1999.

91 An intervention in a field of signification which aims to go beyond the existing oppositions also requires a displacement. See Derrida, *Positions*, pp. 41–3.

92 The OSCE estimates that 1.4 million people from Kosovo had been displaced by 9 June 1999: OSCE, *Kosovo/Kosova. As Seen, As Told*. We have already seen that it is difficult to ascertain precisely how many people were killed. However, the OSCE report argues that violations of the right to life increased dramatically after the withdrawal of observers on 20 March 1999 and further escalated with the beginning of the NATO air campaign four days later. See OSCE, *Kosovo/Kosova. As Seen, As Told*, chapter 5. Moreover, some Kosovars were killed by NATO bombs: see Human Rights Watch, *Civilian Deaths in the NATO Air Campaign* (February 2000), available online: http://www.hrw.org/reports/2000/nato (accessed 18 December 2000).

93 This notion of responsibility is, however, diametrically opposed to what Derrida has to say about responsibility. See Jacques Derrida, *The Other Heading*.

Reflections on Today's Europe, trans. Pascale-Anne Brault and Michael B. Naas (Bloomington and Indianapolis, Indiana University Press, 1992), p. 41.
94 Quoted in Josef Joffe, 'Wir haben keine andere Wahl', *Süddeutsche Zeitung*, 24 March 1999. See also 'Nato ordnet Angriffe auf Serbien an', *Süddeutsche Zeitung*, 24 March 1999.
95 *Ibid.*
96 See, for example, Statement by Federal Chancellor Gerhard Schröder on the situation in Kosovo on 24 March 1999, in Presse- und Informationsamt der Bundesregierung, *Bulletin*, no. 13, 30 March 1999, p. 140. Fischer said this would just take a phone call. Quoted in 'Nato greift Ziele in Serbien an', *Süddeutsche Zeitung*, 25 March 1999.
97 'Everyone had Scruples', interview with Defence Minister Rudolf Scharping, *Der Spiegel*, 29 March 1999.
98 Jenny Edkins and Véronique Pin-Fat, 'The Subject of the Political', in Jenny Edkins, Nalini Persram and Véronique Pin-Fat (eds), *Sovereignty and Subjectivity* (Boulder, CO, and London, Lynne Rienner Publishers, 1999), p. 4. See Wittgenstein, *Philosophical Investigations*, §§114–15.
99 Derrida, *Aporias*, p. 1 (italics in original); see also pp. 3f.
100 Jacques Derrida, *Archive Fever. A Freudian Impression*, trans. Eric Prenowitz (Chicago, IL, and London, The University of Chicago Press, 1996), p. 4 (italics in original).

7 *Andreas Behnke*

'vvv.nato.int.': virtuousness, virtuality and virtuosity in NATO's representation of the Kosovo campaign

> Resist the probability of any image or information whatever.
> Be more virtual than events themselves, do not seek to re-establish the truth,
> we do not have the means, but do not be duped,
> and to that end re-immerse the war and all information
> in the virtuality from whence they come.
> Turn deterrence back against itself.
> Be meteorologically sensitive to stupidity.[1]

Introduction: reading preferences...

The Kosovo war did not take place. Jean Baudrillard's diagnosis of the Gulf War also applies to this latest expression of organised violence in contemporary politics.[2] This is not to deny that death and destruction defined the reality in Kosovo and Serbia in the first half of 1999. After all, NATO planes delivered large amounts of ordnance upon targets in this area, destroying both military and civilian infrastructure; killing civilians as well as soldiers. And on the ground, Serb forces engaged in the mass expulsion and murder of the Albanian population in the province. To deny that a war took place therefore does not mean to deny the exercise of violence and the reality of human suffering in Kosovo. Nor, for that matter, did Baudrillard deny the suffering that was caused by the UN campaign against Iraq. His provocation that 'the Gulf War did not take place' needs, instead, to be understood as the articulation of two distinct, yet related, observations about the nature of organised violence in the new world order. Or, as this term is by now consigned to the dustbin of history, the post-Cold War order (perhaps best abbreviated as PoCoWO). Both observations are relevant for the critical engagement with 'war' beyond the case of the Gulf War. As I demonstrate in this essay, the Kosovo campaign lends further evidence to the suspicion that war as such no longer 'takes place', but that it has transmogrified into a different game with a different logic. There are two central aspects of this strange state of non-war that Baudrillard captures in his own critical reflection.

First, the argument about the Gulf War not taking place expresses the insight that what happened during Operation Desert Storm was not a war in the traditional sense of a duel between two more or less equal antagonists, proceeding 'from a political will to dominate or from a vital impulsion or an antagonistic violence'.[3] For Clausewitz, war was the continuation of (national) politics by other means, a way in which to settle disputes *between* states. The Gulf War and NATO's Operation Allied Force in the skies over Serbia and Kosovo, have changed this logic. Replacing the anarchical logic of war in which no side can claim to fight for more than its own interests, the 'non-wars' of the PoCoWO introduce a *hierarchical* rationale for the exercise of organised violence. Non-war 'operates today on a global level which is conceived as an immense democracy governed by a homogenous order which has as its emblem the UN and the Rights of Man'.[4] The Gulf War and, now, Operation Allied Force thus take on the nature of enforcement actions or police operations against (so-called) 'rogue states' violating the universal consensus which purportedly unites the 'international community' against such perpetrators. Moreover, Baudrillard argues that the hierarchical nature of the exercise of violence is reflected in the way these campaigns are actually conducted. Denying the other side the dignity of the 'enemy' by casting him as a rogue or criminal, 'the Americans inflict a particular insult by not making war on the other but simply eliminating him'.[5] Guided by the principles of precision or 'surgical' strikes, the air campaigns against both Iraq and Serbia do not engage the 'other' as an enemy on a common (battle)ground. Rather, the adversary is turned into the passive object of a methodical administration of violence. As Baudrillard adds: 'We have seen what an ultra-modern process of electrocution is like, a process of paralysis or lobotomy of an experimental enemy away from the field of battle with no possibility of reaction. But this is not a war, any more than 10,000 tonnes of bombs per day is sufficient to make it a war.'[6]

The second observation, expressed in the contention that the Gulf War did not take place, concerns the 'virtualised' nature of the conflict, its representation in a virtual system of signifiers.[7] Unable to fix and localise the Gulf War, we are left with floating, intersecting, contradictory or mutually reinforcing bits and bytes of information 'about' an event, the reality of which itself can no longer be pinpointed and localised. As Paul Patton argues in his Introduction to Baudrillard's *The Gulf War*, virtual war – the war over truth rather than territory – is by now an integral part of modern warfare: 'state-of-the-art military power is now virtual in the sense that it is deployed in an abstract, electronic and informational space, and in the sense that its primary mechanism is no longer the use of force. Virtual war is therefore not simply the image of imaginary representation of real war, but a qualitatively different kind of war.'[8]

Whatever real life 'mudmoving' took place in Iraq and in Serbia/Kosovo is only a part, and perhaps not the most important part, of a wider campaign in which the crucial battleground is the delocalised world of information networks, TV screens, newspaper articles and internet sites. It is on these grounds that the battles over the legitimacy, effectiveness and consequences are fought. Admissions of manipulated videos of Allied Force amount to defeats for NATO, while media reports about mass graves in Kosovo 'confirm' the legitimacy of the Alliance campaign *post facto*.

Some harsh criticism has been launched against Baudrillard's pathomorphology as a typical example of postmodern excess. Christopher Norris, for instance, suggests that Baudrillard's writings represent a kind of political theory characterised by 'cynical acquiescence, ill-equipped to mount any kind of effective critical resistance'.[9] To some extent, these criticisms can be understood as a response to the rhetorical hyperbole in the text and the polemical style in which Baudrillard tends to present his case. Yet this means only that much of the criticism focuses on the *means* of delivery, rather than the message itself, which, if we accept the above paraphrase, is far from revolutionary. The emergence of a hierarchical and discriminatory concept of war, as well as its inherent tendency to produce 'total' warfare, is an insight offered as early as 1938 by Carl Schmitt.[10] Certainly, Schmitt could not possibly have anticipated the development of information technologies that make up the material infrastructure for PoCoWO's virtual war. But he was acutely aware that such a discriminatory concept of war would project the conflict away from the battlefields of armour towards the battlefields of truth, on which the clash between 'us' and 'them', liberal democracy vs. rogue state, would take place. Moreover, Schmitt's discussion of the legal and political consequences of discriminatory war makes it easier to place such critical reflections on the nature of war within an intellectual tradition. Above all, it becomes possible to place both the Gulf War and the Kosovo campaign within the context of a broader, more historically informed, discussion on the nature of liberalism and war. Most notably, Schmitt's critique of the League of Nations and the criminalisation of war suggests that the most significant aspect of the Kosovo experience is not the extent to which the virtualisation of war has by now developed. Rather, the existing media and information technologies offer only a newer and more effective means by which to conduct such an epistemic war. The new quality of virtual war is but the latest phase in a centuries old tradition of conflict over knowledge and truth inherent to the liberal discriminatory concept of war. Obviously, this proposition deserves elaboration.

Loading plug-ins: liberal truth against systemic anarchy

To claim that the international system is anarchical is to give voice to a truism – a truism, however, that easily begs the question of what is meant by 'anarchy'. The usual definition refers to the absence of any superior authority above and beyond the sovereign states that make up the international system. For neo-realists, anarchy is the quasi-objective structural constraint that forces states to maintain their independence and locks them into a perpetual state of war. For constructivists, anarchy 'is what states make of it', i.e. an intersubjective structure of mutually recognised state identities.[11] Anarchy is thus the condition of possibility for a variety of relational complexes between states. In this definition, anarchy can be best understood as the absence of an authoritative voice that preordains the nature of interstate relations.

The notion of anarchy used in this chapter builds on the constructivist reading, and advances it. Constructivists ultimately cling to a realist epistemology within which they ground the proper, 'scientific' nature of their research projects by establishing the identity of states within a presocial atomistic realm. For the purpose of this essay, anarchy is understood as the absence of the very possibility of settling the question of a state's identity beyond its sovereignty. More specifically, while constructivists emphatically assert the prepolitical identity of democracies and authoritarian regimes, the poststructuralist-informed approach, embraced in this essay, holds that the decision about 'democratic' and 'authoritarian' identities are, in fact, political decisions. In other words, they are contestable outcomes of knowledge/power games.

Anarchy as the absence of 'voice' entails the impossibility of any final depoliticised arbitration of claims to, and designation of, identities. The nature of war and its just (or unjust) character cannot be preordained. In an international system ruled by anarchy, wars are to be considered 'just' if they are conducted by recognised entities, i.e. sovereign states. As for the justness of the causes and purposes of war, the absence of 'voice' renders such judgement impossible.

To be sure, the United Nations Charter constitutes a significant intervention into this logic. Article 2.4 of the Charter postulates that states shall refrain from the threat or use of force in their relations. War, in other words, is a breach of international law, and the illegality of the cause and the identity of the perpetrator are ascertained by the UN Security Council, according to Chapter VII of the Charter. In its ultimate consequence, this delegitimises the traditional notion of war as the sovereign prerogative of states. Either war has become illegal as a breach of the UN Charter, or it becomes, as authorised by the UN Security Council, an execution, sanction, or enforcement of international law.[12] War as a duel between states has been replaced by a discriminatory concept in which the warring state becomes a 'criminal' or rogue state.

Although the UN Charter constitutes a major modification of the law of war, the Western imagination goes much further: whereas the Charter allows only the *post facto* identification of a 'criminal' state (namely, *after* it has breached international law), institutionalised Western knowledge attempts to render judgement about the identity of states *before* they act. To simplify and exaggerate the argument found in democratic peace theory and NATO's political discourse, as well as among strategic pundits on CNN *et al.*: some states are evil by nature, regardless of their actual conduct; and while those 'rogue states' cannot do right, the West, as the community that carries the beacon of universally recognised (if not always realised) values, cannot do wrong. The West's intervention in Kosovo expresses this logic in a dramatic fashion: for the first time, a Western security organisation has taken military action against a sovereign country that has not attacked any of that organisation's members. Moral and humanitarian standards, rather than national interest, were offered as the rationale for this campaign.

On one level, this has been discussed as a *prima facie* breach of international law.[13] More relevant for the purpose of this essay, however, is NATO's express claim to represent a superior 'community of values' which would authorise it to conduct such military acts of violence against other, 'lesser', states. NATO presents itself as an agent with a humanitarian purpose and moral values, untainted by politics, power and persuasion, which notions are now replaced by such concepts as morality, authority and force.

NATO has conducted an epistemic war to secure its privileged moral status, fighting against the systemic anarchy of the international system, the inherent ambivalence and undecidability that necessitates and demands the political designation of identity (a demand which even the UN Charter is unable to erase). The vehemence of the Alliance's cyberwar, and its assertive retaliation against any doubts about the virtuousness of Operation Allied Force, should be understood in this context.[14] Cyberwar (as the postmodern expression of epistemic war) is waged in 'an abstract, electronic and informational space', and provides the perfect strategy for this purpose.[15] For power to remain virtuous and exemplary, it needs to be virtual. Virtuousness–virtuality–virtuosity constitute the Holy Trinity of information warfare, a war waged against the ambivalence and undecidability of the anarchical international system. In order to impose order – *its* order – upon the heterogeneity of the international realm of politics, the Western imagination pursues a doubletrack strategy in which 'liberalism' (or 'liberal democracy') is instated as the site and sight of knowledge. Liberalism provides the cognitive vantage-point from which to survey and map global politics, as well as the geopolitical space in which supreme political, social and cultural values and norms have been realised. Liberal theory (which focuses on democratic peace theory) provides ammunition for the first track, supporting the political or politicised representations of 'the West' in its claim to moral and political superiority.

Yet, politics is messy; war is messy. The first victim in war, it is (too) often said, is 'truth'. But this insight should be deepened, since war also demonstrates the very impossibility of truth in the international system as that system defies the possibility of a totalising global regime of ultimate knowledge. If truth is always indebted to power, then the boundaries of sovereignty delineate its realm. It also implies that the universalising impetus of the liberal project sustains a war against those forces that get in the way of its success. Any outside involvement in the messy realities of war has to be purified and made virtuous through virtualisation.

In the following section, I analyse NATO's virtuoso campaign to virtualise Operation Allied Force in order to represent itself as the virtuous actor in the messy reality of war. This analytical strategy thus makes use of the weakest link in the triad of virtuousness–virtuality–virtuosity by appreciating and exploiting the obvious virtuosity of the campaign, its skilful performance in daily press conferences, in the media and, above all, on the internet.[16] The focus of this investigation will be the site where the three V's come together in the most unadulterated fashion, namely NATO's internet site. The target of this investigation is, so to speak, the vvv.nato.int-site. Access is granted, however, only via the alias of www.nato.int.

Looking up host: www.nato.int

On NATO's homepage, under the heading 'NATO's role in Kosovo' and a colour map of the Balkan area with Kosovo designated by a red circle, we find an overview of briefings and background information made available during the air campaign (25 March–10 June) as well as up-to-date (11 June–) information on the UN-mandated international peacekeeping force (Kosovo Force, KFOR).

Host found; waiting for reply . . .

A click on the 'air campaign'-link loads the main page http://www.nato.int/kosovo/all-frce.htm. This page provides hypertext links to 'operational updates', 'morning briefings', 'press briefings', and to 'maps and aerial views'; 'video material and high quality photos are available separately'. More interesting than the listed dates of briefings, however, are the graphic illustrations that are scattered across the page. On top of the page, a banner provides the context of this and connected sites: NATO's emblem on the left side is linked with an image of a stream of refugees on the right side.

Figure 1 *NATO banner*

Figure 2 *F-15/SAMS*

Linking 'NATO' and the Kosovar refugees is a white arc against a blue background, reminiscent of fighter-jet trailers and hinting at the shape of a rainbow. At one end we find the disaster that took place in Kosovo, with the agent that came to set things to rights at the other. The imagery of the pageheader therefore already provides us with the general frame through which Allied Force is represented: the Kosovo crisis as a human disaster, NATO as a distant and aloof organisation working for the good cause, and air power as the means of intervention in the 'Kosovo crisis'. Just below the header, the means of intervention and its successes are proudly displayed: an F-15 takes to the skies, pregnant with weaponry. Under the heading 'Air Operations' the challenge is described: '12 × SAMs Launched'; at the bottom of the picture we find the statement of ultimate success: 'All NATO Aircraft Returned Safely.'

NATO is here represented by one of its finest pieces of weaponry and identified through the apparent impunity with which it was able to execute its strategy. (Although one should note that 12 surface-to-air missile launches as against 37,465 NATO sorties hardly seems to amount to a convincing challenge[17]). Further images depict the actors engaged in their ritualised briefings: Jamie Shea, NATO spokesman; General Wesley K. Clark, SACEUR; and Javier Solana, NATO secretary-general. On this page, NATO puts on its civilised, open face, delivering information rather than explosives, engaging the media audience, rather than its enemy. Its voice comes alive when we click our way through the hypertext links.

First in the offering is a 'historical overview' aimed at setting out NATO's role in relation to the conflict in Kosovo.

Reading file...

Kosovo, NATO tells us, 'lies in southern Serbia and has a mixed population of which the majority are ethnic Albanians'. Until 1989, there had been general peace in the area. However, 'Serbian leader Slobodan Milosevic altered the status of the region, removing its autonomy and bringing it under the direct control of Belgrade, the Serbian capital'. This action by Milosevic, NATO suggests, was at the core of the conflict between the Serbs and the Kosovar Albanians, as the latter 'strenuously opposed the move'. According to this text, the conflict became a matter of concern for the international community in 1998. The escalation of the conflict, its 'humanitarian consequences, and the risk of it spreading to other countries', as well as 'President Milosevic's disregard for diplomatic efforts ... and the destabilising role of militant Kosovar Albanians', forced the West to pay attention and, ultimately, to become actively involved.

In light of these developments, in May 1998, NATO set 'two major objectives', namely, to:
- 'help to achieve a peaceful resolution of the crisis by contributing to the response of the international community'; and
- 'promote stability and security in neighbouring countries with particular emphasis on Albania and the former Yugoslav Republic of Macedonia'.

As the conflict parties were apparently unimpressed by NATO's concern, on 13 October 1998, 'following a deterioration of the situation, the NATO Council authorised Activation Orders for air strikes' in order to make the 'Milosevic regime' withdraw its forces from Kosovo. Under a heavy diplomatic barrage, Milosevic caved in and the 'air strikes were called off'.

The rest of the pre-air-strike narrative provides a tale of institutional networking, with hypertext links to UN Security Council Resolutions 1199 and 1203, to the Contact Group, as well as to the Organization for Security and Co-operation in Europe (OSCE). NATO supported the OSCE by providing a military task force for use in a possible emergency evacuation of members of the Kosovo Verification Mission (KVM), and 'supported and reinforced the Contact Group efforts by agreeing on 30 January [1999] to the use of air strikes if required'. These concerted efforts found their climax in the Rambouillet negotiations in February–March 1999, near Paris. The Kosovar Albanians signed the 'proposed peace agreement, but the talks broke up without a signature from the Serbian delegation'. The NATO website argues that '[i]mmediately afterwards Serbian military and police forces stepped up the intensity of their operations against the ethnic Albanians in Kosovo, [and] tens of thousands of people began to flee their homes'. As a result the OSCE's KVM pulls out of Yugoslavia and NATO aeroplanes take to the skies.

There is nothing intrinsically wrong with this rendition of the Kosovo crisis. But every narrative presents its subject matter in one version rather than another; every narrative is told from a particular perspective, emphasising certain features, while omitting others. In the context of political language, such narratives become resources of power, as they outline the context of political action, assign responsibility, designate identities and legitimise (and, *ipso facto*, delegitimise) certain political strategies. However, their effectiveness as power resources depends on the assumption that they refer to, and properly reflect, a given 'reality'. In order to problematise this status and to highlight the power resources' contingent character, it is 'standard operational procedure' in the critical approach to contrast so-called 'ruling discourses' with alternative ones. One of the purposes of this essay is to demonstrate that a particular narrative provides only one 'construction of reality', which inevitably distributes power, responsibility and agency within a single structure. This strategy is not without pitfalls, since the temptation exists to compile about an event a portfolio of narratives which may produce a meta-narrative of a rather dubious epistemic character.[18] Alternatively, one might easily smuggle in assumptions about a closer proximity to reality when presenting alternative discourses and dismissing the investigated narrative as 'ideological'. To avoid such misunderstandings, let me say here that I do not intend to contrast NATO's narrative about the Kosovo crisis with a 'better', or more 'accurate', one. The following references to alternative texts should serve simply as the background which may bring certain problematic aspects of NATO's rendition of 'Kosovo' into stronger relief.

To begin with, there is the particular timeframe within which NATO's discourse places the events of 'Kosovo'. To argue that the conflict became a concern for the 'international community' in 1998, obviously omits the developments in and around Kosovo before that year, a period in which the 'international community' was heavily involved. One possible way to problematise this omission is to import a discussion of the effects of the Dayton Agreement in our debate about 'Kosovo'. Mark Danner, among others, has argued that the United States government was since 1992 aware of the impending crisis in Kosovo.[19] In April 1993, Secretary of State Warren Christopher stated:

> We fear that if the Serbian influence extends into [Kosovo or Macedonia], it will bring into the fray other countries in the region – Albania, Greece, Turkey ... So the stakes for the United States are to prevent the broadening of that conflict to bring in our NATO allies, and to bring in vast sections of Europe, and perhaps, as happened before, broadening into a world war.[20]

It appears that even before 1998, Kosovo had become a matter of serious concern for the 'international community'. Interestingly enough, the 1995 Dayton Agreement failed to address the issues which were so dramatically identified by Christopher. In Dayton, 'the Americans were in a hurry: they *needed* a Bosnia agreement, only Milosevic could deliver it to them, and he knew it; and he would brook no diplomatic meddling in what was unquestionable "Serb land"'.[21] Dayton's non-decision on Kosovo, and the willingness of the 'international community' to reach an agreement with Milosevic at the cost of ostracising Kosovo from the negotiation agenda, proved to have severe consequences. As Noel Malcolm writes, the Kosovar Albanian leader Ibrahim Rugova had justified his insistence on a nonviolent strategy against Serbia's oppression by 'telling his people, in effect, that they must be patient until the international community imposed a final settlement on ex-Yugoslavia, in which their interests would also be respected. But that settlement ... left the Albanians of Kosovo exactly where they were'.[22]

Consequently, the failure to address the Kosovo issue during the Dayton negotiations contributed to the instability of the area and the subsequent escalation of violence, not least through the strengthening of the Kosovo Liberation Army (KLA). From this perspective, the 'international community' was most certainly involved in the Kosovo crisis long before 1998 – and in a less than helpful fashion.

But there is another aspect of the temporal frame within NATO's historical narrative which deserves critical attention. According to this text, the troubles began in 1989 when Milosevic 'altered the status of the region', taking away Kosovo's autonomy and imposing direct rule from Belgrade. While one need not downplay Milosevic's role in the Kosovo drama, this particular timeframe excludes the long history of friction between Serbs and Albanians in the region, as well as the centuries of Great Power games that have played a part in the region's circumstances.[23] By limiting the historical framework of the conflict from 1989 to 1998, Milosevic's role and responsibility are blown out of proportion: Rather than being one actor in a longstanding conflict with its own dynamic and mythology, he is now rendered as the agent who directly brought about the Kosovo conflagration.

Apart from the temporal framing of the conflict, NATO's institutional networking deserves attention. Although NATO's website wants to create the impression that its air campaign was 'linked' to a United Nations Security Council (UNSC) resolution and has received broad interorganisational support, it should be remembered that a broad consensus exists among legal experts that Allied Force was a *prima facie* breach of international law. To be sure, the UN had identified the situation in Kosovo as a 'threat to peace and security in the region' (UNSC Resolution 1199). Yet, it had also reaffirmed that 'under the Charter of the United Nations, primary responsibility for the maintenance of international peace and security is conferred on the Security Council' (UNSC Resolution 1203). NATO was authorised only to conduct an 'Air Verification Mission over Kosovo' in accordance with an agreement between Yugoslavia and the OSCE. However, even taken together, these resolutions failed to add up to a solid legal basis for NATO's Operation Allied Force.

Finally, the sparse treatment of the Rambouillet negotiations hardly does justice to the political and diplomatic processes that are now known to have taken place there. NATO contrasts the Kosovar Albanians as cooperative signatories to the agreement, with the Serbian delegation stubbornly unwilling to come to an accord. We now know that this is offering a cartoon of what happened in Rambouillet, since from the outset there was very little room for genuine negotiation over the draft agreement presented to the conflict parties. As the representative of the European Union (EU) has declared: '80% of our ideas will be simply whipped through (*durchgepeitscht*)'.[24] Nor did the proceedings resemble the usual negotiation process between sovereign states. The delegations from Kosovo and from Belgrade were 'interned', and contact with the media was prohibited; leaving without signing was forbidden. The Serb resistance to the Rambouillet dictate apparently centred on the military Annex B, which would have granted NATO forces 'unrestricted passage and unimpeded access throughout the FRY including associated airspace and territorial waters'.[25] Bearing in mind this peculiarity in the set-up of the Rambouillet 'negotiations', the Serbian refusal to accept this agreement may be easier to understand. At a minimum, it raises questions about NATO's own responsibility for the failure of the negotiations – questions made impossible by the rendition which NATO offers on its vvv-site.

So much for the prelude to Allied Force. The 'historical overview' goes on to provide hyperlinks to a day-to-day account of the actual air campaign, and a short summary of the aftermath of the Kosovo crisis. Here the narrative once again enmeshes NATO actions within an authorising network of international institutions in which the UN plays a privileged role. A number of UNSC resolutions are available via hyperlink, as are the 'general principles' of the G8 – a group which also includes the Russian Federation – and the 'paper' presented by the representatives of the EU and the Russian Federation in Belgrade on 3 June 1999. Perhaps even more interesting is the narrative's efforts to frame Operation Joint Guardian (i.e. the deployment of military forces following the end of the air campaign and the re-establishment of order and security in Kosovo) as a 'humanitarian effort'. NATO's account of its post-bombing operations focuses on the efforts 'to relieve the suffering of the many thousands of refugees forced to flee Kosovo by the Serbian ethnic cleansing campaign'. Moreover, NATO had 'built refugee camps', moved 'hundreds of tons of humanitarian aid', and coordinated 'humanitarian aid flights'. These 'facts and figures' that conclude the 'historical overview' stand in sharp contrast with the atrocities committed by Serb forces. But, it might be remarked, NATO's current efforts to alleviate the plight of the victims and refugees also stand in sharp contrast to its own earlier bombing campaign.

Again, the point here cannot be to 'prove' NATO wrong, or to present a 'more correct' account of Operation Joint Guardian. But for the purpose of this essay it is important to point out the way in which NATO is removing itself from the ambiguity of the Kosovo reality. To turn the operation into a straightforward humanitarian effort in effect depoliticises it: it bestows upon it a legitimacy that is not immediately available to a military intervention; it silences the political and diplomatic preconditions and consequences of the deployment of NATO-led military forces in a sovereign state; it pacifies the Kosovo population into passive recipients of international humanitarian aid, thus depriving it of political agency. And, finally, it ostracises from the plot the fact that some 500 civilians died in NATO's air campaign, which makes it arguably a somewhat less than humanitarian action.[26]

Cache clean-up . . .

The hyperlink to 'Operation Allied Force' within this narrative takes the reader to the transcripts of seventy-seven days of operational updates, morning briefings and press briefings, as well as the accompanying 'maps and aerial views'. This page also offers access to NATO's densely woven strategic construction of the Kosovo reality. In other words, this page records the daily battles on the frontline of NATO's information warfare. To those interested in strategic discourse as practised at the end of the twentieth century, a plethora of rhetorical strategies, metaphors and analogies here offer themselves for critical study. My purpose here is to identify the distribution of responsibility and the designation of 'evil' in NATO's evolving discourse on the Kosovo campaign. Especially important are NATO's rhetorical gestures to extricate itself from responsibility for the death and destruction in Serbia and Kosovo in an effort to preserve its claim to the moral high ground offered to it by the liberal project. Only by maintaining this high ground can NATO legitimise its actions as the enforcer of humanitarian values that exceed the boundaries of political power and which therefore cannot be restricted or rejected by invoking the privilege of sovereignty. Yet, as Operation Allied Force has demonstrated, enforcing these moral standards by military force also kills innocent people and destroys civilian targets. The reality of 'moral combat' is never as clean as its purpose. This tension has to be resolved in order to avoid the former undermining and debilitating the latter.

One prominent rhetorical strategy used in the press briefings by NATO spokesperson Shea and the representatives of the military is to condense the 'responsibility for evil' within the person of Milosevic. This contraction of responsibility has been a central mechanism by which NATO has sought to morally justify its actions. Firstly, it has allowed the Alliance to blame Milosevic for the death and destruction that NATO has brought to Serbia and Kosovo. Secondly, it has sought to drive a wedge between the Serb people and its leader, allowing NATO to claim that in fact the Serbs themselves are victims of Milosevic. Finally, this individualisation of guilt supports NATO's claim that it did not conduct a 'war' against Yugoslavia: 'NATO is not waging a war against the Yugoslav people, to the contrary' (press briefing [PB], 25 March 1999).[27] NATO's aim is 'to stop the war and to guarantee that peace is a reality for a country that has been suffering from war for many, many, years' (PB, 25 March 1999). Free of the onus of war, NATO's action is the legitimate execution of the 'logic of the UN Security Council'. Given this non-adversarial purpose, 'the great majority of the Serbs would be only too happy to see NATO come in and provide security, stability, stop the fighting, guarantee basic human rights' (PB, 28 March 1999).

NATO has sympathy for the people of Yugoslavia. Ten years ago, when the Berlin Wall came down, any economist looking at the map of Europe would have probably designated Yugoslavia as the country emerging in the post communist period which was most likely to rapidly catch up with the Western European mainstream. It was a wealthy country. People had private bank accounts, they went skiing in Austria and Switzerland, it was a very civilised country indeed and many people obviously went there on holiday and enjoyed it.[28]

In this reading of events, Serbia's fall from grace was at the making of 'Milosevic', who single-handedly turned Yugoslavia into a 'pariah state'. 'It's Milosevic who has isolated a great people from the European mainstream where it belongs and this is a tragedy of course for the whole region but first and foremost for the people of Yugoslavia themselves' (PB, 4 April 1999). Thus, in fighting 'Milosevic', NATO is fighting for the Serbs too – even if the current situation has led to a temporary 'upsurge of nationalism in Serbia itself'. However, once back on the track of rationality, the Serbs would come to realise that NATO will 'help Yugoslavia emerge from this status of a pariah state and take the place in Europe which the people's greatness and ingeniosity [sic] deserves, quite frankly' (PB, 7 April 1999). The price for this prospect of peace and prosperity is to endure the 'strategic bombing' of civilian targets such as power plants and electricity supplies. However, the ensuing 'inconvenience' of power cut-offs 'is nothing compared with the day-to-day misery of that kind of economic meltdown which we have seen at the hands of Milosevic since he came to power'. After all, between 1990 and 1998

Serbian industrial production shrank by 50 per cent . . . Unemployment, the official figure is 27 per cent . . . and more realistically is probably double that. We know that salaries and pensions are paid late . . . 72 per cent of the 1999 budget is planned for defence-related spending. By the way, these are World Bank and IMF figures, I haven't made them up.[29]

Shea could therefore argue that being bombed, day in, day out, was preferable to living a peaceful life in the misery of 'Milosevic's' Yugoslavia.

But the price was paid not only by enduring power cuts and blacked-out TV screens. NATO killed civilians in its bombing campaign; or, in its own terms, NATO was regrettably unable to avoid 'collateral damage'. As NATO explained from the outset, should civilian casualties occur,

the responsibility is on the shoulders of President Milosevic for having manoeuvred, cornered – whatever you like to call it – the international community into a situation where it has had no alternative but to take action and whatever the situation, let's not lose sight of the general context, we are acting because already there have been too many civilian casualties in Yugoslavia, thousands of them dead, and infinitely larger numbers of people who have lost their livelihoods, their incomes, their work, their families, through the violence that has happened and it's in order to prevent this overall situation of a humanitarian catastrophe within the borders, and outside the borders of Yugoslavia because of the refugee overspill, that we are acting, so yes of course and I again stress that we will do everything, everything we can to avoid civilian casualties, but let us at least not lose sight of the overall context which has made this necessary.[30]

The rambling presentation of this case already betrays the discomfort with which this challenge to the basic canons of ethics is being delivered. But NATO has continued to use this argument: the death and destruction caused by NATO bombs were to be blamed on 'Milosevic'. As a consequence, NATO itself bears no responsibility for the death and destruction it has brought to Serbia and Kosovo. Freed of any presumption of malevolence, the 'collateral damage' produced by NATO pilots is represented as a victim of circumstances created by 'Milosevic'. Given the limits of this essay, a discussion of a single case will have to do to demonstrate NATO's strategies of 'ethical cleansing'.

On 14 April 1999, some 70 Albanian civilians were killed and some 100 wounded when NATO pilots bombed a convoy on a road near Djakovica.[31] After initial denials of responsibility and suggestions that this was yet another Serbian atrocity, NATO admitted one day later that one of its own pilots had caused the disaster. Responsibility for the deaths, however, was once again deflected. Firstly, the fact that the pilot was a NATO pilot absolved him from any element of evil. It was argued that he 'dropped his bomb in good faith, as you would expect a trained pilot from a democratic NATO country to do' (PB, 15 April 1999). His identity as a representative of the morally supreme institution obviously immunised him from any taint of responsibility. Bombing the convoy was an *honest* mistake – a mistake that, given the morally superior identity and purpose of NATO, had to be excused. Secondly, this 'mistake' is represented as a contingency of war. After all, 'no conflict in human history has ever been accident free, or will ever be' (PB, 15 April 1999). Regrettable as they are, such accidents will happen, they are part of any conflict. And, finally, culpability is established, as the original source of the evil is once again conjured.

> But I would also like to ask in this connection two questions. First, why was a refugee convoy escorted by Serb military vehicles on the Prizren–Djakovica road at 3.00 o'clock yesterday afternoon in the first place? Why weren't the people in their homes, at their jobs, going about their normal lives? Why were they en route to the border? Because they had been forced from their homes and because they were on their way to joining the 580,000 Kosovar Albanians that have already been expelled from Kosovo. My second question: why was a NATO pilot 15,000 feet up in the air yesterday afternoon over Kosovo? Because along with about 1,000 other NATO pilots, he was risking his life every day to stop human suffering in Kosovo and to allow these 580,000 refugees to be able to go back home.[32]

Responsibility for the deaths of some seventy Kosovar civilians is located, therefore, in the 'force' that drove them out into NATO's bombsights, and not within NATO itself.

The three rhetorical strategies found in this case – the assumption of essential moral superiority; the reference to the contingencies of war; and the projection of culpability for NATO's killings onto 'Milosevic' – represent the structure for NATO's designation of responsibility during Operation Allied Force. Whenever 'collateral damage' threatened to taint the image of NATO as the moral agent in a humanitarian effort, these strategies are used to ethically cleanse the Alliance and to maintain the legitimacy of its actions. After all, in the vast majority of the attacks, legitimate targets were effectively destroyed. Or so the video images that appears hyperlinked in the seventy-seven-day narrative suggests.

'All video sequences are available in MPEG'

NATO's internet site collects 112 of these video sequences. During the daily Press Briefings, these videos were used to provide evidence of NATO's ability to strike at Yugoslav forces in Kosovo and to hamper their genocidal campaign against the Kosovar Albanians.[33] Taken out of this context and accessed via the internet, these videoclips produce their own peculiar narrative of what 'really' happened during the Kosovo war.

It comes as no surprise that the execution of military violence is cleansed of the mishaps and disasters that in the end cost the lives of about 500 civilians. Reminiscent of videogame simulations, NATO's imagery produces the impression of hygienic effectiveness: only military targets are hit, and all targets are destroyed: *Jeder Schuß ein Treffer*.

Figure 3 *Tank attack*

Figure 4 *Tank attack*

As a matter of perspective, the videoclips show the exercise of a just violence in the deliverance from evil. The spectator is in the position of the pilot who is following the laser-guided missile to its target, its bright flash indicating successful delivery. The actual consequences of the attack, the destruction and death it wreaks, cannot be captured by this vantage-point. What we see are blurred and shaky images of tanks, armoured personnel carriers and planes, captured in the crosshairs of the bombsight. Seconds later, these instruments of genocide and death are destroyed. No 'collateral damage' taints the reiterated images of grey shades, crosshairs and the ultimate explosion.[34]

The video images reinforce NATO's claim to have conducted a moral campaign in which 'collateral damage' is the regrettable, if unavoidable, exception to the rule of a just and hygienic war. As the video footage is supposed to prove, NATO aimed to destroy the tools of Milosevic's genocidal campaign, and in the end forced him to surrender. Or maybe not? Perhaps what we see in many of these blurred images is the destruction of rubber decoys and fake bridge constructions. Perhaps Serbian cunning added another twist to NATO's simulation of moral warfare, by also simulating the required destruction of its war machine.

Conclusion: vvv.nato.int: host not found . . .

The Kosovo war did not take place. What did take place was the enforcement of universally held humanitarian values by a morally privileged agent (known as NATO), against a rogue leader (named 'Milosevic'). In this campaign, the lines were clear: liberalism confronted one of the last vestiges of autocracy and dictatorship in Europe; humanitarian values confronted genocide; virtue did battle with crime. And, in the end, morality triumphed over politics. No national or institutional interests, no concern for the balance-of-power or the supply of natural resources, drove NATO's action. As the agent of a community of liberal and democratic states that defines the epitome of civilisational standards, NATO faces no equals against which it can wage 'war' in the traditional sense. Consequently, war is replaced by enforcement; diplomacy is replaced by ultimata; and politics is substituted by moral rectitude.

Yet, to maintain the virtuousness of NATO's actions is only possible within the realm of the virtual. Only when its verbal representation is controlled, structured and disseminated by spin-doctors and clever spokespersons, only when the visual 'evidence' is presented in the form of videogames, only when we stay within the framework of this de-ontologised version of warfare, can NATO's claims be sustained. Outside of this framework, confronted with the consequences of NATO's inscription of universalist order upon Yugoslavia, a different reality emerges.

It was Friday, May 7, 1999, in the city of Nis, in southern Serbia, and Nato had made a mistake. Instead of hitting a military building near the airport about three miles away, the bombers had dropped their lethal load in a tangle of back streets close to the city centre. At least 33 people were killed and scores more suffered catastrophic injuries; hands, feet and arms shredded or blown away altogether, abdomens and chests ripped open by shards of flying metal. This had been no 'ordinary' shelling, if such a thing exists. The area had been hit by cluster bombs, devices designed to cause a deadly spray of hot metal fragments when they explode.[35]

It is this representation that NATO's virtual simulation of virtuous warfare is supposed to suppress in order to maintain the legitimacy of its purpose and action. As Shea admitted: 'This was the first media war: all journalists were also soldiers. Part of my task was to provide them with ammunition in order to demonstrate the sincerity of our motives and actions. After the bomb misses and the death of civilians, this became more problematic.'[36]

Virtuous warfare does not accept any responsibility for evil on its own part. Virtuous warfare is warfare *against* evil. Based on a totalising ideology that invokes universal values and norms as the justification for all its actions, this kind of warfare tends to become total in its conduct. Neither the death of innocent people nor the principles of international law can stand in its way. In this sense, Baudrillard is certainly right: We should be 'meteorologically sensitive' to this development.

Notes

1 Jean Baudrillard, *The Gulf War Did Not Take Place* (Sydney, Power Publications, 1995), pp. 66–7.
2 *Ibid.*
3 *Ibid.*, p. 83.
4 *Ibid.*
5 *Ibid.*, p. 40.
6 *Ibid.*, p. 61.
7 *Ibid.*, p. 41.
8 Paul Patton, 'Introduction' to Baudrillard, *The Gulf War*, p. 9.
9 Cited in *ibid.*, p. 15.
10 Carl Schmitt, *Die Wendung zum diskriminierenden Kriegsbegriff* (Berlin, Duncker & Humblot, [1938] 1988).
11 Alexander Wendt, 'Anarchy Is What States Make of it', *International Organization*, vol. 46, no. 2 (spring 1992).
12 Schmitt, *Die Wendung zum diskriminierenden Kriegsbegriff*, p. 42.
13 See, for instance, Bruno Simma, 'NATO, the UN and the Use of Force: Legal Aspects', *European Journal of International Law*, vol. 10, no. 1 (1999), and Antonio Cassese, 'Ex iniuria ius oritur: Are We Moving Towards International Legitimation of Forcible Humanitarian Countermeasures in the World Community?', *European Journal of International Law*, vol. 10, no. 1 (1999).

14 For instance, Dinner Speech by NATO Secretary-General Lord Robertson, International Institute for Strategic Studies, London, 22 March 2000, where Robertson condemns 'the voice of revisionism' in the media which dares to reject NATO's representation of its Kosovo campaign as a full-fledged success. Text of the speech is available: http://www.nato.int/docu/speech/2000/s000322b.htm
15 Baudrillard, *The Gulf War*, p. 56.
16 The virtuoso nature of this campaign was aptly revealed by its main actor, NATO spokesperson Jamie Shea, in numerous speeches and presentations to think-tanks and PR agencies, where he discussed the problems of 'communications strategy in modern warfare', and 'selling a war'. See, for example, Centre for European Policy Studies, 'Lessons of the Kosovo Conflict: Communication Strategy in Modern Warfare', available: http://www.euronet.be/ceps/Commentary/Webnotes/130300.htm (accessed 3 August 2000); and '"Wie man einen Krieg verkauft"; NATO-Sprecher Shea über sein Konzept', *Der Standard*, 30 March 2000.
17 For the number of sorties, see Wesley K. Clark, 'When Force Is Necessary: NATO's Military Response to the Kosovo Crisis', *NATO Review*, no. 2 (summer 1999), p. 14.
18 David Campbell, 'MetaBosnia: Narratives of the Bosnian War', *Review of International Studies*, vol. 24, no. 2 (April 1998).
19 Mark Danner, 'Endgame in Kosovo', *New York Review of Books*, vol. XLVI, no. 8 (6 May 1999), p. 10.
20 Quoted in Stephen Engelberg, 'Weighing Strikes in Bosnia, US Warns of Wider War', *New York Times*, 25 April 1993.
21 *Ibid.*
22 Noel Malcolm, *Kosovo: A Short History* (New York, New York University Press, 1998), p. 353.
23 Fabian Schmidt, 'Im Griff der großen Mächte. Das Kosovo in der wechselvollen Geschichte des Balkans', in Thomas Schmid (ed.), *Krieg im Kosovo* (Reinbeck bei Hamburg, Rowohlt, 1999); and Tim Judah, 'Kosovo's Road to War', *Survival*, vol. 41, no. 2 (summer 1999).
24 Quoted in Andreas Zumach, '"80 Prozent unserer Vorstellungen werden durchgepeitscht". Die letzte Chance von Rambouillet und die Geheimdiplomatie um den "Annex B"', in Schmid (ed.), *Krieg im Kosovo*, p. 70.
25 'Interim Agreement for Peace and Self-Government in Kosovo, Appendix B: Status of Multi-National Military Implementation Force, Article 8', available: http://www.monde-diplomatique.fr/dossiers/kosovo/rambouillet.html (accessed 28 February 2000). See also Michael MccGwire, 'Why Did We Bomb Belgrade?', *International Affairs*, vol. 76, no. 1 (January 2000).
26 Human Rights Watch, 'Civilian Deaths in the NATO Air Campaign', available: http://www.hrw.org/reports/2000/nato (accessed 7 November 2000); and Amnesty International, '"Collateral Damage" or Unlawful Killings? Violations of the Laws of War by NATO During Operation Allied Force', available: http://www.anmesty.org/ailib/aipub/2000/EUR/47001800.htm (accessed 12 June 2000).
27 One should also point out that NATO did not kill anybody in this war: the Alliance 'degraded', 'disrupted', 'devastated', 'knocked the stuffing out of' and 'destroyed', but never killed. For a further discussion, see Pertti Joenniemi's contribution to this volume.
28 NATO, press briefing, 4 April 1999.

29 *Ibid.*
30 NATO, press briefing, 27 March 1999.
31 Human Rights Watch, 'Civilian Deaths in the NATO Air Campaign', and Amnesty International, '"Collateral Damage" or Unlawful Killings?'
32 NATO, press briefing, 15 April 1999.
33 Subsequent reviews suggest that NATO was bombing more rubber than steel since it hit mostly decoys rather than real tanks. See John Barry and Evan Thomas, 'The Kosovo Cover Up', *Newsweek*, 7 May 2000; and Reiner Luyken, 'Das Täuschungsmanöver', *Die Zeit*, 4 May 2000. The video sequences can be accessed at: http://www.nato.int/kosovo/video.htm.
34 There is one notable exception to this rule: the video sequence accessed at http://www.nato.int/video/990413d.mpg shows the destruction of a train that crosses a targeted bridge at the moment of a NATO attack. Interestingly, NATO showed this video sequence at its daily press briefing at nearly three times its normal speed. At the same time, NATO's Supreme Commander Wesley Clark explained to the audience that the video demonstrated how the pilot of the F-15E conducting the strike had aimed at an empty bridge and that the train appeared 'too quickly' for him to abort the attack. See Roberto Suro, 'Bombing Tape Called Flawed', *Washington Post*, 7 January 2000.
35 Eve-Ann Prentice, 'Nato's Mistakes', *The Times*, 27 March 2000.
36 Quoted in 'Der etwas andere Krieg', *Der Spiegel*, 10 January 2000.

8 Mika Aaltola

Of models and monsters: language games in the Kosovo war

Introduction: Kosovo as a sign

The oddity of 'humanitarian bombing'; the demonic Slobodan Milosevic; the violence of genocide; the darkness of Serb nationalism; the anguish of uprooted Kosovars; the hatred of ethnic cleansing. What took place in Kosovo fascinates us, both because of its many monsters and because of the opportunity it has offered 'the West' to portray itself as a model of altruism and morality. The war over Kosovo is now far enough in the past to view Kosovo as a 'sign', an emblem for things to come. Much as was the case in ancient Rome, where omens and portents were always odd and bizarre, this Kosovo-sign has for us a curious air of ambiguity. For those observing it from the outside, it is either a model or a monster, a sign either of a maturing and perfecting European security framework or of a Europe the fragile stability of which is still under serious threat.

Kosovo's ambiguity is relevant since we now have to come to an appreciation of what this war implies for international relations (IR) theory, international law, normative approaches to politics and the development of European security in general. What makes these examinations both demanding and interesting is that 'Kosovo' is located in a realm where exotic and distant things seem to occur. This essay therefore examines the events of Kosovo not only as a sign of the future, but as a place where 'different' things occurred in a realm beyond the classical local–foreign boundary.

A fascination with freaks of nature – or *lusus naturae* – has been part of Western culture since the ancient accounts of the marginally believable (paradoxography). Explorers like Marco Polo and Columbus, like today's legions of tourists, have helped to incorporate the wonders of our world into the dichotomy of the local and the foreign, and, later, into the domestic–international nexus. The realm of the 'outside' has been inhabited by fascinating and often horrifying things which frequently seemed to test and defy the moral order that could be found at home. At the known world's periphery – a realm that is foreign to us because it is unfamiliar and nameless – the domain of marvels and wonders seems to commence.[1] During peacetime, such foreign oddities are often turned into tourist attractions and TV entertainment. However, war often amplifies the horror and terror of the foreign. Whereas the outside realm displays outlandish customs or curious physical features during normal circumstances, the outbreak of war allows for further freedom of interpretation and freedom of action, going beyond the 'normal' and the 'natural'. It is this sort of freedom that explains seemingly unrestrained behaviour at the borders of the 'known' or, as it is more conventionally called, 'the West'. When war breaks out, this interpretative freedom may turn into a violence that may both breed new life and bring death.[2] From this perspective, we should start to ask how to conduct war under such foreign/international conditions?

In this essay, I try to examine such interpretative freedom, the 'magical' and 'fluid' construction of the Kosovo phenomenon, in both Western and Serbian discourses. In particular, I consider how power can be derived from the art of repetition – i.e. how 'security' can be created and maintained by sticking to a single message and spreading it as widely as possible. To the average spectator, one of the most noticeable features of the Kosovo war has been the non-stop repetition of certain key concepts by all parties to the conflict. One might have expected that such a continual repetition would have become not merely boring but ineffective, and even counterproductive. I argue here that this is a quandary inherent to the nature of repetition. By repetition, all actors risk losing agency. Under these foreign/international conditions, in order to counter enemies – 'monsters' able to change appearances and transform themselves – one has to avoid becoming a mere automaton. So, the question becomes how one might create (or maintain) stable and potent agency?

The answer is inherently problematic since it involves the dilemma of repetition versus variation. In exploring this question, I start from the premiss that reality – and international reality in particular – has a strongly 'magical flavour'.[3] The concept of 'magic' may be new and unsettling to some students of IR, but I wish to argue that it offers a good template for understanding contemporary global politics since it deals with the art of producing and maintaining marvellous, striking and at times also shocking phenomena by ritualistic/performative methods. From this perspective, the rationale justifying ritualistic repetition has to do with the power of words to create (in and of themselves) a new kind of 'reality'. The term 'magic' suggests a strong sense of forcefulness behind explicit words. But this degree of force is not associated only with military power, or with human sacrifice in battlefield. Other sources of power have to be explored.

In doing so, I base my approach on a variety of philosophical traditions ranging from Plato via Giordano Bruno to Wittgenstein. The latter's ideas, for example, are extremely relevant for our discussion since Wittgenstein's notions of the power of language conjure up images of something 'higher', something 'profound', which goes well beyond the actual words themselves. This essay argues that this ability of *mere* words to suggest and stimulate powerful images should be considered an important source of political power. The Kosovo-sign is just one recent illustration of this mechanism, albeit an extremely powerful one.

Repetition, variation and incantation

To begin this exploration of 'Kosovo', I start my philosophical journey with Bruno's thinking on the importance of the hidden qualities in the magic of reality. Bruno believed in what is called the 'magical theory of language'. A key element of this 'theory' is that words can bring matters and events into existence and hence create agency. The power of words to animate is not only connected with existing things: Bruno assumed that uttering something could itself actually change reality. This suggests that language is more than a means of describing reality, that the link between language and reality is deeper, more creative and at times even forceful.[4]

The metaphorical thinking of Bruno suggests that the essential features of a thing or event could be changed, maintained or even created. For example, the powerful use of words could give a ruler characteristics associated with God, thereby reinforcing the state's power. One of the central elements of Bruno's thought is his emphasis on the infinite variance of reality, which, he argues, offers the raw material that can be shaped by the power of words and the imagination. For Bruno, even 'real things' are imaginary. For example, he argues that 'even if there were no hell, the thought and imagination of hell without a basis in truth would still really produce a true hell, for fantasy has its own type of truth. It can truly act, and can truly and most powerfully entangle in that which can be bound.'[5]

In his *On Magic* (*c*.1590), Bruno writes that 'nothing is so incomplete, defective or imperfect, or . . . so completely insignificant that it could not become the source of great events'.[6] This is both the promise and the problem of prosaic politics, which involves the necessity of variance and the impossibility of controlling it. This theme also appeared in Aristotle's writings, for instance when he argues that in a *written text* repetition may soon lead the reader to incredulity and rob the text of its dramatic effect.[7] Repetition is, however, an altogether different matter in *speech*, where the strings of unconnected and constantly repeated words are at times to be recommended for their dramatic effect. Aristotle does not recommend simple repetition, but repetition with variance: 'In this repetition there must be variety of tone, paving the way, as it were, to dramatic effect.'[8] A certain level of variation is required in repetition, just to keep the listener's attention. This theme is continued and given explicitly political content in Bruno's *General Account of Bonding*, where repetition and variance establish the basis for bonding, influence and power.

This brings us to Plato, who had much to say about repetition as a means of 'producing' certain effects, mainly by influencing existing patterns of sympathy and antipathy among people. In his *Laws* (*c*.360 BC), Plato goes as far as to argue that political incantations play a central role in the affairs of the state.[9] For Plato's so-called 'ideal state', the cultivation and strengthening of the skills of calculation, reckoning and consideration – *logismo* – are paramount. However, this *logismo* is considered weak in comparison to the soul's irrational and destructive impulses. Hence, for Plato, there is a need to make these irrational features subservient to the faint voice of reason, paving the way towards the good *polis*. Plato has a solution for that: the use of incantations. He argues that it 'is the duty of every man and child – free and slave, female and male – and the whole State, to use these incantations we have described upon themselves incessantly'.[10] He further defines these incantations as plays and chants which, if taken together, can influence the beliefs and actions of those who are not persuaded by reason alone.[11] In *Laws*, Plato argues for chants and plays which enchant in such a way as to implant harmony through encouraging desirable and 'correct' behaviour in people. These incantations are to teach people what is to be considered 'good', and what is to be deemed 'bad'. He argues that the proper incantations should bind together good and pleasurable things with the correct sort of behaviour.

Before I continue this short journey into the uncharted territory of political 'magic', a reference to Wittgenstein's notion of *language games* is necessary to clarify matters. Wittgenstein uses the term 'family resemblances' (*Familienähnlichkeiten*) to illustrate the often elusive and indeterminate character of language.[12] This elusiveness is due to the variance and indeterminacy which, together with family resemblances, comprise the kaleidoscopic character of everyday experience. This kaleidoscopic character of reality lacks a stable and consistent set of features that would once and for all define any language game or offer a set of qualities common to whatever is included in a language game. Nevertheless, Wittgenstein points out that language games can 'conjure up' a sense of order that goes beyond family resemblances, and which is inherent in the actual *uses* of these games. Using language games often suggests a determinate design that proceeds according to specific rules, and language itself can hint at the more coherent and consistent sense of order that can not be reduced to any specific example of actual usage of the language.

Used in a specific way, language games that 'enchant' may have political implications. Political rhetoric often uses language to give an impression of something higher, or 'spellbound', within the language game. That which is 'spellbound' assumes a quasi-independent existence from the language games with which it is interwoven.[13] Wittgenstein argues that these games can serve two functions: they can be a means of showing how things *could* be, but also a way to indicate how things *should* be. In the former sense, language games can be used to bind things together by invoking patterns of similarity and dissimilarity. Wittgenstein maintains that 'language games are rather set up as *objects of comparison* which are meant to throw light on the facts of our language not only by way of similarities, but also of dissimilarities'.[14] Apart from this enlightening character of language games, they may also have, as in the latter sense, a more dogmatic use, binding and holding captive.[15] Images invoked by a specific language game may hold the 'user' captive, which prompts Wittgenstein to argue that in this way 'we could not get outside of a language game, for it [lies] in our language and language [seems] to repeat it to us inexorably'.[16]

We may therefore conclude that the 'magical' side of language games can be used both to control the social frame of mind, as well as to do battle against the 'bewitchment of our intelligence by means of language'.[17]

Irrespective of whether correctness and legitimacy pre-exist on some metaphysical level (as in Plato's thought) or whether they are embedded in the language game itself (as is implied by Wittgenstein), these incantations/ language games have certain 'magical' qualities. These 'magical' powers are reified in the repetitive and incantatory rituals that bind things and people together into persuasive wholes and render them meaningful – existent as a collective or as a group – through persuasive analogies.

The phantasmal background of political 'magic'

For present purposes, the important element of Wittgenstein's and Plato's thinking is the idea that there seems to be something higher, 'spellbound', in our language games that is essential to the creation of a legitimate political order. In this process, an appreciation of the 'art of memory' is being formed which attempts to arrange images into memorable – or repeatable – order(s). In this way, a certain sense of memory establishes a connection between the practical level of everyday life and behaviour and the 'spellbound' stratum of imaginary constructs.

Throughout history, the place (*locus*) for the ordering of memory has usually been a well-known building such as a theatre, a church or a mausoleum. With the help of such 'mental places', the act and art of memory implies the reading of written signs. This means that finding oneself in a certain *locus* of memory – a place where memorable things and ideas are situated – may allow for their actual recollection. However, in itself, the orderly *locus* has proved to be insufficient to sustain memory and to produce order. What is usually also required are striking images that complete the 'art of memory' with unforgettable and sometimes bizarre details. Specific memories may be contained in, and provoked by, images by using simulacra that offer general representations of specific things/ideas.[18] Thomas Aquinas, for example (in his commentary on Aristotle's *De Memoria et Reminiscencia*), argues that 'if we wish to remember easily any intelligible reasons, [we must] bind them, as it were, by certain other phantasma'. *Phantasmata* enable orderly memory, since 'things that have subtle and spiritual considerations can less be remembered, whereas things are more memorable that are gross and sensible'. Aquinas (whose thinking was admired and followed by Bruno) further claims that intellectual constructs can therefore be better remembered if they are connected with striking emotional *phantasmata*.[19]

It can be argued that over the centuries, 'the art of memory' and *phantasmata* have been used by political elites as a template for the orderly arrangement of political *loci* such as the state itself, as well as to achieve certain political objectives. The state, as an ordered political entity, is used as a memory aid and a *locus* where striking *phantasmata* can be placed to produce recollection, repetition and order. If the state is to be considered a *locus* which produces political order and sustains its organisations, the role of striking and unforgettable details becomes of paramount importance. But what qualifies as a striking image in the state *locus*? Looking at the history of state formation in Europe, we see that most states have traced their origins through a series of miracles, catastrophes, struggles for national determination and recovery, a string of enemies, and, more often than not, a succession of violence and war. It is these *phantasmata*, and the elite's skill in making political use of them, that allows for the 'magical' act of sustaining the existing state order.

Here I wish to consider how the practice of political 'magic' in global politics – based on repetition and the variance of language games – may evoke *phantasmata* that may be capable of producing certain desirable effects. Looking at the Kosovo-sign, it will be essential to identify central language games that have been used; the 'spellbound' *phantasmata* that have been evoked by the warring parties; and the incantations that have served as their context.

Western *phantasmata* and Yugoslavian counter-'magic'

Much like their ancient incantatory templates, contemporary Western political language games are based on the recitation of 'magical' words. During the Kosovo war, the spectrum of these 'divine' words (used by both parties) included such concepts as 'freedom', 'liberty', 'hope', 'peace' and 'unity'. By repetition and variation, these concepts were sublimated and acquired a powerful character reminiscent of the 'spirits' of medieval times. Given that these incantatory language games are at the core of Western texts, one could expect them to be repeated only in order to install desired beliefs, values and the 'correct' spirit within the audience at large. These language

Of models and monsters 151

games were essential in fighting what has been labelled a 'legitimate war' and a 'humanitarian intervention', and reinforcing the Western-dominated *locus* that underlies a specific system of images and keeps this system alive and vibrant.

Obviously, numerous *phantasmata* have helped to sustain this existing political order through the Kosovo-sign, most notably the continual emphasis on 'prosperity' (open markets, high standards of living, investment opportunities and health); 'peace' (security, stability, justice and human rights); 'freedom' (human dignity, life and hope); and 'unity' (the ideas of nation, family and democracy).[20]

Besides these legitimate *phantasmata*, there were powerful *phantasmata* whose status was considered undecided or even negative, such as 'globalisation' and 'interdependence'.

Finally, illegitimate *phantasmata* included 'hate' (genocide and cynical manipulation); 'disorder' (corruption, rogue states, terrorism and economic destruction); 'suffering' (drugs, diseases and environmental decay); and 'despair' (most notably the loss of hope).

In Western rhetoric, peace was oftentimes opposed to suffering; freedom put opposite to despair; and unity opposite to hate. Reading the Kosovo-sign, it becomes clear that this image-pantheon helped to maintain a sense of political order, thereby giving uncertain concepts such as globalisation and interdependence (which were oftentimes used as metaphors and analogies for 'the West'), a more positive and even quasi-legitimate connotation.

Central to repetition and incantation is the factor of time. In the case of Kosovo, the build-up of powerful *phantasmata* did not occur overnight. The NATO-led military operation against Yugoslavia had to be based on broad popular support, which required careful preparation. For one thing, the existing gallery of Western political images had to be rearranged and even transformed so as to avoid the need for a United Nations Security Council mandate which would legitimise the military intervention and overcome the barriers of sovereignty and other established political norms. The emphasis was therefore not only (or even mainly) on the careful military planning and build-up; the West had to prepare its own public to accept the new code of conduct of the emerging New European Order.

Since Western incantations and charms were based on a semblance of consistent and legitimate aims, Yugoslavia's counter-'magic' had to point out the inconsistencies in Western language games and images, while simultaneously interrupting the West's repetitions. In Brunoïan terms, these seemingly insignificant things – the level of variation in the West's repetition – could possibly be turned into a self-defeating force. Belgrade's attempt to underline the weakness of the Western Alliance as such was part of an overall scheme to protect itself from Western *phantasmata*. But the most effective means of counter-'magic' was to highlight the offensive and therefore illegitimate nature of Western actions. However, much of Yugoslavia's counter-'magic' failed since these claims were not able to reach and influence Western public opinion on a daily basis.

For example, Yugoslavia was keen to emphasise the ethnic diversity of Kosovo, claiming that almost half of the Kosovo population was ethnically non-Albanian, whereas much of the Western press reported that the vast majority of Kosovo was of Albanian ethnic origin.[21] The issue of Kosovo's ethnic make-up was important since it queried Western assumptions and similes of 'unity' as opposed to images of 'disintegration' which were already occupied by the Milosevic regime. If Kosovo was not inhabited overwhelmingly by ethnic Albanians, the West could be seen as *de facto* supporting the Albanianisation of Kosovo, which would undermine much of its political legitimacy. The *phantasmata* of the West supporting attempts by the Kosovars to reach ethnic purity – an image frequently evoked by the Yugoslavian side – was potentially disruptive to Western policy.

There were numerous problems with the Yugoslavian system of *phantasmata*. It lacked internal consistency and credibility, but, most importantly, the reactive nature of its counter-'magic' could not resist and compete with Western efforts to capture the Kosovo-sign. The problem was not so much that Yugoslavia did not have powerful images in its arsenal. The main reason why Belgrade appeared so ineffective in its resistance to the West's production of order was that its counter-images could not be 'read' with sufficient ease: they were not produced and consumed with the required regularity. The *phantasmata* evoked by the Yugoslavian leadership were based on specific historical experiences which the Serbian people attach to Kosovo, as well as their ideas of national unity, sovereignty and territorial integrity.

What was needed was a more striking element in the Yugoslav language game, and this was found in the notion of Kosovo as a 'holy' site for the Serb nation. For example, President Milosevic compared Kosovo with the human heart: 'Kosovo is important for us emotionally. As a part of this country, this is the heart of the country. We shall never give away Kosovo . . . it is the worst possible spot in the world for any threats, because of its sensitivity, Kosovo is a sensitive spot in the heart of any Serb.'[22] By using the image of the 'heart', the Kosovo-sign was given a spiritual dimension which was intended to unite a country that may have otherwise fallen apart.[23] The *phantasma* of Kosovo as the Serb 'heart' was kept alive by the continuous references and public incantations in Yugoslavia's official media. For example, the website of Yugoslavia's Foreign Ministry claims that 'Kosovo and Metohia [Kosmet] represented, in the medieval ages, the centre of the Serbian state and of the spiritual and cultural life of the Serbian people.'[24] It further argued that 'in Kosmet, over 250 immovable cultural–historical monuments are protected by the state'.[25] These claims were made to associate Kosovo's spiritual strength with the Serbian right-wing – or, until recently, their actual power – to repel outside forces. One could even suggest that this claim to offer protection to Kosovar monuments may have given Yugoslavia a certain 'magical' power over Kosovo.

By equating Kosovo with Serbia's 'heart', a deliberate connection was made with blood, life and death, and, therefore, with war itself.[26] Since Kosovo had been the site of the 1389 battle between Serb forces (in 'reality' these forces were ethnically mixed) and the army of the Ottoman Empire, it evoked images of violent early death and horror. Although an event of the distant past, the Field of Blackbirds at Kosovo Pole symbolised the cataclysmic defeat in which the flower of the medieval Serbian aristocracy had been destroyed. For the Yugoslavian political leadership, linking Kosovo with blood and violence offered an image which mixed private disaster (death on the battlefield) with public defeat (the defeat of the state itself). In principle, it appears to be impossible to separate private from public matters when one is standing at the grave of a fallen soldier friend, or when the state is constructing monuments and memorials for its war heroes. In these cases, of which there are all too many in Kosovo and Serbia, the public sphere penetrates 'private' emotions in an extremely powerful manner. In this way, the war dead become mediators, connecting the private lives of current and past generations with the public *locus* where their lives have taken place: the state itself.[27] The war dead function as a bizarre societal cement that gives the state a sense of pride and vitality through collective mourning.

During the war over Kosovo, these *phantasmata* have served to emphasise the actor's roots and sense of belonging. In the West, for example, this was highlighted by the continual use of the powerful images of 'unity' and 'union' (e.g. the name 'Operation *Allied* Force' for the NATO air campaign). On the Yugoslavian side as well, it was repeated that the war was all about the 'unity' of the State, claiming that the unity of the Yugoslavian people would be undermined by the actions of the Kosovo Albanians and the West. Unity was therefore at stake for both sides in the conflict. The war over Kosovo was fought not only for territory, but for the 'higher' goal of unity: the unity of Yugoslavia as a state, and the unity of 'the West' and the NEO which it sought to project on the continent as a whole. The Kosovo war was used to produce and sustain political and moral unity; war could both strengthen and alter this unity in a desired way.

Extending political order during the Kosovo war

Another element of the phantasmal nature of global politics is the tendency to construct and support the state as a functional organisation. The idea that the state has a spiritual dimension dates back to the medieval concept of 'heavenly fatherland'. E.H. Kantorowicz claims that the 'community of the blessed and saints was . . . the civic assembly of the celestial *patria* which the soul desired to join', adding that 'Christian doctrine, by transferring the political notion *polis* to the other world and by expanding it at the same time to a *Regno coelorum*, not only faithfully stored and preserved the political ideas of the ancient world, as so often it did, but also prepared new ideas for the time when the secular world began to recover its former peculiar values'.[28] In these cases, the celestial *patria* served as an image and a model for the earthly fatherland.

The images of holy places, monasteries and churches repeatedly promulgated by the Serb authorities during the Kosovo war, should be understood as part of this long-standing tradition of providing the state with a much-needed spiritual extension. The Christian notion of the heavenly *polis* is part of the tradition in which the saint dies for all of us, and becomes our immortal 'ambassador' to the heavenly kingdom, thereby offering ordinary people a connection between the state and heaven.[29] As the power of these venerable dead accumulated through the centuries, their tombs and relics were turned into images providing a 'higher' sanction for the state as well as for the people.[30] Memorials and war cemeteries have been turned into collective 'embassies' of those people who could mediate between the earthly state and its divine and spiritual shape. Through this mechanism, the presence of Serb memorials in Kosovo could be turned into a potential source of power substantiating Belgrade's claim to political order. Yugoslavia therefore read the Kosovo-sign in a distinct Wittgensteinian manner, interpreting monuments as something 'higher', something 'spellbound'.

For a Yugoslavia which found itself on the brink of further disintegration, the spiritual extension of its statal power was considered crucial. Even in the West, this invocation of Serbia's 'ancient dead' did not go fully unnoticed. However, in the West, Serbia's claim to spiritual belonging was not considered a legitimate power resource, but rather as yet another illustration of its propensity to give in to ancient and illegitimate hatred. To nullify their possible effect, Serbia's claims were called 'scars', 'dividers' and 'faultlines'. US Vice-President Al Gore argued in 1999 that the

> tensions and hatreds in Kosovo run very deep. Kosovo sits directly atop some of the deepest and most bitterly drawn ethnic, ideological, and religious fault lines in human history. The border between Rome and Byzantium was drawn there. Bitter battles between Muslims and Christians took place there. Turks and Serbs killed each other there. Communism battled for the minds of the people there. All these struggles have left scars, and each scar has fed a lust for vengeance.[31]

Such words were part of an overall Western strategy to question Belgrade's claim that Kosovo was part of the spiritual core of Serbia. Gore even quoted W.B. Yeats in this context – suggesting that 'too long a sacrifice can make a stone of the heart'[32] – thereby trying to neutralise the idea of Kosovo as Serbia's heartland. This strategy to defuse one of Serbia's most important power resources – its claim to the moral and historically rooted legitimacy of its presence in Kosovo – may explain why the West emphasised the death and destruction inflicted by Serbia on ethnic Albanians, whereas the losses of the Yugoslavian army were reported in terms of military equipment only. Admitting that the Serbs were again sacrificing their lives in and over Kosovo would have reinforced the historical link between private and official suffering, and might thereby have strengthened Serbia's claim to Kosovo. Western rhetoric and the media were focusing mainly on the suffering of the Kosovar people – and there was certainly a lot of that – thereby weakening Serbia's spiritual claim on Kosovo and suggesting that the ethnic Albanian population could now lay their own spiritual claim to the region by spilling their blood during the conflict.

The Western media therefore chose to emphasise the *phantasma* of hate, both individual and collective. The suffering of the Albanian refugees who were driven from their homes in Kosovo was turned into the most striking image of hate and ethnic cleansing. President Bill Clinton argued that the United States and its

> eighteen NATO allies are in Kosovo today because we want to stop the slaughter and the ethnic cleansing; because we want to build a stable, united, prosperous Europe that includes the Balkans and its neighbours; and because we don't want the twenty-first century to be dominated by the dark marriage of modern weapons and ancient ethnic, racial and religious hatred. We cannot simply watch as hundreds of thousands of people are brutalised, murdered, raped, forced from their homes, their family histories erased – all in the name of ethnic pride and purity.[33]

In this way, the *phantasma* of Balkan-style hatred was created, which – together with the notions of 'suffering' and 'despair' making the actual hate visible – soon became the most obvious target of the Western bombing campaign in Serbia and Kosovo.

However, in itself, hatred was not enough, since it had to be embedded in a more coherent set of *phantasmata* that would encompass the complexity of the daily events during war. One way to overcome this was for the Western media to show on a daily basis the suffering of the ethnic Albanians, using the most shocking and striking images. Both sides (i.e. NATO's air forces and the KLA, on the one side, and the Yugoslav army and its militias, on the other) were using violence to achieve political goals. But only Kosovar suffering made Western newspaper headlines and reached Western TV screens, as was illustrated by President Clinton's remarks in May 1999:

> In the last few days we have seen more disturbing evidence of the atrocities committed against innocent Kosovars, including some of the first photographic proof of massacres of unarmed people. In trying to divert attention from these crimes Serbian forces are only committing more by placing civilians around military targets. It's like pushing someone in front of an on-coming train, and then trying to blame the train for running them over.[34]

By applying this language game, the West admitted that its bombing raids could be inflicting minor human suffering, but that this should be considered merely as an unfortunate error, and that the real source of all evil was the Milosevic regime. These language games were meant to construct a *phantasmal* demon which could be exorcised and ultimately defeated in a military campaign.

The massive Western bombing of Serbia to destroy 'hate' in the 'heart of Europe' has historical parallels with the medieval period when demons were exorcised through torture and fire in a 'legitimate' fight of good against evil. Peter Brown argues that for the late Roman Empire, exorcism gave a more 'palpable face to the unseen *praesentia* of the saint than did the heavy cries of the possessed'.[35] He suggests that these torturers of 'evil' were often considered 'good' by definition. In a similar fashion, the death cries of the witch burning at the stake were reminding the onlookers of their own relative goodness. It is only the demon that is crying and dying, but not the possessed human being that one sees 'really' being burned at the stake. Also, when 'evil' is being punished, it is only logical that it should be the 'good' that are doing the punishing. The few images of Serb suffering that reached the Western public therefore resulted not in empathy, but, quite to the contrary, helped solidify the identities of the 'good West' versus the 'evil Serbs'.

Thus, one of the most important goals of the West's incantations was to stress that it was 'evil' that suffered from the NATO bombardments. In these language games, the *phantasmata* of hate and evil were made synonymous to the Milosevic regime which was systematically dehumanised by the media to the point of losing any human quality whatsoever. This was most clearly illustrated by the fact that the destruction caused by Western bombardments was counted only in the loss and damage of military hardware, without any mention of human casualties.[36] The reason for this omission was evident, since mentioning the human suffering inflicted upon Serbia itself might have humanised the face of evil. The *phantasmata* of evil and hatred were therefore legitimately made to suffer by the *phantasmata* of freedom and unity (i.e. 'the West'). Punishing hatred and evil was a means by which to drive out the Balkan demon exemplified by the Serbian people. Causing pain and suffering was, in itself, not the goal; on the contrary, it served to distinguish between the righteous ones and the evil ones, and to identify those who had the legitimate right to punish. Pain and suffering, and the striking images thereof, helped to re-establish a new hierarchy of power in Europe which had become less obvious after the end of the Cold War. The Kosovo-sign helped to reinstate this clarity.

Concluding remarks: security in search of agency

The central theme of this essay has been the power of linkages between different political levels – day-to-day politics and its higher normative appeal.

Of models and monsters 157

Such links can be viewed as either legitimate (the model military actions of the West) or illegitimate (Milosevic's image as 'a monster'). The claims and counterclaims have drawn attention to the legitimate and, thereby, forceful nature of one's own links and the illegitimate and, thereby, weak bonds of the other side. From a theoretical perspective, Wittgenstein's notion of something higher, 'spellbound', in our language games sheds light on the power of these linkages.

For Wittgenstein, these two customary levels – the everyday ('lower') and the more normative ('higher') – are combined in the same magical language. Tapping into the magical resources of power gives the earthly body of the state an air of eternity, but also reifies its more phantasmal level. The *phantasmata* were made physical in many ways during the Kosovo war. For example, the dead were represented through material structures, such as tombs. Meanwhile, in a much more radical sublimation, the nameless dead were turned into *phantasmata* engaged in the fight over Kosovo. Ideas such as honour, pride, brotherhood, sacrifice and unity made no distinction between the dead and the living. The spiritual was understood in material terms (as the ability to destroy the enemy troops), and the material was understood in spiritual terms (the ability to bomb was connected with spiritual superiority). Language games referring to 'love for one's fatherland', 'honour of the war-dead', 'cruel massacres of innocent civilians' and 'genocide', were at once mysteriously intangible and forcefully concrete. These linkages materialised in the power of weapons on both sides; weapons which, just by themselves and detached from the phantasmal, would have been powerless.

All parties to the Kosovo war have aimed their (re)actions at securing their own agency. Both the West and the Serbs wanted to maintain their agency, and their political independence, unrestrained by the other side. It is clear that the orthodox reading of the conflict in Kosovo, based on the interconnectedness of multiple actors and their interests, fails to secure agency either for the West or for Serbia. When the local Serb *phantasmata* are being removed from the Kosovo-sign in the form of burnt churches and fleeing people, and are replaced by the Western *phantasmata* of ballotboxes and peacekeepers, the problem of 'security' (i.e. how to define peace and order in Yugoslavia) remains. However, the West's hegemonic desire for the monotonous repetition of its own *phantasmata* is likely to prevent the necessary variance, and therefore may lead ultimately to the loss of its own agency. The West's grasp for agency may well be futile, since what it has now seems to be slipping out of its hands. In turn, this will lead to a performance of ceremonies and rituals of European security – comprised of such happenings as the war in Kosovo – to which the West will be increasingly dedicated and without which it will not be able to exist.

Notes

1. Lorraine Daston and Katherine Park, *Wonders and the Order of Nature, 1150–1750* (New York, Zone Books, 1998). Daston and Park state: 'Wonders tended to cluster at the margins rather than at the center of the known world, and they constituted a distinct ontological category, the preternatural, suspended between the mundane and the miraculous' (p. 14).
2. The elusive nature of international relations and the difficulties of constructing credible theories may well be related to this conceptual template, which still forces itself upon us. Due to the status given to things inhabiting the 'outside', it remains difficult to define the meaning of 'security'. See Jef Huysmans, 'Security! What Do You Mean? From Concept to Thick Signifier', *European Journal of International Relations*, vol. 4, no. 2 (June 1998).
3. The use of the concept 'magic' may seem somewhat unorthodox in an academic essay like this. However, I use it to describe the power of language in the construction of what we consider to be 'reality'. The main difference with modern discourses such as constructivism is that 'magic' as used here is not so much oriented towards discovering all-encompassing practices and rule structures, as it is inclined to emphasise and accept fluidity and action.
4. D.P. Walker, *Spiritual and Demonic Magic: From Ficino to Campanella* (University Park, Pennsylvania State University Press, 2000). The theory of magical language is related to the so-called 'linguistic turn', which argues that 'philosophical problems are problems which may be solved (or dissolved) either by reforming language, or by understanding more about the language we presently use'. See Richard Rorty, *The Linguistic Turn. Essays in Philosophical Method* (Chicago, University of Chicago Press, 1967). The so-called 'deep structure' of language is related to the quest of Renaissance theorists of magic to find the occult nature of things within language. The practicality with which the theorists of magical language (especially Giordano Bruno and Theophrastus) approached reality is largely unmatched among the writers of the linguistic turn, with the possible exception of J.L. Austin. See S.J. Tambiah, 'Form and Meaning of Magical Acts: A Point of View', in Robin Horton and Ruth Finnegan (eds), *Modes of Thought: Essays on Thinking in Western and Non-Western Societies* (London, Faber, 1973).
5. Giordano Bruno, *On Magic* (*c*.1590), now published under the title *Cause, Principle and Unity: Essays on Magic* (Cambridge, Cambridge University Press, 1998), p. 156.
6. *Ibid.*, p. 111.
7. Aristotle, *Rhetoric* book III, part 12, available: http://www.public.iastate.edu/~honeyl/Rhetoric/ index.html (accessed 16 November 2000).
8. *Ibid*.
9. For Plato's ideas about the connection between magic (*goeteia*) and reasonable politics, see Jacqueline de Romilly, *Magic and Rhetoric in Ancient Greece* (Cambridge, MA, Harvard University Press, 1975). See also Elizabeth Belfiore, 'Elenchus, Epode, and Magic: Socrates as Silenus', *Phoenix*, vol. 34 (1980), and William Welton, 'Incantation and Expectation in Laws II', *Philosophy and Rhetoric*, vol. 29, no. 3 (1996).

10 Plato, *Laws*, in *Plato in Twelve Volumes* (Cambridge, MA, Harvard University Press, 1988), book II, p. 665c. Aristotle's argument in favour of repetition ties it in with the notion of dramatic effect. The structure of spoken language is arranged so that it generates harmony within the listener, not only because of what is spoken but because *how* it is said. The pleasurable way of saying something captures the imagination of the listener, which makes what is actually being said more powerful.
11 William Welton, 'Incantation and Expectation', p. 659d–e.
12 Ludwig Wittgenstein, *Philosophical Investigations* (Oxford, Basil Blackwell, 1968), §§23, 67.
13 Ludwig Wittgenstein, *Philosophical Occasions* (Cambridge, Hackett Publishing Company, 1993), p. 117.
14 Wittgenstein, *Philosophical Investigations*, §130.
15 *Ibid.*, §115.
16 *Ibid.*, §105.
17 *Ibid.*, §109.
18 In his *De Anima*, Aristotle deals with imagination (as well as 'mental images') as the intermediary between sense perception and intellect. In other words, the intellectual faculty does not directly use and work on perceptions, but on perceptions arranged and represented by imagination.
19 Thomas Aquinas, *Summa Theologica* (New York, Tabor Publishing, 1981), II, ii, question 49, states: 'First, when a man wishes to remember a thing, he should take some suitable yet somewhat unwonted illustration of it, since the unwonted strikes us more, and so makes a greater and stronger impression on the mind; and this explains why we remember better what we saw when we were children. Now the reason for the necessity of finding these illustrations or images, is that simple and spiritual impressions easily slip from the mind, unless they are tied as it were to some corporeal image, because human knowledge has a greater hold on sensible objects.'
20 US President Clinton has argued that the 'United States has the opportunity and . . . the solemn responsibility to shape a more peaceful, prosperous, democratic world in the 21st century . . . We cannot assume it will bring freedom and prosperity to ordinary citizens . . . we must work hard with the world . . . to defeat the dangers we face together and to build this hopeful moment together, into a generation of peace, prosperity, and freedom. That's why I've worked hard to build a Europe that finally is undivided, democratic and at peace . . . a community that upholds common standards of human rights, where people have the confidence and security to invest in the future, where nations cooperate to make war unthinkable.' Remarks by the President on Foreign Policy, 26 February 1999, available: http://www.pub.whitehouse.gov/uri-res/I2R?urn:pdi://oma.eop.gov.us/1999/3/1/3.text.1 (accessed 16 November 2000).
21 President Milosevic has answered the question whether Kosovo will always be part of Serbia with the argument that it '[a]lways has been and always will be. Why would it be any different in the future. Only in Kosmet, there are 1800 Serb, Christian churches . . . This is where different national communities live – Serbs and Montenegrins, Albanians, Muslims, Egyptians, Romanies, Turks. The approach of the Serb Government and all political parties and citizens of Serbia

is that nationalities living there have to be equal.' Interview with Slobodan Milosevic, *Washington Post*, 13 December 1998.
22 *Ibid.*
23 In this context, the notion that Kosovo is the holy land for Serbia is highlighted also by the term *Metohija*, which, in Serbo-Croatian, refers to church property. See also the website of Serbia's Ministry of Information: http://www.serbia-info.com/news/1999-07/25/13536.html (accessed 16 November 2000).
24 Yugoslav Federal Ministry of Foreign Affairs, *The Cultural Heritage in Kosovo and Metohia*, available: http://www.gov.yu/Kosovo_facts/enter5.html (accessed 16 November 2000).
25 *Ibid.*
26 Thomas Emmert has argued that the 'legend of the battle became the core of what we may call the Kosovo ethic, and the poetry that developed [among Serbs] around the defeat contained themes that were to sustain the Serbian people during the long centuries of foreign rule'. Thomas Emmert, *The Kosovo Legacy*, available: http://www.kosovo.com/history/dorich_kosovo/kosovo11.htm (accessed 16 November 2000).
27 Michael Roberts writes in this connection that 'power emanates from the location of the martyr's tomb in ever-widening circles until it embraces the whole world'. Michael Roberts, *Poetry and the Cult of the Martyrs: The* Liber Peristephanos *of Prudentius* (Ann Arbor, University of Michigan Press, 1993), p. 25.
28 E.H. Kantorowicz, *The King's Two Bodies: A Study in Mediaeval Political Theology* (Princeton, NJ, Princeton University Press, 1957), p. 234.
29 This association drew a parallel between the martyrs dying in defence of the kingdom of heaven and those dying in defence of holy soil of one's own *patria*. One marked difference is illustrated by the pagan repugnance towards the Christian way of connecting the world of the living with the world of death through the cult of saints: 'The profane was pervaded by the supernatural, and the sacred was impregnated with naturalism.' See Philippe Ariès, *The Hour of Our Death* (New York, Vintage Books, 1982).
30 *Ibid.*, p. 72.
31 Remarks by Vice-President Al Gore, 50th Anniversary of NATO, 21 April 1999, available: http://www.pub.whitehouse.gov/urires/I2R?urn:pdi//oma.eop.gov.us/1999/4/22/10.text.1 (accessed 16 November 2000).
32 *Ibid.*
33 Remarks by President Clinton upon departure for Littleton, Colorado, 20 May 1999, available: http://www.pub.whitehouse.gov/urires/I2R?urn:pdi//oma.eop.gov.us/1999/5/21/30. text.1 (accessed 16 November 2000).
34 *Ibid.*
35 Peter Brown, *The Cult of the Saints* (Chicago, IL, University of Chicago Press, 1981), p. 108.
36 US President Clinton has argued: 'At the beginning of the operation, we focused, properly, on Serbia's highly-developed air defences, to reduce the risks to our pilots. There are still significant air defences up and, therefore, there is still risk with every mission. But we have degraded the system to the point that now, NATO can fly 24 hours a day, not simply at night. We've struck at Serbia's machinery of repression, at the infrastructure that supports it. We've destroyed

all of Serbia's refineries, half of its capacity to produce ammunition. We've attacked its bridges and rail lines and communications networks to diminish its ability to supply, reinforce and control its forces in Kosovo. Increasingly now, we are striking the forces themselves, hitting tanks, artillery, armoured personnel carriers, radar missiles and aircraft.' Remarks by President Clinton to the American Society of Newspaper Editors, 15 April 1999, available: http://www.pub.whitehouse.gov/urires/I2R?urn:pdi//oma.eop.gov.us/1999/4/16/8.text.1 (accessed 16 November 2000).

9 Mikkel Vedby Rasmussen

'War is never civilised': civilisation, civil society and the Kosovo war

Introduction

'War is never civilised', British Prime Minister Tony Blair declared on 10 June 1999, 'but war can be necessary to uphold civilisation.'[1] On that day, seventy-eight days of war were brought to an end by the assertion that they had secured the principles on which the post-Cold War European order was founded. For that reason the Kosovo war provides an opportunity to study what the West believes to be the foundation of a new European order.[2] This opportunity should be used because the reflexive confusion which followed the end of the Cold War finally seems to have settled into a new kind of political order. To appreciate how the West is constructing this order should be of concern to anyone who wants to understand what the twenty-first century has to offer European politics.

In the context of the debate on the futures of European order, Blair's construction of the Kosovo war may be seen as an illustration of Samuel Huntington's scenario of some forthcoming 'clash of civilisations'.[3] Was Blair not arguing that, while war has ceased to be a means of politics in the relations between Western states, the West's relations with *other* civilisations do – at least occasionally – involve war? However, the construction of the Kosovo war as a defence of civilisation does not seem to vindicate such a reading of the emerging post-Cold War world. On the contrary, Huntington's conception of civilisation is merely the culmination of a long tradition of conceiving government – as well as relations between governments – in terms of civilisation. This tradition began with the philosophers of the Scottish Enlightenment (particularly Adam Ferguson), and culminated in Immanuel Kant's conception of the pacific federation of liberal governments as the cosmopolitan purpose of history. The centrepiece of this tradition is the construction of government in terms of civil society. In order to understand how the West came to see the Kosovo war as necessary for the upkeep of civilisation, both the concept of civilisation and the notion of international politics it constructs should be carefully analysed.

Civilisation and civil society

Adam Ferguson coined the term 'civil society' in *An Essay on the History of Civil Society* (first published in 1767). In today's idiom, Ferguson described how modern society, with its elaborate division of labour, shapes both domestic and international order. The division of labour, he argued, was a prerequisite to an organic society that allowed social institutions independent of the state. In their turn, these institutions would produce a truly free society, whose organic nature was believed to encourage creativity and progress.[4] Ferguson's work, therefore, implied a clear link between the notion of civil society and the concept of 'civilisation'. Ferguson suggested that civil society was the vehicle of civilisation, being the result of what Norbert Elias was to term the 'civilising process'.[5] Civilisation is an understanding of society as history, an understanding which developed from the same Enlightenment belief in progress and freedom through social organisation by which Ferguson defined civil society. Kant developed and sharpened these ideas of the Scottish Enlightenment, and argued that the peaceful nature of civil society could be preserved only if the liberal governments of civil societies would join in what he labelled a 'pacific federation'.[6]

In 1999, the West believed itself to have realised such a pacific federation, and its bombing campaign was supposed to defend this cosmopolitan peace. French Prime Minister Lionel Jospin could therefore wholeheartedly agree with his British counterpart that intervening militarily in Kosovo was the answer to a profound challenge to Europe's identity:

> For decades Europe, at any rate our Europe, has been being rebuilt on new foundations of peace, respect for human rights. To accept the flouting of these values on the European Union's doorstep would have meant betraying ourselves. What is at stake in today's conflict is a certain conception of Europe. Do we accept the return of barbarism on our continent or do we rise up against it? For us, the choice is clear.[7]

This makes it obvious that 'Europe' is constructed as more than a matter of geography. To Western leaders like Jospin and Blair, 'their' Europe represents a certain monopoly of civilisation. By challenging this Western claim, the Milosevic regime not only came to represent 'barbarism' in the eyes of the West, but was questioning the very mechanisms by which the West defined 'Europe'. In other words, the conflict in Kosovo did not threaten the physical borders of Europe, but it seriously challenged the West European notion of 'Europe'.

But who were Jospin and Blair to define the nature of Europe? As Huntington would be the first to point out, 'European civilisation', on behalf of which they were speaking, was only one voice in a cacophony of civilisational identities. Serbia ostensibly fought for the interests of the 'Orthodox' civilisation, and Russia half-heartedly supported its 'Slav brothers'. From this perspective, one might argue that the Kosovo war was not the triumph of civilisation (as proclaimed by Blair), but the first, nasty glimpse of a world in which political (and occasionally armed) conflict stems from mutually exclusive identities. Huntington argues that the West cloaks its particular civilisation interests in universalism, which makes Western political leaders (including the likes of Jospin and Blair) blind to the fact that their interests, values and norms are at odds with those of many other Europeans – not to speak of peoples in other parts of the world. However, there is no such thing as an objective or stable identity. If a community of nations constructs its (collective) identity around the notion of 'the West', defining it in universal terms, then this is certainly relevant and 'true' for that community. Other states and peoples may construct other (and competing) identities, but these do not make the construction of 'the West' less relevant and 'true'. What matters for our discussion here, is whether Huntington's assertion that any identity (including the Western one) is inherently in conflict with other identities is correct. If Huntington is right, then the fight against 'barbarism' inevitably follows from Western identity, and the Kosovo war is the prelude to a new century of civilisational conflict. However, if Huntington is wrong, the Kosovo war may show that Europe is on its way to a cosmopolitan peace which may well rule out war as a means of international politics.

This essay pursues these questions by adopting a constructivist conception of international relations (IR).[8] Huntington meets the constructivist argument half way, since he claims that politics is shaped by the cultural identities of governments. He differs from constructivists by arguing that the basis of these identities can be objectively defined in terms of the concept of 'civilisation'. Huntington's argument works according to what James March and Johan Olsen term 'the logic of consequentiality'.[9] For Huntington, the purpose of IR theory is to establish categories (such as 'civilisations') that are supposed to explain and even predict the future development of global politics.[10] Constructivism rejects the viability of this kind of universal theory, arguing that agents do not follow a pre-programmed schedule but are influenced by the events and rules of action which constitute social institutions.[11] Constructivist studies therefore survey what March and Olsen term the 'logics of appropriateness'.[12]

The study of IR is – primarily, but not exclusively – the study of governmental actions.[13] Constructivism asks by what rules states define 'appropriate action'. Huntington argues that different civilisations cherish different notions of what is 'appropriate', explaining these differences by referring to the impact of civilisation. As I argue below, that position is untenable, but for now it is important to notice that Huntington's assertion is basically of a constructivist nature. The question therefore remains whether there is some other way to conceptualise political appropriateness. Michel Foucault's notion of 'governmentality' offers *a* solution. 'Governmentality' assumes that the governmental system is constructed and that it is possible to study this construction as a totality. Foucault rejects the notion that politics should be segregated from other social institutions in order to gain insight into the workings of government. On the contrary, he argues that government does not only concern politics, but also the government of the self: the way a nation is governed and the way individuals govern their own behaviour are parts of the same construction. This observation springs from a study Foucault conducted on the historical sociology of the state in which he points out that the development of the modern sovereign state has gone hand in hand with the separation of the public from the private sphere.[14] By conceiving 'the West' as a configuration of governmentality rather than as a civilisation, we may better understand that the notion of civilisation is the manifestation, rather than the explanation, of the West's construction of appropriate government in post-Cold War Europe.

This essay, first, describes the way Huntington constructs civilisation. It then argues that this construction is the manifestation of the governmentality of civil society; and it concludes that this governmentality can explain the Western construction of the Kosovo war.

'Who are you?'

Like other constitutive texts of the post-Cold War world (such as Francis Fukuyama's *The End of History and the Last Man*[15]), Huntington suggests that the end of the Cold War has been a moment of becoming. But whereas Fukuyama argues that the collapse of communism has made states essentially similar, Huntington claims that states are becoming essentially dissimilar, mainly because they define their interests by virtue of collective identities that are mutually exclusive. He argues that during the ideological confrontations of the twentieth century, the identity of an agent (be it the individual or the state) was defined by the answer given to the question 'Which side are you on?' In the post-Cold War world, that question has been replaced by the much more complex and ambiguous question 'Who are you?'[16]

Working within the realist understanding of IR, Huntington suggests that the sources of (armed) conflict remain basically unchanged, although the construction of these conflicts is now increasingly driven by identity. This is bad news, according to Huntington, because identity is constituted by conflict: 'Identity at any level – personal, tribal, racial, civilisational – can only be defined in relation to an 'other', a different person, tribe, race, or civilization.'[17] Now that the history of ideological struggle has come to a close, the state and its political system are no longer able to dominate people's identity, opening up new possibilities for personal, ethnic, religious and other, non-state-centred, processes of identity formation.[18] For Huntington, civilisation has become the defining level of identity. He defines civilisation as follows: 'The civilization to which he [the individual] belongs is the broadest level of identification with which he strongly identifies. Civilizations are the biggest 'we' within which we feel culturally at home as distinguished from all the other 'thems' out there.'[19]

The Cold War provided the West with an 'other' through which it could clearly define itself. But now that the Cold War has been 'won', Huntington fears that the West will succumb to complacency because it believes that its 'universal values' will inevitably come to dominate global politics.[20] The West may no longer see itself as a subject of history, he argues, but many other peoples are defining their identities in juxtaposition to 'the West'. Huntington lists the usual suspects: Islamic fundamentalism, Chinese revivalism and Russian revanchism.[21] Since these 'civilisations' can define themselves only in conflict with their Western 'other', the West itself will have to overcome its complacency and re-engage itself in history. Otherwise, he argues, the West will cease to be a subject of history and become an object of the history of others.

Huntington therefore considers Western attempts to enlarge the geographical scope of European integration as at best futile, at worst a process that may weaken Western civilisation. 'Europe', he claims, can not be (and therefore should not be) redefined by politics, since politics has to be based on the 'fact' that Europe's (geographical) west is part of a different civilisation than Europe's east. The enlargement of NATO and the EU may try to redress this situation, but 'Europe' (as a civilisation) can never include the Slavs: 'Europe ends where Western Christianity ends and Islam and Orthodoxy begins.'[22] Huntington therefore suggests that EU membership will be awarded to states within the Western Christian sphere, but that the defining act of political organisation will be NATO enlargement: 'NATO is the security organisation of Western civilization. With the Cold War over, NATO has one central and compelling purpose: to ensure that it remains over by preventing the reimposition of Russian political and military control in Central Europe.'[23]

Huntington's thesis suggests that the conflict of identity between self and other which defines civilisation almost inevitability leads to political and armed conflict. This 'logic' has been strongly criticised. Stephen Walt, for example, rightly complains that 'Huntington never explains why conflict is more likely to arise between civilisations than within them'.[24] The explanation, I would suggest, is that Huntington conceives of civilisation in terms of peace. States within a civilisation may not feel the same need to resort to war as to a 'continuation of politics' because they (are supposed to) act in a conforming manner and do not present each other with an 'other' which needs to be resisted and contested. Following Huntington's logic, this suggests that within each civilisation there is a relatively good chance of peace. This interpretation explains Huntington's rather peculiar conjecture that Africa is the only continent without a distinctive civilisation. With sub-Saharan Africa riveted by war within and between states, the continent hardly qualifies as a 'realm of peace'. This point is underlined by the fact that sub-Saharan Africa does not have a common religion which could hold the region together.

Religion is an important element (though not the exclusive factor it is sometimes claimed to be) of Huntington's definition of civilisation. Huntington constructs religion as a gospel of peace, as it preaches harmony and reconciliation among its followers. If people share a religion, they are also likely to share an understanding (or at least have compatible understandings) of peace. Indeed, in the case of Christianity and Islam, the realm of the faithful has traditionally been defined in terms of peace, whereas relations with the infidels were defined in terms of war.[25] To Huntington, civilisation is thus a community of peace achieved through conflict with 'others'. But why does Huntington believe peace depends on collective values?

The civilisation of civil society

The reason why Huntington defines civilisation in terms of peace becomes apparent when one turns to his definition of Western civilisation. He makes a distinction between the material and pop-cultural elements of Western civilisation and what he calls 'core values', those elements of civilisation that make the West 'the West'. 'The essence of Western civilisation', he holds, 'is the Magna Carta not the Magna Mac.' Arguing along these lines, Huntington places himself firmly within the German conception of *Kultur* (culture), especially in the way it was presented by Oswald Spengler. Nevertheless, he goes to great lengths to disassociate his concept of 'civilisation' from *Kultur*. This contradiction in Huntington's thought demonstrates his purpose for the concept of civilisation and how it reflects a very Western concept of political identity.

Huntington defines 'the West' in terms of social and political values:
- the classical legacy;
- Catholicism and Protestantism;
- the separation of spiritual and temporal authority;
- the rule of law;
- social pluralism;
- representative democratic bodies; and
- individuality.[29]

Huntington has been criticised for dismissing the state as an agent of international relations.[30] Given his broad definition of Western civilisation, this is hardly fair.[31] One could even argue that Huntington makes an effort to define what makes Western states unique. This uniqueness is the product of history, and his list of Western characteristics can therefore be read as a timeline describing how the West starts off in antiquity, solidifies in Christendom, matures in the Renaissance and the Enlightenment, and culminates in the democratic societies of NATO. Reasoning along these temporal lines, Huntington reproduces what David Gress has identified as the grand narrative of 'the West'.[32] The West, Gress tells us, is an ancient reference to the land of promise in European culture. The West is not constructed as a *subject* of history, but rather as an entity that can shape its *own* history by virtue of its superior values. As such, the notion of the West defines what is best in the civilisation Huntington terms 'Western'.

Gress argues that it was through the First World War I that 'the West' acquired its current meaning, as a reference to the north Atlantic community of democratic nations.[33] After Russia had left the war and the United States had joined it, it was possible to give the endless battles in Flanders meaning by constructing them as a struggle of democratic nations against German 'autocracy'. US President Woodrow Wilson, for example, argued that the war had been brought about by a German governmentality in which the use of force was considered a legitimate extension of politics. At the beginning of the war, Wilson believed that the ultimate source of the conflict could be found in the balance-of-power system and that the war could be stopped by revising that system. However, when Germany rejected his peace proposals and had stepped up its submarine warfare, Wilson came to believe that the war was the result not so much of the workings of the balance of power as of the very nature of German governance. Where the US and its allies came to see 'the Kaiser' as the symbol of an aggressive society, 'democracy' was deemed to be the culmination of an historical process. As such, it was not the European order that had to be changed: it was Germany itself which had to be forced to adopt democratic principles of government which had progressively generated freer and more peaceful societies. The conclusion to be drawn was that democracies were peaceful *not* because they were democracies, but because democracy as a system of government was the culmination of a long-term civilising process.

As mentioned earlier, this notion of a 'civilising process' has been developed by Elias, who described the same practice as does Foucault in his concept of governmentality: the historical process whereby a public sphere is created which sets new standards for how individuals are supposed to govern their behaviour and how the state is supposed to govern its subjects. One of the clearest examples of such a (joint) process is how the state has tried to monopolise the exercise of violence within society. In seventeenth-century Europe, most men of standing were carrying side-arms and were allowed to use them under certain circumstances. This practice showed that violence was a right, and occasionally even a duty of private persons, mainly because the lack of public order, and state-organised violence – ranging from standing armies to the actions of police forces – made it necessary for individuals (as well as for society in general) to depend upon private violence. In the course of the seventeenth century, this situation changed as the state gradually assumed the monopoly of violence.[34] The state assumed the responsibilities hitherto held by individuals, who were now compelled *not* to use force against each other. This process is continuing to this very day, as more and more acts of violence are delegitimised in the private sphere. The right of the head of a household to punish servants, as well as his wife and children, has disappeared to the point where some governments have prohibited parents from physically disciplining their own children.[35]

In 1767, Ferguson described the development of the monopoly of violence as a constitutive part of the division of labour within the emerging 'civil society' of Britain.[36] Through Hegel's use of this term, civil society is now widely regarded as the private elements of society (e.g., the economy or social movements).[37] But, as Ernest Gellner, John Hall and John Keane have pointed out, Ferguson originally used the notion of civil society to delineate the separation of public and private functions as the unique characteristic of a new kind of society.[38] Ferguson described a certain Western governmentality based on an increasing division of labour which allowed for the diversification of society's resources, a process that would in turn result in increased wealth.[39] As a former military chaplain, he was interested in the relationship between the norms of army and society, and considered it crucial that each man was no longer required to defend himself and his family, since this would allow him to specialise in other professions. The state's monopoly of violence therefore produced a civil nation in which political and military power were separated. Such a civil society, Ferguson argued, was characterised by 'peace and regular policy'.[40] Civil society was peaceful because the monopoly of violence had made warfare the monopoly of the state, thus allowing the domestic relations of citizens to be guided by peace. As Elias would later point out, both the manners of people and the manner in which individuals relate to each other were being transformed, thus making society ever more civil. As the state was no longer dominated by a violent struggle for power, domestic policy was stabilised, allowing for cultural sophistication, commerce and progress, which all depended heavily on law and order. Civil society was thus characterised by an evolution which accumulated ever more civility. This notion of a society striving for perfectibility is the link between civil society and civilisation.

Ferguson was one of the first thinkers to use the English term 'civilisation'.[41] To him, civil society was the sociological manifestation of civilisation. Civil society was a description of the nature of a given society and the dynamics by which that society developed. As civilisation, civil society represented 'an ideal order of human society', an order which was considered 'ideal' because it was supposed to have history on its side.[42] Kant described the culmination of history as the realisation of a true civil society, and argued that war could be abolished since the increasing civility of and among states would guarantee the peaceful settlement of disputes.[43] When civil societies had created a 'pacific federation', Kant concluded, they would be able to look back on history as if its very purpose had been to create a 'cosmopolitan system of general political security'.[44]

To summarise: the West is not a civilisation. But it may define itself as civilisation, and this definition constitutes a governmentality. After the First World War, the West was defined in terms of civil society, which in turn was defined in terms of civilisation. Gress shows how the West became constructed as the culmination of civilisation: 'the West' was constructed as the system of cosmopolitan security which Kant had argued would be the culmination of human history. Therefore, the alliance of democracies that came into being after the Second World War was regarded not only as an alliance of states but as the culmination of Western civilisation.[45] History, Gress ironically points out, was constructed as a progression 'from Plato to NATO'.[46] Therefore, when NATO acted as it did on the Kosovo issue, it acted on the belief that its bombing campaign was enforcing Kant's idea of a 'cosmopolitan system of general political security'.

The cosmopolitan soul of Europe

The West will have to realise, Huntington argues, that 'its Europe' is fundamentally different from 'Orthodox Europe', the Europe of Russia and, indeed, of Serbia. Between these 'two Europes' there is either conflict (of all sorts) or mutual recognition, but never the possibility of comprehensive and peaceful integration. The war over Kosovo showed that the West did not construct Europe that way. As I mentioned earlier, Prime Minister Jospin constructs 'Europe' as a governmentality rather than as a geographical or geo-political notion. To Jospin, Europe is the result of a civilising process which started in the West after the Second World War and by 1999 had resulted in a definition of Europe as a cosmopolitan political system. The Kosovo war was therefore not a way of drawing the line between this cosmo-political Europe and the 'barbarians' (the 'other'). On the contrary, the Kosovo war was undertaken to secure the civilising process in Central and Eastern Europe. Robin Cook, Britain's foreign secretary, argued in *The Guardian* that there

> are now two Europes competing for the soul of our continent. One still follows the race ideology that blighted our continent under the fascists. The other emerged fifty years ago out from behind the shadow of the Second World War. The conflict between the international community and Yugoslavia is the struggle between these two Europes.[47]

Cook obviously agrees with Jospin that the West could not accept 'barbarism' in one part of Europe and have civilisation in another. There could be only one Europe, and this Europe had to be civilised. But what did this manifestation of 'barbarism' signify? Jospin as well as Cook defined 'barbarism' as a lapse into the 'Europe of the past'. In 1999, the West had become used to the construct of the Second World War as the close of its past barbarity, a barbarity now left behind by the civilising process.[48] The Second World War had brought out the evil of human society in the shape of fascism, and the West had barely been able to defeat it. Fascism had been able to flourish because of the ongoing confrontation between European states, and, in the words of the former British Foreign Secretary Douglas Hurd, 'a Europe of nation-states always signified a Europe of war'.[49] Only by removing the state as the sole source of government in Europe could a new governmentality be introduced, one that did not automatically lead to war. This argument shows a remarkable consistency in the way the process of European integration has been conceived from the time of the Schuman plan to the 1990s. 'The European Common Market', Christopher Coker remarks, was 'a "civilising process" that was intended to render Europe at peace with itself for the first time.'[50] In the late 1990s, this civilising process was believed to have produced a new European governmentality, a new 'Europe'.

In 1999, Western governments believed that this civilising process had delivered them from their past and had introduced a 'cosmopolitan system of general political security'. The end of the Cold War had ensured that the civilised ways of the West were the only game by which European politics could be played. However, the Serbian regime had shown otherwise, and by doing so it denied entirely the claim that European politics had been truly transformed. This would not have been the case had Serbia been constructed as part of an antagonistic 'Orthodox' civilisation. In that case, Serb violence against 'Muslims' within Kosovo would have proved that civilisations were indeed in conflict, and that very conflict would have constructed 'Orthodox' Serbs and 'Muslim' Kosovar Albanians as the West's 'other'. However, as it turned out, the West had no 'other' in Europe. There was no other Europe for the West but the Europe of the past. The methods of the Serb army and militias therefore constituted a more massive and serious provocation than the atrocities in Rwanda (a few years earlier), or the conduct of the Russian army in Chechnya (a few months later). The notion of Europe's own non-civilised past was so present in the Western construction of its own European political project that, faced with the non-civilised ways of the Serbian government, the West felt it had to act in order to secure its own future.

There was no 'other' in the construction of European identity because that identity was defined in terms of cosmopolitan integration. The West believed itself to have moved beyond the Europe of the nation state, but what rules of government ('governmentality') constituted this 'modern Europe'? During the Kosovo war, Prime Minister Blair probably came closest to defining this new governmentality when he spoke, in April 1999 in Chicago, about 'a wider context' in which the events of Kosovo should be placed, a context he defined as that of 'globalisation'.[51] The interdependence of the world's economies, Blair argued, was only the 'most obvious' manifestation of the new governmentality since we 'are all internationalists now'. The West could no longer define itself only as a community of nation states as the very governmentality of these Western states themselves had become cosmopolitan. Blair agreed with his Foreign Secretary that cosmopolitanism had been created during the Cold War, but that it was only at that time, during the Kosovo campaign, that this historical civilising process had come into its own:

> We are witnessing the beginnings of a new doctrine of international community. By this I mean the explicit recognition that today more than ever before we are mutually dependent, that national interest is to a significant extent governed by international collaboration and that we need a clear and coherent debate as to the direction this doctrine takes us in each field of international endeavour. Just as within domestic politics, the notion of community – the belief that partnership and co-operation are essential to advance self-interest – is coming into its own; so it needs to find its own international echo.[52]

By arguing that in today's Europe the national interests of states are defined by 'liberal' cosmopolitan rules, Blair's Chicago speech offers a fine description of what Alexander Wendt has termed a 'Kantian culture'.[53] Although 'national interests' are routinely invoked by Western leaders, the states to which these interests attach are believed to have gone through a civilising process. West European societies have transcended their past war-like nature and have adopted a practice of 'international collaboration'. International action is no longer guided by the transhistorical notion of 'national interests', but is instead dominated by the 'international echo' of domestic politics. In a sense, the civilising process has created 'a new Europe'.

Arguing along these lines in his Chicago Speech, Prime Minister Blair thus invoked Ferguson's notion that individual societies would gradually transform into an international community. Western governmentality is now constructed in cosmopolitan terms and the formulation of national interests has become subject to the rules of a new cosmopolitan system. 'If we can establish and spread the values of liberty, the rule of law, human rights and an open society', Blair argued, 'then that is in our national interest too.'[54] Taken together, the values he was referring to are constitutive of a true civil society. But why should the West want to spread civil communality? Because, Blair argued, 'the spread of our values makes us safer', since states that share civil values will eventually integrate into a democratic community and, following the logic of his new international community, will subscribe to 'the belief that partnership and co-operation are essential to advance self-interest'. This system of cosmopolitan security would make armed conflict extremely unlikely because 'the principle of international community applies also to international security'.[55]

To Blair, globalisation allows the 'domestic peace and regular policy' of civil society to become the constitutive elements of European politics. Globalisation is thus constructed as a process of transcendence, a process which replaces the old rules of power politics with the novel rules of a cosmopolitan community.[56] As such, globalisation is a late-modern concept which invokes the Enlightenment belief in the possibility of integrating civil societies into a cosmopolitan system. To the West, globalisation is proof that history is coming to an end and that a cosmopolitan system is emerging. Since history has been defined by war, as Kant has argued, history would end if civil societies would translate their 'domestic peace and regular policy' into such a cosmopolitan system. In this context, the notion of globalisation signifies that the West now seems to believe that this transcendence of international anarchy is currently being constructed, and that this cosmopolitan system in the making is both possible and desirable. When Blair argued that the Kosovo war was fought to protect civilisation, he was arguing that this was a war against the 'Europe of the past', a war to ensure the continuation and completion of a post-historical Europe. The Kosovo war was a key part of the civilising process securing the future for a 'cosmopolitan system' of civil societies in Europe.

Concluding remarks

One might argue that the West constructed the Kosovo war in terms of civilisation by default. As the bombing campaign had only the shakiest of foundations in international law, the West realised that its legal arguments were weak and that it was therefore time to use the heavy rhetoric of civilisation. This illustrates the political importance, rather than the emptiness, of the concept of civilisation. If the notion of civilisation can justify illegal military actions, then civilisation holds a very powerful position in the minds of Western political leaders and apparently also in the minds of the peoples they represent. And as war allegedly starts in the minds of men, civilisation is a concept that should be given serious attention.

Huntington has, almost single-handedly, placed this question of civilisation on the agenda of IR. Most students of IR are likely to turn to Huntington in order to explain Prime Minister Blair's statement that 'war can be necessary to uphold civilisation'. According to Huntington, civilisations are basically identities of peace, but conflict (including armed conflict) with an 'other' is necessary for civilisations to define the values which render them at peace among themselves. Following this argument, one is left to conclude that the Kosovo war showed peace in Western Europe to exclude peace with states in Eastern Europe and beyond. The West's rejection of the universal values of international law thus shows that the time for the particular identities of civilisation has come. It also suggests that this time will be one of war.

This line of argument has forced many students of IR to reply that the very notion of civilisation is the problem. For those critics, the Kosovo war proves that civilisation is a very dangerous concept because it excludes political solutions that go beyond established categories of exclusion and is obviously unable to include Western civilisation's 'other'. This, so these critics argue, is a mechanism leading directly to war. This essay has argued that while Huntington's conception of civilisation is basically flawed, 'civilisation' nevertheless remains important for the way the West understands international politics. One will therefore have to focus on civilisation on its own terms in order to understand the emerging post-Cold War order.

This essay has argued that civilisation is a manifestation rather than an explanation. Huntington essentially replaces the neorealist concept of 'the state' as the unit of analysis with 'civilisation', in the belief that every international occurrence of importance can thereby be explained. This line of argument only works if all international agents belong to a unit of civilisation. The fact is that they do not, mainly because civilisation is a uniquely Western concept. It is a concept developed during the Enlightenment as a way to express the belief that society could only be understood in terms of history and progress. Western societies '*had* civilisation' because they – or so it was believed – had a hold on the future due to their progressive modernity. Civilisation is the expression of a certain conception of society and can be understood only in light of that conception. It is also a conception of modern society as a civil society.

So when Tony Blair argued that 'war is never civilised', he was invoking the conception of a civil society that is constituted by 'peace and regular policy', internally and externally defined by cosmopolitan peace between civil societies. Within this conception, war is not a civil mode of interaction. On the contrary, war limits the possibility of a regular policy of peace on which civil society depends, nationally as well as internationally. Blair feared that if war or coercion were seen to be effective in Europe, it would come to threaten the regularity by which European politics had developed through integration since the end of the Second World War. That war has become a symbol of the end of European history as defined by armed conflict; European integration was constructed as a civilising process which was to establish a 'cosmopolitan system of general political security'. The Milosevic regime, Cook argued, was threatening the 'peace and regular policy' of that European system and had thereby defined itself as 'barbaric'. The Serb government was deemed to be uncivilised because it did not engage in the political discourse of civil society and was blatantly using violence and military force as a means of politics. In doing so, it had placed itself beyond politics in the mind of the West. War was the only possible answer to its actions, and therefore Blair could argue that 'war is sometimes necessary for civilisation'.

This leads me to conclude that the notion of civil society offers us the best explanation for the Western response to 'Kosovo'. It is not civilisation, but civil society that should be the unit of analysis in an account of why the West considered the Kosovo war necessary and inevitable. But how is one to conceptualise a construction of politics as a unit? In this essay, I have suggested that Foucault's notion of governmentality may provide a conceptual framework for understanding a construction of politics as the basis of collective action. As such, governmentality serves the same analytical purpose as Huntington's notion of civilisation. However, governmentality is not based on *a priori* assertions of how collective identity is (supposed to be) created. Because governmentality is an analytical category, it also rejects the *a priori* notion that identity is necessarily conflictual. On the contrary, this essay has tried to show that the West has not pursued 'others' in order to remake its collective identity after the end of the Cold War. The post-Cold War order is created on the basis of inclusion, rather than exclusion. To the West, the Kosovo war was necessary to maintain the development of the 'cosmopolitan system of general political security' that European civil societies have constructed as the beginning of a new political order.

Notes

I would like to thank the Copenhagen Research Project on European Integration for funding the research upon which this essay is based. An earlier version was presented at the Annual Convention of the International Studies Association in Los Angeles (March 2000). I am grateful to Christopher Coker, David Gress and Ole Wæver for their comments on previous incarnations of the ideas presented here. I would also like to thank the editors, Peter van Ham and Sergei Medvedev, for their useful suggestions. Any errors and omissions are, as always, mine alone.

1 Tony Blair, Prime Minister's Speech on a New Beginning for Kosovo, 10 June 1999, available: http://number10.gov.uk/public/info/index.html (accessed 16 November 2000).
2 In a conflict of identities no concept is innocent and even the spelling of the name of the site of the conflict is contested. The Serb spelling translates to Kosovo and the Albanian to Kosova. As the former is the more commonly used in the West, I have adopted it acknowledging that in the absence of a neutral term the only term to use is the one used by other people trying to be neutral. See chapter 6, by Maja Zehfuss, for a further discussion of this problem.
3 Samuel P. Huntington, *The Clash of Civilizations and the Remaking of World Order* (London, Touchstone Books, 1998).
4 Adam Ferguson, *An Essay on the History of Civil Society* (Cambridge, Cambridge University Press, [1767] 1995).
5 Norbert Elias, *The Civilizing Process* (Oxford, Blackwell, [1939] 1978).
6 Immanuel Kant, 'Idea for a Universal History with a Cosmopolitan Purpose', and 'To Perpetual Peace: A Philosophical Sketch', in *Kant's Political Writings*

ed. Hans Reiss and trans. H.B. Nisbet (Cambridge, Cambridge University Press, 1970 [1784, 1795]).
7 French Prime Minister Lionel Jospin, Speech to the National Assembly (Paris, 26 March 1999, available: http://diplomatie.-gouv.fr//actual/dossiers/kosovo/kosovo12.bg.html (accessed 16 November 2000).
8 The purpose of this essay is neither to develop constructivist theory nor to discuss its merits *vis-à-vis* other theories of international relations. Instead, this essay seeks to analyse the Kosovo war and – in this case – a constructivist approach must prove its worth on its analytical merits rather than on its ontological and epistemological credentials. For discussions of credentials, see Emanuel Adler, 'Seizing the Middle Ground: Constructivism in World Politics', *European Journal of International Relations*, vol. 3, no. 3 (September 1997). For a general assertion of the constructivist position, see John Searle, *The Construction of Social Reality* (London, Penguin Books, 1995).
9 James G. March and Johan P. Olsen, *Rediscovering Institutions. The Organizational Basis of Politics* (New York, Free Press, 1989), pp. 160–1.
10 Huntington, *Clash of Civilizations*, pp. 13–14.
11 Anthony Giddens, *The Constitution of Society. Outline of the Theory of Structuration* (Cambridge, Polity Press, 1984); and Searle, *The Construction of Social Reality*.
12 March and Olsen, *Rediscovering Institutions*, p. 161.
13 Alexander Wendt, *Social Theory of International Politics* (Cambridge, Cambridge University Press, 1999).
14 Michel Foucault, 'Governmentality', in Graham Burchell, Colin Cordon and Peter Miller (eds), *The Foucault Effect. Studies in Governmentality* (London, Harvester Wheatsheaf, 1990). For an introduction to the concept of governmentality, see Mitchell Dean, *Governmentality. Power and Rule in Modern Society* (London, Sage, 1999). Within IR, Michael Dillon has used 'governmentality' to explore questions of world order. See Michael Dillon, 'Sovereignty and Governmentality: From the Problematics of the "New World Order" to the Ethical Problematic of the World Order', *Alternatives*, vol. 20, no. 3 (July–September 1995).
15 Francis Fukuyama, *The End of History and the Last Man* (London, Penguin Books, 1992).
16 Huntington, *Clash of Civilizations*, p. 128.
17 *Ibid.*
18 Zygmunt Bauman, 'Forms of Togetherness', in his *Life in Fragments: Essays in Postmodern Morality* (Oxford, Blackwell, 1995).
19 Huntington, *Clash of Civilizations*, p. 43.
20 Samuel Huntington, 'No Exit: The Errors of Endism', *Parameters. US Army War College Quarterly*, vol. 19, no. 4 (December 1989). On post-historical conceptions, see Lutz Niethammer, *Posthistoire. Has History Come to an End?* (London, Verso, 1994).
21 Huntington, *Clash of Civilizations*, pp. 155–79.
22 *Ibid.*, p. 158.
23 *Ibid.*, p. 161.
24 Stephen M. Walt, 'Building Up New Bogeymen', *Foreign Policy*, no. 106 (Spring 1997), p. 184.

25 Hedley Bull and Adam Watson (eds), *The Expansion of International Society* (Oxford, Clarendon Press, 1985).
26 Huntington, *Clash of Civilizations*, p. 58.
27 Oswald Spengler, *The Decline of the West* (Oxford, Oxford University Press, [1918–22] 1991). The distinction between *Kultur* and civilisation originated in the revival of German nationalism which wanted to distinguish the traditions of the German bourgeoisie from the French-speaking aristocracy (see Elias, *The Civilizing Process*, pp. 7–24). Kant presented one of the first arguments for this distinction in 'An Answer to the Question: "What Is Enlightenment?"', in *Kant's Political Writings*. For an encyclopedic introduction to the distinction between civilisation and culture in German political discourse, see Jörg Fisch, 'Zivilisation, Kultur', in *Geschichtliche Grundbegriffe. Historisches Lexikon zur politisch-sozialen Sprache in Deutschland* (Stuttgart, Klett-Cotta, 1972–82).
28 Huntington, *Clash of Civilizations*, pp. 41–2.
29 *Ibid.*, pp. 69–72.
30 Walt, 'New Bogeymen', p. 187.
31 This is, however, understandable as Huntington himself insists that civilisations are not political (Huntington, *Clash of Civilizations*, p. 44). However, Huntington focuses on reasons for acting rather than the units of action themselves. When identifying civilisations as the units of world politics in the twenty-first century, Huntington is not saying that civilisations will become agents themselves, but that civilisation will be the reason for acting. The state will remain the main agent but will no longer be capable of generating identity on its own accord.
32 David Gress, *From Plato to NATO. The Idea of the West and its Opponents* (New York, Free Press, 1998), pp. 24ff.
33 *Ibid.*, pp. 31ff.
34 Max Weber, 'Politics as a Vocation', in H.H. Gerth and C. Wright Mills (eds), *From Max Weber: Essays in Sociology* (London, Routledge, 1991).
35 For an analysis of the relationship between violence and civil society, see John Keane, *Reflections on Violence* (London, Verso, 1996).
36 Ferguson, *An Essay on the History of Civil Society*.
37 G.W.F. Hegel, *Elements of the Philosophy of Right* (ed.) Allen W. Wood and trans. H.B. Nisbet (Cambridge, Cambridge University Press, [1821] 1991). The concept of civil society is becoming increasingly fashionable within IR. See, for example, Robert Cox, 'Civil Society at the Turn of the Millennium: Prospects for an Alternative World Order', *Review of International Studies*, vol. 25, no. 1 (1999); Ronnie D. Lipschutz, 'Reconstructing World Politics: The Emergence of Global Civil Society', in Rick Fawn and Jeremy Larkin (eds), *International Society After the Cold War. Anarchy and Order Reconsidered* (London, Macmillan, 1996); and Nicholas Greenwood Onuf, *The Republican Legacy in International Thought* (Cambridge, Cambridge University Press, 1998).
38 Ernest Gellner, *Conditions of Liberty. Civil Society and its Rivals* (London, Penguin, 1996); John A. Hall (ed.), *Civil Society: Theory, History, Comparison* (Cambridge, Polity Press, 1995); John Keane, *Civil Society. Old Images, New Visions* (Cambridge, Polity Press, 1998).
39 Ferguson, *An Essay on the History of Civil Society*, p. 254.
40 *Ibid.*, p. 214.

41 Oz-Salzberger, 'Introduction', in *ibid.*, p. xxii.
42 Christopher Coker, *Twilight of the West* (Boulder, CO, Westview Press, 1998), p. 14.
43 'The greatest problem of the human species', Kant argued, 'is that of attaining a civil society'. But in isolation, a civil society could not create the 'peace and regular policy' referred to by Ferguson because of the 'distress which every state must eventually feel within itself, even in the midst of peace'. Or, 'the problem of establishing a perfect civil constitution is subordinated to the problem of law-governed external relationship with other states'. See Kant, 'Idea for a Universal History with a Cosmopolitan Purpose', pp. 45–7.
44 *Ibid.*, p. 49.
45 To the West, the peaceful nature of the democratic alliance is so deep-seated that democratic peace theory has been developed to explain the alleged causal relationship between democracy and peace. See Michael E. Brown, Sean M. Lynn-Jones and Steven E. Miller (eds), *Debating the Democratic Peace* (Cambridge, MA, MIT Press, 1997).
46 Gress, *From Plato to NATO*, pp. 16ff.
47 Robin Cook, 'It Is Fascism that We Are Fighting', *The Guardian*, 5 May 1999.
48 Compare Ole Wæver, 'Three Competing Europes: German, French, Russian', *International Affairs*, vol. 66, no. 3 (1990).
49 Douglas Hurd, *The Search for Peace. A Century of Peace Diplomacy* (London, Warner Books, 1997), p. 6.
50 Coker, *Twilight of the West*, p. 106.
51 Tony Blair, Prime Minister's Speech to the Economic Club of Chicago (23 April 1999), available: http://number-10.gov.uk/public/info/index.html (accessed 16 Novemer 2000).
52 *Ibid.*
53 Wendt, *Social Theory of International Politics*, pp. 297–308.
54 Blair, Prime Minister's Speech to Economic Club of Chicago.
55 *Ibid.*
56 On the notion of globalisation as transcendence, see Jens Bartelson, 'Three Concepts of Globalization', *International Sociology*, vol. 15, no. 2 (2000).

10 Christoph Zürcher

Chechnya and Kosovo: reflections in a distorting mirror

This is not a text about who was wrong and who was right; neither is it a text which aims to establish the true figures of those killed and displaced by Russian or NATO bombs. It is a tale of two conflicts that share some remarkable similarities and which are to some extent archetypal for our globalised post-Cold War world. It is, above all, an essay about two conflicts which are, *nolens volens*, tied like twins, because they became the focal point of three fundamental, at times competing, principles of how to organise the world. These are: the claims, rights and capacities of the nation state; the claims, rights and capacities of identity groups; and the claims, rights and capacities of international regimes. It is in the discourse and debates about these organisational principles that the outlines of a European (global?) security landscape must be found or will be lost.

Prologue

1230 hours, 24 March 1999: NATO airfields in Italy and the United Kingdom

Eight American B-52 bombers, each carrying twenty cruise missiles in its bomb bay, leave their UK base in Fairford and head towards Serbia. From NATO airfields Aviano and Istrano in Italy, allied aircraft leave at short intervals. The British frigate *HMS Splendid* fires a salvo of cruise missiles. These events are broadcast in real time by satellite links all over the globe. These are the pictures that the public has been told to expect for weeks. It is the beginning of NATO's Operation Allied Force, the long-announced answer of the international community to ethnic cleansing in Kosovo. From 24 March until 3 June, the images of aircraft taking off from airfields in the UK and Italy, and returning home after the completion of their missions become a regular part of TV news programmes. They will gradually replace the images of Kosovar refugees trying to escape the Serbian assaults. Now the former refugees are shown mainly as a cheerful crowd, applauding NATO's decisive actions. These bombs will pave the way for a safe return to their homeland.

Meanwhile, over the Atlantic...

The Russian Prime Minister Yevgeni Primakov is on his way to Washington, DC. His mission is to obtain a much-needed financial infusion for the crumbling Russian economy. Russia is hoping for new credits from the International Monetary Fund: its external debts need to be restructured and Russian steel exporters need to increase their exports to the highly protected American market. The Russian space industry needs American satellites to be launched from its space centre in Baikonur. However, in a dramatic gesture, upon learning of NATO's attack on Serbia, Prime Minister Primakov orders his plane to return to Moscow. He does not wish to be on the Potomac at a time when American cruise missiles are hitting targets in Serbia, so he tells the reporters waiting at Moscow's Vnukovo Airport on his arrival. Although this seems to be an expensive decision (according to the liberal daily *Kommersant*, it cost the Russian economy up to US$15 billion[1]), it is certainly a popular one: NATO's attack on Serbia has led to an unprecedented outburst of public emotion in Russia.

In Moscow and some other big cities, there are spontaneous anti-American demonstrations. The façade of the American Embassy suffers slight damage; a pub in Moscow, which is unfortunately named *U Djadi Sema* (Uncle Sam's), is less lucky and is partly demolished. The political entertainer Vladimir Zhirinovski begins to enlist volunteers for the fight against NATO. NATO's Moscow office is shut down and its director expelled. START II and START III are declared virtually dead.

The Russian public's emotions are running high these days, as if the NATO bombs are actually hitting Russia. After a few days, the public's mood cools down somewhat. But a deep conviction of the public and the *classe politique* remains: NATO's action in Kosovo is ultimately threatening the very idea of state sovereignty.

One night of NATO bombing has achieved what ten years of nation building had not: a remarkable consensus between the public and the *classe politique* has emerged. Leaders and public have become close as never before, united in the vociferous condemnation of NATO's operation. They agree that NATO (for the Russians, basically an instrument of US hegemonic ambitions) has finally shown its arrogance and unchecked power aspirations. The cruise missiles of the Alliance are not only hitting targets in Serbia: they are destroying the pillars of a multipolar world. These missiles target the very essence of the United Nations, the peaceful concert of equal nations. They amount to an assault on the idea of state sovereignty. Ultimately, they are hitting Russia.

August 1999: the Caucasus Mountains, border between Chechnya and Daghestan

Two long columns of bearded fighters cross the border between Chechnya and Daghestan. They are on their way to carry the Islamic anti-Russian rebellion from Chechnya into Daghestan. They are lightly armed, mainly with AK-47s, some machine guns, a couple of mortars and a few RPG-7s – Russian shoulder-held anti-tank grenade launchers. Shamil Basaev and Emir Khattab, two of Chechnya's most famous warlords, veterans of the first Chechen war, lead the two columns.

For Russia, the first Chechen war in 1994–96 was meant to be a short and victorious one, which would boost the badly damaged reputation of President Yeltsin. Instead, it had turned into a bloody disaster, leaving more that 10,000 Russian soldiers and over 50,000 civilians dead. The Chechens, surprisingly enough, had won on the battlefield, but had made little political progress since then. In the 1996 'peace agreement' of Khasavyurt, which was actually a ceasefire, the opposing sides agreed to postpone the murky question of Chechnya's status until 2000. During the following years, neither side showed any inclination for compromise. In August 1999, Basaev and Khattab decided to take the struggle for Chechnya's independence into Daghestan. They hoped to trigger an uprising of the Daghestani population against the Russians, thus probably deciding the question of Chechnya's status. In their view, the final stage in the war for the liberation of the Islamic population of the North Caucasus from the Russian yoke had just begun.

Three years later . . .

The Russian army is still fighting a bloody and costly war against the Chechen rebels. More than 100,000 Russian troops are engaged against the Chechen's small forces. After driving the units of Khattab and Basaev out of Daghestan, the Russian army launched a full-scale war against the Chechen forces in Chechnya. The capital, Grozny, has been completely destroyed; the rebels have been driven into the mountains, where they continue to engage the Russians in a guerrilla war that neither side can win. Almost 300,000 Chechens have become refugees and are internally displaced. For Moscow, this war is a 'policing operation' on a huge scale. Its objective is to protect Russia's state sovereignty and territorial integrity from criminal and terrorist assaults.

The Europeans accuse the Russians of gross human rights' violations in Chechnya. The Parliamentary Assembly of the Council of Europe (PACE) has suspended Russia's voting rights. Russia's political elite, however, refuses to discuss what it sees as an internal affair. Any reference by Western politicians to international norms and regulations are dismissed as hypocrisy.

After all, it was NATO that bombed Serbia in clear violation of international norms and regulations – and now these same international norms are invoked to prevent Russia from defending itself against a terrorist assault on its territorial integrity.

In the Balkans, Kosovo has *de facto* become a protectorate, governed by the EU and protected by KFOR.[2] The official currency of Kosovo is the Euro, and the UN is struggling hard to establish a working administration. KFOR is struggling hard to protect its monopoly of violence, but the KLA, far from being disarmed, continues to exercise considerable influence. Most of the Kosovar refugees have returned home, and most of the Serbian population have become refugees. They are not especially welcome in Serbia, which has to rebuild almost its entire infrastructure. Slobodan Milosevic has been defeated in the election and displaced through popular protests, but his regime and repressive machine have stayed largely intact, and his popularly elected successor Vojislav Kostunica does not seem to be too accommodating to the West's policy on Kosovo.

The high-intensity military operations in Kosovo and Chechnya are over, and the dust has settled. But there a war of interpretation is still going on. At stake is the 'correct' interpretation of what happened in Kosovo and Chechnya. Did NATO bombs protect and promote human rights, or did they violate international norms and regulations, and the rights of a sovereign state? Do Russian bombs defend Russian territorial integrity and sovereignty, or do they violate human rights? What about the collective rights of the Chechens and the Kosovars? What will become of Kosovo when KFOR leaves? What will become of Chechnya when Russia wins?

NATO's interpretation of the events in Kosovo has clearly won the day in Europe. The notion of 'humanitarian intervention' has given a remarkably high degree of legitimacy to the Alliance's Kosovo policy during the war and in its aftermath. European politicians and the public seem to agree that there are situations where protecting human rights is more important than respecting a state's sovereignty, and that in such cases the use of force even without a UN resolution is justified.

On the other hand, the 'humanitarian intervention' interpretation has failed in Russia. Here, the dominant interpretation is that NATO's action will undermine the principles of state sovereignty and weaken international regulations. This latter interpretation in turn has helped to legitimise the Russian war in Chechnya – a war that Russia fights in order ultimately to protect her sovereignty and territorial integrity. In Russia, the political elite and the public seem to think that the state's sovereignty must be defended by all means, even if the price is an occasional violation of human rights.

The creation of a dominant interpretation has always been an important part of politics. In the cases of Kosovo and Chechnya, interpretation *is* politics. Chechnya and Kosovo are so closely tied together that any interpretation of one case ultimately affects the other. Both NATO and Russia went to war for the sake of principles, and both made their points with bombs. Indeed, both went to war for principles that seem to be mutually exclusive.

At the core of each of these wars of interpretation is the crucial question of how to reconcile the competing claims of the sovereign states and identity groups concerned. Neither Russia nor NATO has offered a viable answer. But they better had, because 'Kosovo' can happen elsewhere, in Kashmir, in the Philippines, in East Timor, in Sri Lanka, in Punjab – and in many places in the former Soviet Union, like Nagorno-Karabakh, Abkhazia, Tatarstan or Chechnya, to name only the notoriously 'hot' spots.

This chapter proceeds by offering an anatomical comparison of the conflicts in Chechnya and Kosovo, emphasising the remarkable similarity between the two. I then move on to the responses of Russia and NATO to the respective Chechen and Kosovo problems, discussing which rationales and motives can, in the absence of any convincing Realist interests, best explain NATO's and Russia's decision to go to war. In the final section, I show how Chechnya and Kosovo are linked, both by *Realpolitik* and, perhaps more directly, by each being the focal point of an on-going war of interpretation. The outcome of each of these wars of interpretation may influence the European security landscape more than the 'hot war' in Kosovo ever could.

Chechnya and Kosovo: the similarities

Both the Chechen and the Kosovo conflict are essentially a by-product of the breakdown of the Soviet and Yugoslav ethno-federations. The Soviet Union and the Socialist Federal Republic of Yugoslavia (SFRY) were multi-level federations, consisting of ethno-territorially defined units with different status. On the first level were fifteen Soviet republics and six republics of the SFRY. They had all the institutional prerequisites of statehood, that is, political institutions, political symbols, constitutions and borders. Within those units, there were units of the second level, the autonomous republics, which also were ethno-territorially defined. While they enjoyed lesser privileges than the first-level units, they nevertheless possessed similar institutional prerequisites for statehood. Both Chechnya within Russia and Kosovo within Serbia were autonomous republics within first-level subjects of the federation.

After the implosion of the Soviet Union and the SFRY, the first-order subjects of the federations became independent. Thus, the fifteen Soviet republics and five republics of the Yugoslav federation became sovereign nation states, recognised by the international community. Second-level territorial units, however, were denied independence, even in cases where they actively sought it. The international community reacted pragmatically to the problem of how to deal with crumbling empires: all first-level republics were, according to the principle of the self-determination of nations, recognised as sovereign states. The second-level units, i.e. the former autonomous republics, on the other hand, were not. Here, the principle of the inviolability of borders was invoked.

After the dissolution of the federations, the borders of these second-level units became the fault line for conflict: most hot spots in the former Soviet Union and the former Yugoslavia have emerged over the question of the status of these second-level units. Chechnya, Kosovo, Nagorno-Karabakh, South Ossetia and Abkhazia were all ethnically defined territorial units within the Soviet or Yugoslav republics. All of them turned violent, when they started seeking greater autonomy or even independence. Thus, the legacy of the socialist ethno-federalism proved to be especially prone to conflict. When the empire broke down, the Chechens reacted by declaring their independence, thus unilaterally seceding from the Russian Federation. After two years of an incompetent and inconsistent Russian policy toward the breakaway republic this move led to the first Chechen war.[3]

The situation was slightly different in the former Yugoslavia. Milosevic used an aggressive Serb nationalism to build up and stabilise his power within Serbia. Already, in 1989, he had accused the Kosovars of separatism and anti-Serb politics, and removed Kosovo's autonomous status. The social system he installed proved to be the perfect breeding ground for inter-group violence: Kosovars were under-represented in political and economic key positions, and denied access to educational and business opportunities, while the use of Kosovar cultural symbols was restricted in public spaces. The amount of inter-group violence was much higher in Kosovo than it was in Chechnya. The Kosovars and the Serbs have been engaged in a low-intensity internal conflict ever since 1989. By March 1998, the conflict had escalated into an open guerrilla war between the Serbian police and army units and the KLA. By the autumn of 1998, ethnic cleansing on a massive scale was going on, and NATO began to threaten Milosevic with air strikes.

In the cases of Chechnya and Kosovo, there were additional permissive conditions that made conflict highly probable.[4] The Chechens and the Kosovars had, prior to the actual outbreak of violence, a highly developed sense of otherness in relation to the dominant group of each state, that is, respectively, the Russians and the Serbs. Russians–Chechens and Serbs–Kosovars are separated by language and religion. Chechens–Russians and Kosovars–Serbs have, furthermore, complex histories of grievance – the Chechens remember well the Tsarist wars and Stalin's deportation of the entire Chechen nation to Kazakhstan; and the Kosovars have not forgotten the continuous politics of Serbisation of their homeland by administrative measures or violence, dating back to the beginning of the twentieth century.

Chechnya and Kosovo can thus be labelled post-socialist conflicts. These conflicts were shaped by the institutional legacy of the socialist ethno-federations, and triggered by the collapse of the Yugoslav federation and the Soviet Union. However, these conflicts share another set of similarities, one often overlooked. The type of violence that has emerged in Kosovo and in Chechnya resembles in many ways the violent conflicts in Africa or Latin America of the last decade. They belong to a type of violence that Mary Kaldor has labelled 'new wars', that is a type of organised violence that blurs the distinction between war (defined as violence between states or organised political groups), organised crime and the large-scale violation of human rights.[5] Such wars involve not only state actors and state armies, but myriad other actors, like paramilitaries, the warlords, militias, international aid or human rights organisations, mass media and international organisations. Therefore, such wars are by definition transnational, since most, if not all, of these actors are embedded in transnational networks.

'New wars' may have been common in Africa; but Chechnya and Kosovo became the first new wars that were fought and broadcast in Europe. Chechnya and Kosovo are thus not only examples of post-socialist conflicts: they may be the first manifestation of a new type of violence, one that is on the rise globally and will not stop at the fuzzy borders of Europe, and which calls for new responses.

Such new wars share at least four common features:
- they are conflicts between identity groups and the state;
- they take place in an environment where the state in question is at best 'weak' or at worst all but absent;
- they often lead to the emergence of a 'market of violence';[6] and
- the conflicts, and the actors, are embedded in transnational networks of images, resources and politics.

Violence between the state and organised identity groups has become a worldwide phenomenon, and the number of violent conflicts of this type has been growing since 1950.[7] There are three broad sets of reasons for that growth. The first has to do with the steadily increasing acceptance of, and concern for, collective rights, which is part of the (Western) cultural evolution since the 1960s. The second set has to do with cultural globalisation, which threatens to replace indigenous cultures with the globally proliferating McCulture. The greater the loss of specificity to a given culture, the more people tend to stress or reinvent the remaining distinctiveness, building cultural communes of resistance. As the information technology of today makes it cheap and easy to disseminate cultural markers, group-building processes are becoming faster and cheaper than ever. The third set relates to the processes of de-colonisation after World War II and the collapse of empires after 1989, which have triggered many conflicts of this type, among them the conflicts in Chechnya and Kosovo.

Like most originally internal conflicts, both the Chechnya and Kosovo conflicts have their roots in an environment that is characterised above all by dramatic *state weakness*. I define state weakness here as little or no capacity to provide collective goods, and little or no coercive power. State weakness may have many sources, and the on-going discussion of the diminishing role and capabilities of the nation state in our current globalised era points at one. However, in the cases of the Russian Federation and Serbia, there is no need to look at the process of globalisation in order to explain their dramatic state weakness. Both the Russian Federation and Serbia are the successor states of imploded socialist federations, and each is trying to establish its statehood on the ruins of an empire. This task at times clearly overloads these new states. The result is state weakness, and its most dangerous symptom is loss of the monopoly of violence. After the collapse of the socialist federations, the Balkans and the post-Soviet space saw a proliferation of weapons of all kinds, from small firearms to tanks, aircraft and artillery. Most of the hardware came from the stockpiles of the Red Army and the Yugoslav Army. What was needed in addition was provided by international arms dealers, to whom the numerous new and quite permeable international borders posed no serious hindrance.

State weakness also means that the state is no longer able to penetrate the territory with its institutions, and part of the state's territory becomes *de facto* governed by alternative institutions, such as clans, criminal networks, rebel governments or local potentates. In such 'lost territories', social security is provided by family ties, education by grandparents and protection by private 'firms'. In short, state weakness fosters the creation of parallel or alternative institutions, which tend to be more private and more criminal than the crumbling state institutions. In the mid-1990s, both Kosovo and Chechnya had become, from the perspective of the central state, such 'lost territories'. In Chechnya, between 1994 and 1999, the Russian state was all but absent and the Chechens have, though with no success, tried to establish their alternative state structures. In Kosovo, the Serbian state maintained its presence, though only by means of violence and at a considerable cost. The Kosovars reacted by establishing parallel 'shadow' institutions, and by 1998 they had had their shadow state fully in place.

In both cases, low-intensity conflicts were well under way since the early 1990s, and restricted but organised violence became part of daily life. Prolonged violence paves the way for the emergence of *markets of violence*. By 'market of violence' I mean a situation where violence is both politically and economically profitable for a handful of successful entrepreneurs of violence. The organisation of violence, however, is expensive, and sustained violence needs continual investment: warlords have to buy weapons for their soldiers, soldiers need vehicles and vehicles need fuel. Therefore, entrepreneurs of violence engage in a sort of economy of war which characteristically blurs the border between legal economic activities, organised crime and warfare. This economy tends to be integrated in transnational networks of trade and investment. Entrepreneurs of violence engage in drug or weapon trafficking, kidnapping, extortion, or in the black economy. Profits are reinvested or kept in offshore banks. More often than not, sustained markets of violence consequently become trading routes for goods with a very high value per weight, such as drugs, gold, diamonds or weapons. In addition, markets of violence often serve as a hub for duty-free importation–exportation. Other sources of revenues include profits from kidnapping or, where it is available, the squandering of humanitarian aid.[8] Lastly, when local production and logistics are destroyed, the black economy booms, controlled by those who have the monopoly of violence.

Both Chechnya and Kosovo, together with places like Afghanistan, Kashmir, Somalia, the Philippines and numerous others, qualified at a certain stage as markets of violence.[9] The 'core' of these conflicts is still political; but for the entrepreneurs of violence there is an important economic rationale for prolonging the conflict. This rationale has to be addressed analytically and practically before any sustainable end to violence can be negotiated between, or forced upon, the actors involved. Thus, any political solution to such conflicts must be preceded by a strategy of raising the costs for violence, which can only be achieved by closing the borders for supply, denying the entrepreneurs of violence access to financial markets and/or establishing a monopoly of violence by external powers. All of these measures, however, are usually costly, dangerous, time-consuming and very difficult to achieve: drying up markets of violence is a difficult task. Nation states are often incapable of handling it, and external intervention is often not a good instrument with which to tackle it either.

New wars tend to be geographically restricted, but they are *embedded in transnational networks* which link these local wars with the globalising world. The entrepreneurs of violence depend on the transnational ties of trade and investment; on the other hand, international organisations such as the UN, the Council of Europe and the Organisation for Security and Co-operation in Europe are monitoring the conflicts, pointing at violations of international norms and regulations, and occasionally making attempts at conflict regulation. Once the violence has reached a certain level, all sorts of 'internationals' enter the scene. International non-governmental organisations provide help, gather information or sponsor developments they think desirable. They act locally, but they use the resources of their international sponsors. Newsmakers and image distributors bring the war, as soon as it becomes an 'event', to the attention of audiences all over the world. And then journalists, international relief organisations, human rights activists, press officers and supporters of identity groups in conflict all flock to the place, ready to provide their selection of facts to an international audience. At times, this selection is so gruesome and compelling that the international community is forced to respond.

Chechnya and Kosovo: the responses

War used to be the ultimate domain of high politics, and high politics used to be ruled on the basis of Realist considerations. According to this body of literature, states go to war if their survival is at stake (or when there is a dominant perception that this might be the case), or if they think that relative gains *vis-à-vis* other states can be made. However, both Russia's Chechen campaign and NATO's Kosovo campaign are characterised by a distinct lack of Realist interest. Realism, the self-evident traditional interpretative key to international relations, fails to explain these developments: neither NATO nor the Russian Federation went to war because its survival was actually threatened, or because of relative gains to be made. Rather, one of the main objectives of these wars was to satisfy the expectations of domestic audiences, on the one hand, and to 'send the right message' to the 'villains', on the other. Both NATO and Russia wanted to make a point with bombs. Winning these wars not only meant to outgun the enemy – it meant above all 'selling' the conflict to the consumer, i.e. having the monopoly of interpretation.

If this reason seems unconvincing, one can take a brief look at alternative Realist explanations. As for Russia's war in Chechnya, there have been three sets of Realist argument: the oil argument; the domino argument; and the geopolitical argument. None of them seems compelling.

The *oil-argument* sees the main motive for the war over Chechnya in the Chechen oil-wells. The oil argument is usually supported by reference to Chechnya's importance as a transit route for oil from the Caspian to the Russian terminal in Novorossiysk. There are, however, problems with this argument. To begin with, the quantity of Chechen oil is insignificant. It has no strategic importance, and the profits to be made are too small to warrant activating the state's military machine. During the final decade of the Soviet Union, Chechen oil accounted for approximately 2 per cent of the overall Soviet production. Since then, oil production in Chechnya has dramatically decreased. What is more, if the war were really about oil, then it would make no sense for Russian bombs to destroy most of the infrastructure. Finally, Chechnya is not important as a transit route for the Caspian oil, since the main export route will anyway go through Georgia and Turkey to the Mediterranean port of Ceyhan.

The *domino argument* suggests that Chechnya is the first domino to fall, causing a chain reaction all over the Caucasus and probably reaching the ethnic republics in Siberia and the Volga regions. The international community and, certainly, states which themselves have fought a war against 'falling dominoes' tend to meet this argument with understanding. However, this line of reasoning fails any empirical test. The first Chechen war, although won by the Chechens, has not produced a growing quest for independence from Russia within the ethnic republics. On the contrary, Chechnya's fragmentation in the inter-war period has strengthened the inclination of ethnic elites in the republics to stay within the Russian Federation, especially so within Chechnya's Islamic neighbour republics Ingushetia and Daghestan.

The *geopolitical argument* combines the oil argument and the domino argument, and places both into the broader context of geopolitical rivalry between Russia, Turkey, Iran and the US, with the Caucasus as the battlefield.[10] There is no denying that geopolitics plays an important role in the Caucasus, and it certainly does so in the minds of the political elites. However, during the last ten years Russia's politics in the Caucasus has amounted to nothing but a more or less orderly retreat. Russian influence in Georgia and Azerbaijan is continually decreasing; Russia has maintained a significant military presence only in Armenia, with the consent of the Armenians themselves. On the other hand, Iran and Turkey, both potential rivals to Russian regional hegemony, have kept a relatively low profile towards the events in Chechnya. Iran needs Russia as a supplier of weapons and nuclear technology, and also in order to balance the hegemonic aspirations of the US. Thus, Iran's official support for its Islamic brethren in Chechnya is moderate. Turkey, on the other hand, has a deeper understanding of the 'internal affairs' argument because of its own Kurdish problem. It is clearly unwilling to take any political risks for the sake of the Chechens, although public support in Turkey for the Chechen cause is high and prominent Chechen politicians operate from Istanbul.

Realist explanations of Russia's war in Chechnya are, therefore, less than convincing. What about NATO's motives and interests? Here, Realists seem to face even more obstacles. In the Balkans, there are no significant resources that would make a war worthwhile. There is no potential challenger to NATO's hegemony in the region, and Milosevic's Serbia was definitely no threat to NATO member states. There are, however, two Realist arguments worth considering.

According to one argument, the aggressive nationalism of Serbia posed a threat to the stability of the whole region, with possible effects for NATO's southern flank. The Serbian policy of repression and ethnic cleansing of the Kosovars could have spread to Albania and Macedonia. Macedonia has a significant Albanian minority, so that refugees from Kosovo could have changed the ethnic balance there, leading to internal conflict. In another scenario, the Albanians of Kosovo, Macedonia and Albania would have revitalised the idea of a Greater Albania. Either way, the territorial integrity of Macedonia would have been endangered. Were Macedonian statehood put under question, Greek, Turkish and Serb interventions would have become a real possibility, constituting a threat to NATO's southern flank.

The second argument posits that the Serbian policy of repression and ethnic cleansing created refugee flows which would, sooner rather than later, reach EU countries. As is well known, accommodating refugees is expensive and politically sensitive. In order to prevent this from happening, NATO decided to force Serbia to halt its policy of aggression.

Both arguments have some credibility, but share one big flaw: a rational actor chooses the cheapest and safest plan to achieve its objectives. A full-scale air operation against Serbia was neither cheap nor without risk. In order to contain Serbia, the cheapest and safest way would have been to engage the Extraction Force, to keep the refugees in the neighbouring countries, and to negotiate their return in exchange for political concessions.

To sum up: neither Russia's war in Chechnya nor NATO's war against Serbia can be explained by Realist interpretations and motives alone. Yet both wars have taken place, so how do we explain them? If we follow the official discourse of NATO, the reason for war was the protection of the Kosovars against the criminal assaults of the Serbian state. Moscow's official line cited the defence of the territorial integrity of the Russian Federation and the restoration of law and order in the 'lost territory' of the breakaway Chechen Republic as reasons for the 'anti-terrorist operation' in Chechnya.[11] Both Russia and NATO had some good arguments: Milosevic's Serbia was without doubt guilty of gross violations of human rights; and breakaway Chechnya had, especially after the first Chechen war, indeed become a place where crime was rampant.

However, NATO had not gone to war in all cases of human rights' violations in recent history, and Russia had seen too many challenges to its state sovereignty from organised crime and obstinate regional elites without going to war over any of those issues either.[12] The official discourses grasp only some of the reasons for war; these were merely necessary, but certainly not sufficient, conditions.

I argue here that the decision to go to war had been shaped, apart from the stated principles ('protection of the human rights' for NATO, and 'protection of the territorial integrity and sovereign rights' for Russia), by the following reasons:

1 the need and opportunity to respond to the expectations of domestic audiences;
2 the opportunity to 'send a message' to targeted audiences – whereas the 'decision' to go to war has been eased by –
3 a blurred chain of command and by an almost complete lack of democratic control mechanisms in both cases.

I start with the third of my reasons. Russian policy is for structural reasons incoherent: at best it is polyphonic, at worst cacophonous. Russia's institutions are still weak, political elites are engaged in endless power struggles, and there is a strong tendency to use foreign and security policies mainly for their symbolic value on the domestic front.[13] The second Chechen war began as a limited defence operation. The Russian army pushed the units of the Chechen commanders out of Daghestan. This defence operation then gradually developed into a full-scale war against the Chechen guerrillas. There are some credible assertions by former Prime Minster Sergei Stepashin that the military plans for such operations had already been in place in early spring 1999, and that the army had just waited for an opportunity to strike. The opportunity came when the limited defence operation against the Chechen invasion in Daghestan proved to be successful, and hugely popular with the public. However, there had never been a formal decision by the president;

there had been no ultimatum to the Chechens, and there had been no parliamentary debate. President Yeltsin took responsibility for the war only after the war had become a huge public relations success for Prime Minister Putin.

The decision-making process during NATO's war was similarly blurred, and had a very questionable popular legitimacy. Here, decision making and democratic legitimisation got all but lost in a thicket of delegated decisions and pre-emptive legitimisation acts, and in evoking the spirit, but not the letter, of the UN Security Council's resolutions. In the end, the NATO Council took the decision alone. It did so in the spirit of the UNSC Resolutions 1199 and 1203, in the spirit of the declaration of the Contact Group prior to the Rambouillet talks, and in the spirit of the NATO Council's threat from October 1998. However, it had no explicit mandate from the UNSC, since Russia and China would have vetoed it, and there had been no prior debate in the national parliaments of member countries.

A second objective of both wars was to meet public expectations. It is hard to say what comes first, images, public expectations, political action or active image manipulation. At the start there was probably an image, e.g. a picture of a refugee who had barely escaped from ethnic cleansing, with a burning house in the background. This image created public expectations: 'Somebody must do something about it!' Public expectations prompted political action, and, in order to sustain the public mood, creative management of the information flow was generating more images. The image, the expectation, the action and information management formed a self-sustaining process. Once the circle begins to spin, each component reinforces the others.

The images of Kosovar refugees fuelled public indignation. Ethnic cleansing in Europe? Never again![14] The indignation was rising, and with it the legitimisation and acceptance of war, fought by European nations in Europe against another European state, without a UN mandate. Preparations for war, and the war itself, were accompanied by a media campaign, skilfully orchestrated by NATO spokesman Jamie Shea and his colleagues. Its main actors were the Kosovar refugees, and NATO's clean and smart high-tech weapons. Both images contributed to the legitimisation of war – the refugees were standing evidence that someone had to do something, and a display of weapons certified that NATO could do the job, with high efficiency and minimal collateral damage.[15]

Things were somewhat different in the case of Chechnya: Russia had lost not only the first Chechen war on the battlefield, but the information war itself. Images of a demoralised army, of senseless destruction and the vandalised corpses of Russian soldiers had forced a sharp anti-war turn in the Russian public opinion, finally leading to the cease-fire of Khasavyurt in 1996.

In the first war, the Russian army had made the same mistake as the Serbs during their war against the Kosovars: they had treated journalists as enemies and tried to keep them out. Journalists sneaked into Chechnya and

Kosovo anyway with the help of the locals. Consequently, they reported from the Chechen and the Kosovar side, and media coverage often reflected only Chechen and Kosovar views.

By August 1999, the Russians had learned their lesson: during the second Chechen war, journalists were guests of the Russian army, witnessing its 'police operation', while the Chechen victims' perspective was hardly noticeable in the Russian papers and TV screens. Instead, it was the images of tortured and executed hostages of the Chechen criminal gangs that were widely disseminated and presented to the European politicians.[16]

These manipulated images conveyed the impression of a highly motivated and technically up-to-date Russian army successfully conducting a police operation against the Chechen bandits. These images catered to the principal demand of the Russian population, as was revealed by numerous polls: a quest for *poryadok*, order. It also played into the hands of Vladimir Putin, the previously unknown KGB *apparatchik* chosen by Boris Yeltsin and his entourage to become Russia's next President. When Putin became Prime Minister in August 1999, only a few Russians knew him, and even fewer liked him. However, skyrocketing approval ratings soon rewarded his decisive and tough stance on Chechnya. On 1 January 2000, he became acting-president, and on 26 March 2000 he easily won the presidential elections in the first round. Without the war in Chechnya – which gave Putin ample opportunity to demonstrate his determination, decisiveness and toughness – there probably would have never been a President Putin.

Images of the second Chechen war easily captured the minds and hearts of the electorate. They proved to be a powerful message, saying Putin = *poryadok*. By the same token, images of NATO aircraft taking off and landing, and images of refugees gradually turning into cheerful crowds, applauding NATO's war efforts, sent the message to domestic audiences in Europe and the US: 'NATO is doing something about it, *and* it is fair.' Ten years after the end of the Cold War and the virtual loss of its principal *raison d'être*, the Alliance had finally found a new mission: the Europeans had found a sort of common identity in a common war, and the 'West' had finally showed to the 'rest' that it would stand up and fight for its principles.

While domestic audiences in both cases were important recipients, they were not the only ones. Images of war are polysemantic: on the one hand,

Russian bombs in Chechnya	Nato bombs in Serbia
To self: Putin = order	To self: We protect human rights
To other: No breakaway	To other: Do not mess with NATO

Figure 5 *Polysemantics of war images*

they must target domestic audiences in order to synchronise domestic moods with the political actions taken by the elite; on the other hand, they must deliver a message to the 'other'. Thus, NATO aircraft were delivering a message to Milosevic, and also to potential Milosevics. The message read: 'Those who do not respect the basic principle of human rights face a determined response from NATO.' Operation Allied Force just drove that point home, restoring NATO's 'credibility' after months of empty threats. The same is true of the Russian bombs: they were meant to bomb into submission the Chechen guerrillas and/or to prove Putin's toughness; but they also carried a message to other potential 'breakaway' republics.

The problem, however, is that messages can be unwittingly or deliberately misinterpreted, and read by others than the intended recipients. Thus, NATO's message, originally meant for Milosevic and intended for domestic consumption, was received by and deciphered in Russia. To Russia, it said: 'NATO is willing to violate the principle of sovereignty, without consent of the United Nations.' On the other hand, the message Russia sent to domestic consumers and would-be separatists said to NATO countries: 'Russia is willing to violate human rights on a large scale for the sake of her imperial ambitions.' The result was an on-going war of interpretation, a cooling down of East–West relations and the fallout in 'real' Russian politics.

Epilogue: reflections in a distorting mirror

The conflicts in Chechnya and Kosovo are in many ways closely linked. There is a remarkable similarity between the two cases. Both are post-socialist and post-imperial conflicts, and both share the characteristics of 'new wars'. The responses of Russia and NATO were also in many ways similar: both have been largely influenced by domestic considerations and by the need and the opportunity to 'send messages'. Another similarity lies in the fact that pure Realist approaches are not well suited to explain these wars.

Chechnya and Kosovo are also linked because these twin conflicts serve as an interface between Russia and the West. It is not that Russia has any Realist interests in Kosovo, or that 'the West' has any similar interest in Chechnya. Nor, for that matter, is it that 'the West' has any significant influence on the events in Chechnya, or Russia any significant influence on the events in Kosovo.[17] However, it is *over* Chechnya and Kosovo that Russia and the West engage in debates: it is here that both test the actual market value of their principles and measure their actual weight in *Realpolitik*. It is primarily over Chechnya–Kosovo that Russia and the West are playing the game of mutual integration/insulation.

Prior to the Kosovo crisis there were numerous attempts at integrating Russia into the West's Balkan policy, for example as a member of the Contact Group for Bosnia, as co-chair of the Dayton Conference, and as a participant of SFOR and KFOR. These attempts at integrating Russia in the Western policy were, however, a facilitation for East–West relations rather than a significant contribution to European policy on the Balkans. At present Russia has neither the resources for nor any serious interests in being a key player in the Balkans. Russia's primary interest in the region is, above all, in defining its position *vis-à-vis* the West. Before the outbreak of the Kosovo crisis, Russia took a flexible and pragmatic stand on Western policy on the Balkans: it was generally supportive, but in certain symbolic matters ostentatiously kept its distance. For example, it wished, and obtained, some sort of autonomy for the Russian units within SFOR.

The outbreak of the Kosovo crisis changed that situation. The more the West (NATO and EU member states) sought Russian support for its policy towards the Milosevic regime, the more reluctant Russia became. When NATO aircraft demonstratively carried out manoeuvres over the former Yugoslavia in June 1998, the Kremlin no less demonstratively received Milosevic for talks in Moscow. Although Russia supported UNSC Resolution 1199, it tried to slow down the efforts of the Contact Group to implement decisive action on Serbian non-compliance, and made it clear that it would under no circumstances support NATO air strikes.

Russia's reluctance to support Western policy paralysed the UN. As a result NATO emerged as the key player in the Kosovo drama, and signalled that it would act without a UN mandate, if necessary. This, in turn, stiffened Russian resistance to what, in the end, became unilateral NATO policy in the Balkans. When NATO started Operation Allied Force, diplomatic and public reactions in Moscow were extremely harsh, and Russian top politicians gloomily spoke about a new Cold War, or even hinted at the possibility of a third world war.[18] The Kosovo crisis suddenly showed a deep rift between Russia and the West, and it seemed that the policy of mutual integration and accommodation had proved a failure. It had indeed been a pet idea of Russian foreign policy to integrate and thus constrain NATO into international regimes, such as the UN or the OSCE. Until 1997, one of Russia's favourite ideas was to put the OSCE in charge of NATO. Likewise, the West had attempted to integrate and constrain Russia in Western institutions and policies. The Kosovo crisis has demystified these mutual attempts at integration for what they were – benevolent and useful simulations.

NATO air strikes were seen in Russia, and not without good reason, as an arrogant demonstration of power, a violation of international norms and regulations, and ultimately as a threat to Russian national security and to international stability in general. Consequently, paragraph 3 of the new Russian National Security Doctrine, adopted in April 2000, states:

> [A] destabilizing impact on the military–political situation is exerted by attempts to weaken the existing mechanism for safeguarding international security (primarily, the United Nations and the Organisation for Security and Cooperation in Europe) . . . [and] by the use of coercive military actions as a means

of 'humanitarian intervention' without the sanction of the UN Security Council, in circumvention of the generally accepted principles and norms of international law.[19]

NATO air strikes ended in June 1999. A month later, the second Chechen war began. When the West expressed disapproval and protest over the gross violation of human rights by the Russian army, this criticism was widely rejected in Russia as hypocrisy.

The high-intensity conflicts in Chechnya and Kosovo are over, but the war of interpretation is still going on, and binds the two cases even closer together. Russia claims that NATO's action was a violation of the international norms, especially of the UN Charter. NATO declares that its actions were justified, because they were aimed at the protection of the human rights of the Kosovars. On the other hand, Russia claims to be defending its territorial integrity and sovereign rights in Chechnya, while the West maintains that Russia is violating the international norms, especially the human rights of the Chechen civilians. The debates on what Kosovo was about, and what its implications really are, are also crucial for an understanding of what Chechnya is about, and vice versa. Kosovo and Chechnya have become synonyms, two signs forced to share a single referent – while that referent is actually contested. Chechnya is the reflection of Kosovo. But this mirror is a distorting mirror.

NATO probably feels no urge to look into the mirror for the time being. It has won the war, and while the UN is working hard to restore a civilian administration in Kosovo, NATO is busy managing its impressive collection of pictures from the war: here a happy refugee, there a clean cockpit video. For Russia, the distorting mirror will not go away any time soon, and she feels dizzy. In order to find a hold, Russia gladly embraced a new president. He has a black belt in Judo, and he is likely to abolish all mirrors.

Notes

1 *Kommersant Daily*, 24 March 1999.
2 With Resolution 1244, the UNSC has externalised administration and security of Kosovo. Based on this resolution, UNMIK (United Nations Interim Administration in Kosovo) was established. Formally, the UN is responsible for UNMIK, but the EU bears the bulk of the financial and organisational burden of the interim administration.
3 Until 1990, Chechnya together with Ingushetia formed the autonomous Chechen–Ingushetian Republic within the Russian Federation. In 1991, the two separated. Ingushetia remained within the Russian Federation, Chechnya declared independence.
4 For a useful overview of permissive factors for ethno-political conflict, see Michael E. Brown, 'The Causes of Internal Conflict: An Overview', in Michael E. Brown, Owen R. Cote, Steven E. Miller and Sean M. Lynn-Jones, (eds), *Nationalism and*

Ethnic Conflict. An International Security Reader (Cambridge, MA, and London, MIT Press, 1997).

5 The term was coined, to the best of my knowledge, by Mary Kaldor in *New and Old Wars. Organized Violence in a Global Era* (Stanford, CA, Stanford University Press, 1999).

6 As far as I am aware, this concept was developed by Georg Elwert of the Free University of Berlin. See Georg Elwert, 'Gewaltmärkte. Beobachtungen zur Zwecksrationalität der Gewalt', in Trutz von Trotha (ed.), *Soziologie der Gewalt, Sonderheft 37 der Kölner Zeitschrift für Soziologie und Sozialpsychologie* (Köln, Westdeutscher Verlag, 1997). See also François Jean, Jean-Christophe Rufin (eds), *Économie des guerres civiles* (Paris, Hachette, 1996).

7 Ted Robert Gurr and Barbara Harff, *Ethnic Conflict in World Politics* (Boulder, CO, Westview Press, 1994), p. 11. I prefer the term 'identity group' to the narrower labels 'ethnic groups' or 'minority groups', because not all groups in conflict are minorities, and not all organised groups are bound together by ethnicity. In today's globalising world, cultural communities often transcend the 'natural' borders of territory, language, religion or local customs, but form communities nevertheless, bound together by selected markers of difference. After all, in conflicts identity is what people choose to fight over.

8 Ann Auerbach-Hagendorn, *Ransom. The Untold Story of International Kidnapping* (New York, Henry Holt & Co., 1998); Kaldor, *New and Old Wars*, p. 103.

9 It is well known (and duly stressed by the Russian media) that kidnapping, extortion, drug and weapon trafficking are booming industries in Chechnya. Less well known is that Kosovo has become an important hub for drug trafficking and that the KLA, also thanks to its military muscle, has become a key player in the Balkan narco-business. This is a serious problem which KFOR needs to deal with. Cf. Sunil Ram, 'NATO in Kosovo: In Bed with a Scorpion', *The Globe and Mail*, 9 August 2000.

10 This argument comes sometimes in the Huntingtonian guise, that is the war in Chechnya is fought between the Orthodox world and Islam.

11 For NATO's official discourse, see e.g. 'NATO & Kosovo: Historical Overview', available: http://www.nato.int/kosovo/history.htm (accessed 5 December 2000; see chapter 7, by Andreas Behnke, in this volume). The Russian official discourse is harder to localise, for two reasons: it is still in the making; and Russia, as a rule, speaks with many voices. However, for a good overview, see the homepage of Rosinformtsentr, run by the Russian Federation's Ministry for Press, Television, Radio Broadcasting and Mass Communications, a site exclusively dedicated to the events in and around Chechnya, as seen by the official Russia: http://www.infocentre.ru (accessed 5 December 2000). Rosinformcentr is an attempt at a more effective and centralised information policy, and it clearly shows that Russia has learned a lot from NATO.

12 It is estimated that over 50 per cent of regional laws in Russia contradict federal laws.

13 Christoph Zürcher, 'Krieg und Frieden in Tschetschenien: Ursachen, Symbole, Interessen', *Arbeitspapiere des Osteuropa-Instituts*, no. 2 (1997)

14 This 'Never again' found a special resonance in German ears. The German *Nie wieder*, the ultimate moral imperative central to German politics and society, underwent a semantic dilation: prior to Kosovo, 'Never again' meant 'Never

again will ethnic cleansing and genocide start in Germany', that is in Europe. Now, impelled by such images, it means also 'Never again will Europe allow ethnic cleansing and genocide'. Already in October 1999 the German Bundestag had decided that it would support an armed NATO operation if Milosevic did not give in to diplomatic pressure and if there was no other way to prevent a humanitarian catastrophe in Kosovo. With that decision, the Bundestag gave up a central piece of post-war (West) German policy.

15 The informational side of NATO's war in Kosovo was impressive indeed. Courtesy of NATO, selected images are available online for further examination (see also chapter 7 of this volume). A collection of NATO videos is available at http://www.nato.int/kosovo/video.htm (accessed 5 December 2000). A collection of photographs, maps, aerial views and pre- and post-strike cockpit videos used during the press conference by General Wesley Clark is available at http://www.nato.int/kosovo/slides/m990916a.htm (accessed 5 December 2000).

16 The Chechens, having 'lost' the TV presence in Russia, make increasing use of the World Wide Web for distributing their perspective. The website http://www.kavkaz.org (accessed 5 December 2000) is the mouthpiece of Movladi Udugov, information minister of the Chechen Republic; and http://www.qoqaz.co.za (accessed 5 December 2000) is a fundamentalist website which presents the Chechen war as a *Jihad*. This website hosts a broad selection of especially gruesome and detailed pictures of 'destroyed aggressors', martyred mujahiddin and killed civilians. The Western press, interestingly enough, has started to read and quote Chechen statements from Kavkaz.org as counterpoints to Russian statements.

17 One of the most prominent myths about the Kosovo war, especially in Germany, is that Russia has had some influence on Milosevic, influence which made 'peace without Russia impossible'. Actually, Russia had no influence whatsoever on Milosevic's surprising capitulation to NATO demands; Russia mainly jumped on the Ahtisaari mission as soon as it became clear that Ahtisaari would present the G-7/G-8 peace plan with or without Russia. See also the interview with Marrti Ahtisaari, 'Così ho convinto Milosevic a cedere', *La Repubblica*, 25 July 2000.

18 On 9 April 1999 President Yeltsin said in an interview: 'I have told the NATO people, the Americans, the Germans: "Don't push us into military action. Otherwise there would certainly be a European, and perhaps a world war."' See Gwynne Dyer, 'Behind Yeltsin's Threat', *The Moscow Times*, 13 April 1999.

19 Text of the Military Doctrine of the Russian Federation, approved by a presidential decree dated 21 April 2000, published in *Nezavisimaya gazeta* on 22 April 2000. For an English translation, see *David Johnson's Russia List*, no. 4269, 26 April 2000.